Making Meaning out of Mountains

Making Meaning
out of Mountains

The Political Ecology of Skiing

MARK C.J. STODDART

UBCPress · Vancouver · Toronto

21 20 19 18 17 16 15 14 13 12   5 4 3 2 1

Printed in Canada on FSC-certified ancient-forest-free paper
(100% post-consumer recycled) that is processed chlorine- and acid-free.

Library and Archives Canada Cataloguing in Publication

Stoddart, Mark C. J., 1974-
    Making meaning out of mountains : the political ecology of skiing /
Mark C.J. Stoddart.

Includes bibliographical references and index.
Also issued in electronic format.
ISBN 978-0-7748-2196-4 (bound); ISBN 978-0-7748-2197-1 (pbk.)

    1. Skis and skiing – Environmental aspects – British Columbia. 2. Skis and skiing
– Social aspects – British Columbia. 3. Mountain ecology – British Columbia. I. Title.

GV854.8.C3S76 2012   796.93'09711   C2011-908338-8

Canadä

UBC Press gratefully acknowledges the financial support for our publishing program of the Government of Canada (through the Canada Book Fund), the Canada Council for the Arts, and the British Columbia Arts Council.

This book has been published with the help of a grant from the Canadian Federation for the Humanities and Social Sciences, through the Aid to Scholarly Publications Program, using funds provided by the Social Sciences and Humanities Research Council of Canada, and with the help of the K.D. Srivastava Fund.

UBC Press
The University of British Columbia
2029 West Mall
Vancouver, BC V6T 1Z2
www.ubcpress.ca

For my wife, Kumi, for her generosity and support.

Contents

Figures

Acknowledgments

This research has been shaped through the generous assistance of many people. I would like to acknowledge David Tindall, Thomas Kemple, Brian Wilson, Howard Ramos, Dawn Currie, Bruce Miller, and Harris Ali. Throughout this project, Justin Page proved to be an invaluable colleague and friend.

I would like to thank Randy Schmidt, Graeme Wynn, and the anonymous reviewers at UBC Press for their thorough work and assistance.

Conference papers based on this material were presented at the 2006 Congress of the Humanities and Social Sciences, 2006 International Symposium on Society and Resource Management, 2006 Annual Meeting of the North American Society for the Sociology of Sport, 2007 Congress of the Humanities and Social Sciences, 2007 Nature Matters Conference, 2008 World Congress of the International Sociology of Sport Association, 2008 Congress of the Humanities and Social Sciences, 2008 International Sociological Association World Forum of Sociology, 2008 Annual Meeting of the North American Society for the Sociology of Sport, and 2009 Congress of the Humanities and Social Sciences. Holly Thorpe, Jason Laurendeau, Aaron Doyle, and Jen Wrye provided particularly valuable feedback in this context.

I would like to acknowledge the Social Sciences and Research Council of the Humanities (SSHRC) for financial support for this research.

Making Meaning out of Mountains

Introduction
The Attractive Economy of Skiing

Skiing brings to mind images of snowy mountains, sunshine, and athletic men and women having fun. In the classic film *White Christmas*, the ski resort is synonymous with the magic of winter, about which Bing Crosby croons. Ernest Hemingway, icon of literary masculinity, was an avid skier, as was Sir Arthur Conan Doyle. Through mass media images of resorts in the European Alps and American Rockies, skiing remains linked to images of celebrity and luxury. Skiing, however, is not only for the rich and famous. A 1990 survey of ski market trends notes that a third of Canadian households own downhill or cross-country ski equipment, highlighting the importance of the sport to Canadian social life.[1] The cover of a book titled *How to Be a Canadian* shows a rosy-cheeked young woman with skis and red-knit sweater posed against a mountain background.[2] These images depict skiing as a benign form of human-nature interaction that is far removed from the world of politics. However, skiing should be examined within the context of ecopolitics, a perspective that joins together the microsocial and macrosocial dimensions of environmentalism. These include environmental values, environmentally friendly behaviours, and environmentalist identities, as well as environmental movement political action and debates over ecological sustainability.

Skiing, as a recreational form of interaction with mountain environments, connects humans and non-human nature. Skiing also intersects

with First Nations activism, global climate change, mass media representations of nature, and (partially) global flows of tourism and migration.
At its core, skiing is marked by an ecopolitical ambiguity. Although the
ski industry positions itself as an exemplar of "sustainable development,"
environmental groups and First Nations protesters accuse it of spreading
into wilderness areas and displacing valuable wildlife habitat. Skiers
value the sport precisely because it brings them into embodied relationships with mountainous nature, yet many are also concerned about
skiing's negative environmental impacts. Social and historical studies of
skiing and snowboarding rarely touch on environmental issues, and this
book addresses that gap by examining how playful interactions with
mountain environments are part of our "political ecology," where nature,
politics, economics, and culture intersect.[3]

In British Columbia, nature has been valued primarily as a source
of raw materials for capitalist production. Forestry, mining, and fishing
make up a staples economy that dominated the province in the past
and continues to inform the present. Environmental conflict over forestry practices and the protection of old-growth forests was a major
element of BC politics in the 1980s and 1990s. There were repeated
protests, blockades, and instances of civil disobedience in the Carmanah
Valley, Walbran Valley, Clayoquot Sound, Elaho Valley, Great Bear
Rainforest, and Slocan Valley. The Clayoquot Sound protests of 1993
focused international environmental concern on the province. Vancouver media termed this period the "War in the Woods," while NDP
premier Glen Clark called environmental protesters "enemies of British
Columbia" for questioning the ecological legitimacy of provincial
forestry practices.

Similar environmental movement campaigns around ski resort expansion and new development likewise produced civil disobedience and
mobilized thousands of people through letter writing, petitions, and
protests, but these conflicts were generally sporadic and local in scale.
For the most part, skiing is seen as a benign mode of interaction with
mountain environments, a so-called attractive development that reinforces images of rural British Columbia as a space that is more natural than
social, where wilderness is as important a resource as lumber or minerals.[4]
This renaturalized rural landscape is disengaged from the traditional

staples economy and re-embedded in an economy of global tourism. The symbolic value of the landscape becomes as important as the value of the material resources it contains. Shifts from extractive to attractive development are often assumed to be environmentally beneficent, but there are environmental ambiguities and points of tension inherent in the attractive economy.

The 2010 Winter Olympics, the ongoing development of new ski resorts, and the provincial government's plans to increase the accessibility of the province's backcountry are only a few signs of the importance of the attractive economy in British Columbia. Skiing is an important part of this tourist economy. Since the 1970s, the province has seen "the development of Whistler [into] a truly world-class destination, and the advent of several fine regional destinations in the interior of the province."[5] Whistler Blackcomb, Big White, and Whitewater are only a few of the downhill ski resorts that draw locals and tourists into the mountains every winter. Backcountry skiing and cross-country skiing are also available across the province. Canada's oldest and largest heli-ski company, Canadian Mountain Holidays, is based in British Columbia, and Cypress Mountain, a short distance from downtown Vancouver, boasts that it is the most popular cross-country ski destination in Canada.

Four main themes structure my discussion of skiing in the pages that follow. First, the meaning of the skiing landscape is not a fixed thing. It is actively constructed by a variety of social actors. The ski industry draws upon images of the mountainous sublime to link skiing and nature. Environmental and First Nations groups, by contrast, challenge the ecological and social legitimacy of skiing. Environmentalists argue that skiing transforms pre-existing wilderness and wildlife landscapes into cultural spaces for mass tourism. Similarly, First Nations protesters argue that new skiing development infringes on contested territories. The development and expansion of ski resorts often brings these divergent meanings into conflict with each other. I touch on several examples of this, including Jumbo Pass (in southeastern British Columbia near the town of Invermere) and Sun Peaks (near the city of Kamloops). Cultural constructions of skiing landscapes have political effects, as they determine who controls mountain environments and who belongs in these "contested natures."[6]

Second, skiing is not only a social activity, where the non-human environment serves as a scenic background or set of symbols. It entails material interactions between human skiers, mountains, weather systems, trees, and animals. Skiers' experiences of mountain environments are also mediated by the skis, boots, and specialized outdoor clothing required to participate in the sport. Machines are used to shape the physical landscape to make it more appealing to skiers. Chairlifts carry skiers up mountains; cars, buses, and airplanes connect local skiing landscapes to nearby urban areas and broader networks of tourist travel. A long-standing debate in the environmental social sciences pits environmental "realists" against environmental "constructionists."[7] In very simple terms, environmental realism assumes the existence of a physical environment outside the social realm, which can be accurately known through environmental science. By contrast, environmental constructionism emphasizes the ways in which environmental knowledge is always mediated by systems of discourse. From this perspective, the claims of environmental scientists, environmentalists, and others should be analyzed as social constructions rather than taken as unproblematic accounts of the environment. I circumvent the divide between realism and constructionism by exploring how humans and non-humans "co-construct" skiing as a practice that is mediated by discourse but which is fundamentally about embodied interactions between skiers and non-human nature. Rather than speaking of skiing as a site where nature and society meet, I find more productive to examine how skiing produces mountain environments as hybrid "actor networks," "naturecultures," or "technonatures."[8]

Third, skiing is a site of power relations between humans and non-human nature. There is a tension between interpretations of skiing as a form of sustainable development and skiing as an environmental problem. The ski industry presents itself as a pro-environmental steward of mountain environments. By adopting habitat management programs, eco-efficiency standards, and new technologies, the ski industry appears to be engaged in a project of "ecological modernization" aimed at achieving sustainability within the existing economic and political framework of consumer capitalism.[9] Skiers similarly value their sport because it allows them to engage in embodied relationships with mountainous nature. However, social movement groups highlight the negative environmental impacts of skiing's relationship with non-human nature. Skiers' reflections on the ecopolitics of their sport also illuminate several ecological ironies.[10] These are gaps between the ski industry's use of pro-environmental discourse and its negative ecological impacts. These include wildlife displacement; energy use to power chairlifts; or the intimate connections between skiing, car use, and global climate change. A Foucauldian theoretical framework highlights the power relations that work through playful interactions with mountainous nature. The ecopolitics of skiing plays out within the microsocial environmental subjectivities of skiers, as well as through larger-scale relations of biopower between the ski industry and non-human nature.[11]

Finally, skiing is not only about having fun in the snow. It is also characterized by flows of power based on gender, ethnicity, class, and other social factors. These are relations of power that operate through everyday interaction, rather than through grand acts of exclusion or repression. These relations of power often pass unnoticed or are taken for granted. For example, ski industry discourse links images of the mountainous sublime to normalized whiteness and masculinity. This produces gendered and racialized versions of the skiing landscape. Participation in skiing is also influenced by gendered norms and expectations, which privilege a "guys' style" that is more aggressive and oriented toward risk-taking. Skiing villages like Whistler Blackcomb are also constructed as sites of rustic luxury. An analysis of social power relations within skiing builds upon prior research on how outdoor sports such as skiing, mountaineering, and surfing are shaped by the dynamics of gender, ethnicity, and class.[12] Analyzing how flows of power oriented around gender, class, and racialization work through skiing allows us to see which social groups are positioned as the natural inhabitants and legitimate managers of mountain environments. As certain traits are particularly valorized within skiing (e.g., risk-seeking, youthful masculinity), the experience of those who do not meet these criteria may be devalued and marginalized.

In the end, of course, this is a study of skiing in British Columbia. My findings are broadly consistent with other research on skiing in western North America, such as Coleman's history of skiing in Colorado and Rothman's discussion of the growth of ski resorts in the western United States, but may be less applicable to eastern North America or other regions of the globe.[13]

Since its inception in the 1970s, environmental sociology has been concerned with environmental movements, the spread of environmental values, and social conflicts over access to natural resources. Despite Dunlap and Catton's early assertion that wildland recreation should be a key research area, recreational forms of land use have generally received less attention.[14] At the same time, the sociology of sport has examined outdoor recreation through snowboarding, rock climbing, mountaineering, and windsurfing. This work typically examines how outdoor sport is shaped by gender, class, or ethnicity, while bracketing out the role played by non-human nature in constituting outdoor recreation.[15] The separation of environmental sociology from the sociology of sport produces a double lacuna: the marginalization of sport in environmental sociology and the marginalization of non-human nature in the sociology of sport. An analysis of the political ecology of skiing highlights the salience of outdoor sport for environmental sociology, as well as the importance of non-humans for the sociology of sport. It encourages further research and theoretical dialogue across these two areas of inquiry.

The Social Context of Skiing in British Columbia

This study combines textual analysis, interviews, and field observation. Skier interviews were conducted in two areas of British Columbia: the Vancouver to Whistler corridor and the Nelson region, in southeastern British Columbia. Field observation was similarly split between the Whistler Blackcomb ski resort, near Vancouver, and the Whitewater resort, near Nelson. Different as they are, these two regions and resorts present rich contrasts.

The Vancouver-Whistler Region

More than half the skiers in British Columbia live in Vancouver, the largest city in the province.[16] The city is also a gateway for tourists to Whistler Blackcomb, the flagship resort of the BC ski industry that accounted for 6.1 million skier days during the winter of 2003/2004. Three smaller ski hills – Cypress Mountain, Mount Seymour, and Grouse Mountain – are located in close proximity to Vancouver.

Whistler Blackcomb operates more than two hundred ski runs over 3,307 hectares of skiable terrain on Whistler Mountain, with an elevation of 2,182 metres, and on Blackcomb, with an elevation of 2,284 metres.[17] The longest runs exceed eleven kilometres in length. On average, Pacific weather systems bring over ten metres of snow a year to the resort. A substantial infrastructure has been built up, including thirty-eight chair-lifts and gondolas, with a combined capacity to move up to sixty-five thousand skiers per hour. There are also seventeen lodges and restaurants spread over the two mountains. Whistler Village sits in the valley below the two peaks. Indicating the status of Whistler Blackcomb as a place of tourism and consumerism, the village contains several hotels, including high-end luxury hotels like the Fairmont Chateau Whistler. The village also has several cafés, bars, restaurants, tourist memorabilia shops, clothing stores, and sports gear stores. The cost of lift tickets is relatively high. Day passes for the 2009/2010 ski season cost as much as $91; season passes cost up to $1,500 (early bird passes were available for $1,100). Whistler Blackcomb also hosted several events during the 2010 Olympics, cementing its reputation as a global skiing destination.

Skis – or "Norwegian snowshoes" as they were then called – began to appear in the mountains around Vancouver in the 1920s. As in Colorado and California, skiing was introduced to the Coast Mountains by Norwegian immigrants. In a history of Hollyburn Mountain (the present home of Cypress ski resort), Francis Mansbridge writes,

> Until the early years of the past century, snowshoeing was the trad-itional Canadian way of navigating the winter wilderness, conjuring up images of *coureurs du bois* in colourful garb singing rousing French-Canadian folk songs. But once the Scandinavians began arriving, skiing, at this time a new sport in Canada, and particularly suited to the mountainous terrain of British Columbia, took hold. Attracted to BC by work in logging and mining, Scandinavians brought with them both their skis and their philosophy of sport and camaraderie.[18]

Skiing gained popularity with Vancouverites, who travelled to Hollyburn and other peaks in the North Shore Mountains, often as members of outdoor clubs. During this period, recreational skiing was frequently a form of relief from mining and forestry work. Kaare Hesgeth, an early skier in the Hollyburn area, sums up this relationship when he says, "Mining is our bread, and skiing our soul."[19] Although many skiers saw their sport as compatible with forestry or mining, tensions between recreational and extractive uses of the Coast Mountains emerged early on. For example, skiers were prominent among those who rallied in Vancouver in 1939 to call on the provincial government to protect the recreational landscape of the North Shore Mountains from logging.

Skiers gradually moved northward in their exploration and use of the Coast Mountains. Garibaldi Chalet was opened by Norwegian immigrants in 1946 as the first private ski lodge in British Columbia. The lodge was located at the base of Mount Garibaldi in what is now Garibaldi Provincial Park. It was not until 1960 that skiing came to London Mountain, which was renamed Whistler Mountain after the marmots (that make a high-pitched whistling sound) that live in alpine areas of the Coast Mountains. Garibaldi Lifts Ltd. began development in the area in 1960, and Whistler ski hill officially opened in February 1965. This began a rapid process of transforming the small rural community into a global skiing destination. In 1974, Whistler was serving up to five thousand skiers per day. Although the Roundhouse Lodge provided shelter and a place to eat lunch, services were still relatively undeveloped. In the 1960s and 1970s, there were two distinct cultures at Whistler. The business-oriented resort developers and tourism boosters shared the skiing landscape with a subculture of squatters who inhabited makeshift cabins and who combined their love of skiing with a back-to-the-land ethos and counterculture political values.[20]

Skiing and tourism continued to develop in the 1980s. Blackcomb Mountain opened in 1980, and new hotels, stores, and restaurants were built in Whistler Village. Between 1986 and 1991, the full-time population of Whistler Village doubled to 4,460. This growth was symptomatic of larger trends toward attractive development in British Columbia. In 1986, the city of Vancouver hosted a category II world exhibition (Expo '86), which has been seen as a turning point that "asserted the province's entry onto the world stage."[21] As historian Jean Barman writes, "The attributes of natural beauty and opportunities for outdoor recreation that exist in abundance across the province became increasingly valued around the world, heightening British Columbia's appeal as a holiday destination."[22] Intrawest was one of the companies that took advantage of the bourgeoning attractive economy by purchasing Whistler Mountain in 1986 in its first move into the ski industry.

Whistler Blackcomb became a global tourism destination during the 1990s. In the 1996/1997 ski season, there were 1.74 million skier visits, making the resort the most popular in North America.[23] Intrawest took over the operation of Blackcomb Mountain in 1996. During the same period, possibilities for golf, hiking, and mountain biking expanded, and the mountain became increasingly well known as a year-round tourism destination. The process of rapid growth and the globalization of Whistler as a tourist destination changed the feeling of the community. Stephan Vogler, Toshi Kawano, and Bonny Makarevicz describe this process as follows:

> The irony of it all was that the relaxed, laid-back lifestyle of the previous decade proved the most marketable commodity of all: mountain lifestyle, an elixir that could be bottled and sold with the ever-increasing real estate. Throughout the 1980s and 1990s Whistler was the glamorous young starlet of the ski-resort scene. Accolades were heaped upon it year after year in the form of No. 1 rankings in the ski magazines. Movie stars and pop stars came to revel in the buzz of the happening new resort.[24]

Whistler had been transformed over a relatively short period from a small village in a forestry-dependent region into a rural, mountainous version of a "fantasy city," and Whistler Blackcomb led to the reimagination of the Sea to Sky corridor, once dominated by the forest economy, as "sports country."[25] This shift has been accompanied by a growing environmental sensitivity within the region. Whistler Village adopted the Whistler 2020 sustainability plan as well as the Natural Step Framework, both of which link skiing to a project of local sustainability. The Association of Whistler Area Residents for the Environment

(AWARE) seeks to "improve the quality of life in Whistler and surrounding areas, protect and restore the natural heritage and maintain our resources and ecosystems, and achieve environmental sustainability through community education and advocacy."[26] These connections between skiing and ecopolitics echo broader shifts toward environmentalism and outdoor recreation as key components of a distinctive lifestyle of twenty-first-century British Columbians.[27]

Nelson and Whitewater

Whitewater Winter and Ski Resort is located in the subalpine basin below Ymir Mountain (elevation 2,400 metres), in the Selkirk Mountains of southeastern British Columbia. It is approximately seven hundred kilometres east of Vancouver via the mountainous Highway 3. At Whitewater, two old two-seat chairlifts move skiers up the north (Summit) and south (Silver King) sides of the Ymir basin, where forty-six runs encompass 478 hectares of skiable terrain.[28] The elevation gain from the Whitewater lodge building to the top of the Summit chairlift is only 396 metres, far less than the 1,530-metre elevation gain at Whistler or the 1,609-metre gain at Blackcomb. Whitewater is much smaller than Whistler Blackcomb, but the resort chairlifts are frequently used by skiers to access expansive and popular backcountry skiing routes to Ymir Peak, White Queen, and Five Mile Basin. The average annual snowfall at Whitewater – in excess of thirteen metres per year – is comparable to that at Whistler Blackcomb, but in this Interior location, the snow at Whitewater is often lighter and drier than the heavy, wet snow typical of the Coast Mountains.

Whitewater has only one lodge building, which houses a ski shop, cafeteria, pub, clothing store, and daycare. There is no "village" at the base of the ski hill. Hotels, restaurants, cafés, bars, and shops are all located in the nearby town of Nelson, which has a population of approximately ten thousand people. In general, tourism facilities in Nelson do not compare to the high-end luxury hotels or restaurants of Whistler Village. Even though hiking, rock climbing, and mountain biking are all popular in the Nelson region, Whitewater has not developed the summer activities that are incorporated into Whistler Blackcomb as a "four-season resort." Consistent with the smaller size and less-developed character of Whitewater, access is also more affordable than at Whistler Blackcomb. During the 2009-10 ski season, a full-price day pass cost $57; a season pass cost $700 (with an early bird price of $580).

Skiing in the province's Interior began in the 1880s, well before it emerged in the North Shore Mountains outside Vancouver. Scandinavian miners in the towns of Revelstoke, Kimberley, and Rossland (near Nelson) were the province's first skiers.[29] Nelson was established as part of the silver mining boom in the Interior during the 1880s. The town quickly evolved into a supply centre for the regional mining industry. Two years after its formation in 1932, the Silver King Skiers set up a basic ski lodge and rudimentary rope tow, which was powered by the engine of a Ford.[30] In 1961, the club – then known as the Silver King Ski Club – built a new lodge and rope tow on the site of the abandoned Silver King Mine.

The club began work on a ski hill in the Whitewater area in 1974. The group sought to create a ski hill that would "prevent [the] unnecessary upset of the natural environment" and avoid the "barren *pistes*" characteristic of the European Alps by leaving much of the local forest intact.[31] In 1986, Whitewater resort was bought from the ski club by a group of private Nelson entrepreneurs. Ownership of the resort changed hands again in 1997, when Mike and Shelley Adams became the sole owners. The Adamses managed the resort until 2008, when it was bought by Calgary-based Knee Deep Development, which plans to expand the amount of skiable terrain at Whitewater. The recent sale moves ownership of the resort outside the Nelson area for the first time. Since the 1990s, ski magazine and film coverage has built a reputation for Whitewater as an alternative to the larger resorts.[32] Attempts to create cultural distance between Whitewater and larger resorts like Whistler Blackcomb are captured by its slogan: Pure, Simple and Real.

The attractive economy, based on tourism and outdoor sport, has grown in importance in the West Kootenay region, which also has a strong history of environmental activism. The Valhalla Wilderness Society is widely known for its successful campaigns to protect Valhalla Provincial Park and Goat Range Provincial Park. The Slocan Valley

Watershed Alliance, along with members of the Sinixt First Nation, has protested against clear-cutting in the region and has sought to implement alternative models of ecosystem-based forestry.[33] West Kootenay EcoSociety, based in Nelson, organizes local farmers' markets and car sharing and is also active on land use issues.

Although environmentalism and attractive development coexist in the Nelson area, there are some points of tension. As backcountry skiing and other winter sports become more popular, some environmentalists question the wildlife impacts of increased helicopter, snowmobile, and snowcat traffic (snowcats are large vehicles that travel on treads, used to transport backcountry skiers) in remote alpine environments. Local environmentalists have mobilized against the proposed Jumbo Glacier Resort, planned for the Purcell Mountains northeast of Nelson. For environmentalists, the ski resort risks transforming a wilderness landscape inhabited by grizzly bears and other sensitive wildlife into a place for mass tourism. EcoSociety has also recently mobilized against the planned expansion of skiable terrain at Whitewater, which the group says will compromise caribou and grizzly bear habitat in the area.[34]

The BC Ski Industry as an Economic Network

The structural differences between Whistler Blackcomb and Whitewater ski resorts are well illustrated by network analysis, which describes how members of social networks are connected with each other.[35] Networks can range from small groups of individuals to large-scale relationships, such as those between corporations or nation states. Figure 1.1 is a sociogram (social network diagram) of the ownership relations among key ski resorts in British Columbia. The black circular nodes represent individual ski resorts; the white square nodes represent ownership companies that are tied to more than one resort. Node size reflects the centrality of ownership companies in the network.

As this figure illustrates, the economic network of skiing in British Columbia consists of a few independent star structures, in which several ski resorts have common ownership. A few other resorts are members of small networks, with only one or two ties. The remainder stand alone as isolates within the network. These are privately owned resorts, usually

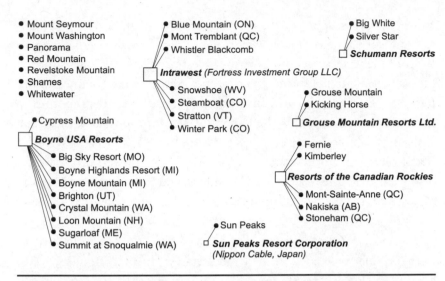

- Mount Seymour
- Mount Washington
- Panorama
- Red Mountain
- Revelstoke Mountain
- Shames
- Whitewater

- Cypress Mountain

Boyne USA Resorts
- Big Sky Resort (MO)
- Boyne Highlands Resort (MI)
- Boyne Mountain (MI)
- Brighton (UT)
- Crystal Mountain (WA)
- Loon Mountain (NH)
- Sugarloaf (ME)
- Summit at Snoqualmie (WA)

- Blue Mountain (ON)
- Mont Tremblant (QC)
- Whistler Blackcomb

Intrawest *(Fortress Investment Group LLC)*
- Snowshoe (WV)
- Steamboat (CO)
- Stratton (VT)
- Winter Park (CO)

- Sun Peaks

□ **Sun Peaks Resort Corporation**
(Nippon Cable, Japan)

- Big White
- Silver Star

□ *Schumann Resorts*

- Grouse Mountain
- Kicking Horse

□ *Grouse Mountain Resorts Ltd.*

- Fernie
- Kimberley

□ *Resorts of the Canadian Rockies*
- Mont-Sainte-Anne (QC)
- Nakiska (AB)
- Stoneham (QC)

Figure 1.1   The BC ski industry as an economic network (June 2010)

the property of a single family or private investment company. At a glance, the network structure appears fragmented; this fragmentation is confirmed by network density measures that compare the number of ties in a network with the number of possible ties between all members of the network. The density of the network depicted in the sociogram is 0.138 (on a spectrum ranging from 0 to 1.0), indicating a low level of network cohesion or corporate concentration in the BC ski industry.

Cliques are subsets of nodes within a network. The two largest cliques in this network centre on Intrawest and Boyne Resorts. Whistler Blackcomb is a member of the Intrawest clique, along with Blue Mountain in Ontario, Mont Tremblant in Quebec, and several resorts in the United States. Intrawest was established in 1976 as a "residential and urban real estate firm."[36] The company entered the ski industry when it bought Whistler resort in 1986. Between 1991 and 2002, Intrawest expanded to become one of the largest ski industry companies in North America through the purchase of several resorts in Canada (Ontario, Quebec, and British Columbia) and the United States (Colorado, Vermont, and New Jersey). Intrawest also expanded beyond the ski industry into resort tourism in Florida, Hawaii, and "other exclusive locations around the world."[37] Intrawest remains headquartered in Vancouver, although the company was bought in 2006 by Fortress Investment Group, an American investment firm based in New York. In the aftermath of the Lehman Brothers debacle, which hit Fortress Investment hard, creditors moved to force an auction of Intrawest properties. Several weeks of uncertainty followed. During this time, Intrawest sold several resort properties to generate capital, including the Panorama resort in southeastern British Columbia. The company also rejected a bid by Vail Resorts for Whistler Blackcomb, described as the crown jewel of the Intrawest properties. A deal was eventually reached with creditors, and Intrawest remains a key organization in the North American skiing economy, though with fewer resort properties.[38]

The second large clique centres on Boyne Resorts. Most of the resorts in this clique are located in the United States. The exception is Cypress Mountain, one of three ski resorts located close to the city of Vancouver. As part of Cypress Provincial Park, the Cypress ski area was managed by the provincial government until 1984. At this point, the ski area was privatized by the Social Credit government and sold to Wayne Booth's company, Cypress Bowl Recreations.[39] Cypress was sold to Boyne Resorts in 2001, marking the company's entry into the Canadian ski industry. Boyne Resorts began with the 1947 creation of Boyne Mountain ski hill in northern Michigan. Since then, Boyne has expanded by buying and developing ski resorts in Maine, New Hampshire, Montana, Utah, and Washington. At present, the company claims that it is the largest privately owned ski and golf corporation in the United States.[40]

A third noteworthy clique centres on Resorts of the Canadian Rockies. Besides Fernie Alpine Resort and Kimberley Alpine Resort, both located in southeastern British Columbia, this clique includes resorts in Alberta and Quebec. The ski hill in Fernie started in 1964 as a "weekend operation for local families."[41] Fernie Snow Valley remained a small, locally run ski hill until 1997, when it was bought by Resorts of the Canadian Rockies, which already owned several resorts in Alberta and Quebec. Charlie Locke, the Albertan owner of Resorts of the Canadian Rockies, expanded the skiable terrain, upgraded the resort infrastructure, and renamed the area Fernie Alpine Resort. Kimberley Alpine Resort was developed by Resorts of the Canadian Rockies in 2000 as part of a push toward attractive development following the demise of the Cominco mine in the small town of Kimberley. In 2001, after a season of poor snowfall, Resorts of the Canadian Rockies was on the verge of bankruptcy. The company was bailed out by Calgary financier Murray Edwards, who became the majority shareholder in the company. Unlike Intrawest or Boyne, Resorts of the Canadian Rockies defines itself as proudly Canadian, while claiming to be the largest private ski resort operator in North America.[42]

These three cliques are the result of a historical process whereby local ski hills have been bought up by ski industry corporations. This process of corporate concentration is relatively recent, beginning with Intrawest's acquisition of Whistler in 1986 and accelerating throughout the 1990s. Only time will tell whether the recent sale of Intrawest holdings, including Panorama, marks the beginning of the decentralization of ski industry economic networks in British Columbia. However, these three cliques illustrate that the BC ski industry is embedded within broader North American economic networks, involving flows of capital between British Columbia, Alberta, and the United States.

Beyond these cliques, there are several dyadic and triadic clusters. Silver Star and Big White, both located in the Okanagan region of the province, are connected through their common ownership by the Schumann family (which has owned Big White since 1985 and Silver Star since 2001). Grouse Mountain Resorts has ownership ties to the Grouse Mountain resort, near Vancouver, as well as to Kicking Horse Mountain Resort in the Rockies. Sun Peaks is a notable anomaly within this network. Originally called Tod Mountain, the resort was purchased by Sun Peaks Resort Corporation in 1992.[43] Since then, it has undergone a considerable – and contentious – expansion program. It is the only BC resort that has significant ownership ties outside North America, as it is a subsidiary of Nippon Cable, a large Japanese corporation that manufactures chairlift equipment for ski hills and also has ownership ties to several Japanese ski resorts.

Several BC ski resorts are privately owned, often by investment groups based outside the province. They are isolated nodes within this network. Whitewater Winter Resort is one of these. Red Mountain, located in southeastern British Columbia near the town of Rossland, was established in 1947. It has been owned since 2004 by a San Diego investment group.[44] Panorama, located near the East Kootenay town of Invermere, was owned by Intrawest until 2010 but was sold to an independent group of investors with ties to the region. Mount Seymour ski resort, located in the North Shore Mountains near Vancouver, has been privately owned by the Wood family since 1984.[45] Other isolates in this network include Mount Washington Alpine Resort on Vancouver Island, Revelstoke Mountain Resort, and Shames Mountain Ski Area in the northern part of the province.

Network analysis highlights several characteristics of the BC ski industry. First, processes of corporate concentration accelerated during the 1990s, but the ski industry is not marked by a high level of economic cohesion. Second, there is a marked divide within the ski industry. The majority of resorts are isolated nodes or members of dyadic or triadic clusters. A smaller number are parts of larger national and continental economic networks. If the globalization of ownership networks is a nascent phenomenon, as sociologist William K. Carroll suggests, the BC ski industry is not yet a major part of this process.[46] For the most part, BC resorts exist within regional, national, and continental economic networks. Finally, in structural terms, Whistler Blackcomb is a central resort in the BC ski industry. Even with the recent restructuring of Intrawest, it remains part of one of the largest cliques in the industry, which is defined by economic ties that span North America. Whitewater, by contrast, is an isolate within this network.

The BC ski industry is also linked to global networks of "tourism mobilities."[47] Tourist flows to the province are strongest from the United States and the rest of Canada. To a large degree, skiing tourism is a continental social phenomenon. Through tourism, however, British Columbia is also connected with the United Kingdom, Japan, Australia, and New Zealand. Local and continental ski resort ownership ties are coupled with continental and global flows of skier tourism. Just as Whistler is more firmly integrated into a North American economic network than is Whitewater, so is it more deeply intertwined with (partially) global tourist flows. Whistler is accessible from Vancouver International Airport and is second only to downtown Vancouver for tourism accommodation revenue in the province, but Whitewater is distant from any major international airport and it attracts relatively few skier-tourists.[48] Whistler is a central nodal point in a (partially) global network of skier-tourist flows, whereas Whitewater is on the periphery.

Skiing, Authenticity, and Sustainability

The Waning Authenticity of Skiing

Histories of skiing frequently suggest that the sport has lost authenticity during the twentieth century. In *From Skisport to Skiing*, the historian E. John B. Allen describes the modernization and disenchantment of skiing as it evolved from a mode of transportation imported to North America by Norwegian immigrants.[49] In his view, the Norwegian ideal of *idræt*, the belief that skiing develops a strong sense of morality, character, and personal well-being, was an important component of "skisport" as a pre-modern social practice. Described as "a life philosophy," it holds the promise of a "regenerating effect on individual body [sic], soul ... and even nation."[50] Skisport (a form of cross-country skiing) prevailed in North America until the twentieth century, when an Austrian style of alpine skiing using a fixed-heel binding and a parallel posture grew in popularity. Endurance-testing cross-country ski races gave way to skiing competitions that emphasized jumping and short downhill races that some see as negating the spirit of *idræt*. The "heady lure of the thrill of speed" came to dominate the sport, and a way of life was translated into "merely a leisure time amusement" as mechanized ski hills and formal competition displaced the more supposedly authentic engagement with nature represented by *idræt*.[51]

According to Hal Rothman, an historian of tourism development in the American West, ski resorts are part of a twentieth-century trend toward the development of tourist landscapes, including Las Vegas casinos, California theme parks, Rocky Mountain ski resorts, and ersatz Old West towns across the western United States. In the process, "places evolved into caricatures of their original identities ... Tourism did not really destroy; it created the new, promised fresh myths, responded to the poignant pleas of a changing culture, in the process making towns that looked the same ... but felt different."[52]

According to Annie Coleman's account, skis first appeared in Colorado in the 1890s as a utilitarian technology used by mailmen to travel between remote mountain towns. Recreational skiing began soon afterward in the Aspen area. For many people, the sport offered escape from industrial modernity and the opportunity to interact with wild nature: "Skiers could enter a landscape that felt wild and natural – they could gain access to something fundamental, pristine, and authentic – and they did it during a century when 'nature' grew both increasingly appealing and elusive."[53] The sport embodied a "natural" freedom that many felt was disappearing from the modernist, industrial landscape of early-twentieth-century America.

In Coleman's view, modern skiing abandoned the desire for authentic connections with non-human nature. Postwar affluence and increased car ownership made tourist travel to ski resorts accessible to a larger segment of the American population. Ski resorts also became increasingly technologized in places, through the ongoing development of chairlift and snow-making technologies. Changes to ski design and lift technology made it easier to ascend and descend the mountain. This broadened the appeal of skiing and transformed skiers' relationships to mountain landscapes. As Coleman writes, "Presenting an empty, pristine, wild, and natural landscape paradoxically became a business, with mechanization not just a necessity but a boon."[54] Images of nature are still associated with skiing, but technology mediates, ever more significantly, skiers' embodied interactions with mountain environments. Contemporary ski resorts are themed, artificial environments, much like Disneyland, and may be thought of as rural, mountainous versions of the fantasy city dedicated to consumerism and "riskless risks."[55]

The increased mechanization of skiing and the parallel development of mountain towns for a "tourist gaze" has prompted environmentalist critiques of the sport.[56] The Earth Liberation Front's arson at Vail resort – where a chairlift, patrol lodge, and restaurant were set on fire in response to the resort's planned expansion into lynx habitat – is the most dramatic example of ski development protest.[57] Pressure from environmentalists has led to a stricter regulatory regime on public lands leased by the ski industry and has highlighted the question of skiing's relationship with environmental sustainability.

Sustainable Development and Skiing

One definition of sustainability is "the notion that an aspect of the environment or practice can be managed into the foreseeable future."[58] This sounds relatively simple, yet attempts to translate the principle of sustainability into policy and practice have often been contested. While paying limited attention to environmental criteria, weak versions of sustainability privilege ongoing economic growth. Strong models of sustainability, by contrast, emphasize the need to make ecological considerations central to economic policy. Strong models of sustainability require the inclusion of social justice as a key component of development and stress the need to redefine development so that it is not synonymous with economic growth.[59] The notion of sustainability may be linked to struggles for ecological well-being and social justice. However, as Laurie Adkin notes, the language of sustainability is easily – and more often – linked to projects of eco-capitalism that incorporate environmental concerns only to the degree that they fit into the ongoing operation of consumer capitalism. Several critics reject the language of sustainability altogether, arguing that ecological well-being is inherently incompatible with the growth logic of economic development. For example, Timothy Luke uses the term "sustainable degradation" to describe the reality of the economic and political policies that emerge from demands for sustainable development.[60] Bearing in mind the inherent limitations of sustainability as a contested and slippery concept, we might speak of a practice as either absolutely or relatively sustainable in the strong sense. In an absolute sense, skiing can continue indefinitely without destroying its ecological basis, or it cannot. Alternatively, we might consider how sustainable skiing is relative to other recreational (mountain biking, hiking) or industrial (mining, logging) uses of the same landscape. In previous work that addresses the ecopolitics of skiing, a division emerges between work that supports the notion that skiing can be a relatively sustainable form of interaction with non-human nature and work that is more pessimistic.

Although John Fry acknowledges the environmental ambiguities inherent in the modern "Disney-World-full-service ski village," he is generally positive about the environmental dimensions of skiing. He writes, "Among the foremost reasons that people give for wanting to ski is the desire to be in a natural environment and to enjoy the mountain scenery."[61] Beyond an interest in skiing as a way of enjoying the outdoors, many skiers also hold memberships to environmental groups. The ski industry trade publication *Ski Area Management* has published research that documents this connection between skiing and environmentalism. Fry uses survey data on ski industry workers, skiers, and environmentalists to compare environmental values among these groups. A large majority (85 percent) of skiers see skiing as an environmentally friendly/compatible sport, whereas a minority of environmentalists (39 percent) express this opinion. Despite this gap, the two groups share several beliefs: that real estate development is a particularly harmful component of ski area development, that existing ski areas should expand instead of new areas being developed, and that water management in ski areas should prioritize wildlife needs rather than snowmaking. David Rockland uses survey data to compare skiers with the general public on their commitments to environmental values. He concludes that skiers rank at least as high as the general public. Neither the public nor skiers tend to see skiing as an environmental problem, especially in comparison with other forms of outdoor recreation (such as golf and powerboating).[62]

Ski resorts in the European Alps have been criticized by local communities and environmental groups to a greater degree than elsewhere. Environmental concern typically centres on soil erosion and pollution of the mountain environment. Otmar Weiss and his colleagues use survey research to examine the relationship between skiing and environmental values in Austria, where skiing is the national sport. Although skiing accounts for half of the country's tourism, environmental organizations target its impact on alpine ecosystems and the urbanization of natural areas that results from resort development. In this research, skiers score relatively high on environmental values scales. Skiers appear to prefer green tourism, yet they also demand all the bells and whistles of a modern ski resort. The authors conclude that the ski industry should pursue an ecotourism strategy by integrating environmental values into its operations. Simon Hudson similarly argues that an environmentally responsible ski industry would look to trends in tourism that consider the "environmental track record of both holiday company and destination when booking a holiday."[63]

Despite several authors describing a convergence between skiing and environmental values, the sport produces its own ecological impacts, including water withdrawal for snow-making, erosion from ski runs, loss of wildlife habitat, and impacts on vegetation. The ski industry causes environmental damage, but it has the potential to mitigate its impacts through "eco-efficiency" and improved management practices. David Chernushenko suggests several courses of action, including limiting new development to address animal habitat destruction, improving ski hill design to reduce impacts on soil and vegetation, limiting snow-making, and using more efficient technology to conserve water and energy. Bob Sachs argues that the American ski industry has been a leader in greening tourism through voluntary initiatives like the Sustainable Slopes Program (SSP), which sets out environmental guidelines for participating ski resorts.[64]

Whereas Sachs offers a positive assessment of the Sustainable Slopes Program, Jorge Rivera, Peter de Leon, and Charles Koerber are critical, asserting there is no correlation between SSP participation and environmental performance.[65] Under the SSP, the ski industry has adopted strategies that are the easiest to implement and that are most visible to the public. As Rivera and de Leon write, "Ski areas enrolled in the SSP program appear to be displaying rather opportunistic behavior expecting to improve their 'green' reputation without actually implementing SSP's [sic] beyond compliance environmental management principles and practices."[66] Ski resorts that sign on to the program are less likely than non-signatories to address issues of growth management, animal habitat loss, or pollution from ski operations.

Hal Clifford's *Downhill Slide* is a particularly damning critique of claims to environmental sustainability within skiing.[67] According to Clifford, a subculture that valued wilderness as an important part of the skiing experience has been displaced by Disneyesque simulations of wilderness at resorts like Whistler Blackcomb, Aspen, and Vail. The increasingly simulated experience of nature through skiing is connected, for Clifford, with skiing's impacts on wildlife through habitat fragmentation, as well as roadkill from increased highway traffic. Soil erosion, pollution, deforestation, energy use, and water use are also among the litany of environmental problems Clifford associates with ski resort operations.

In general, skiers adhere to environmental values, and there is a degree of value convergence between skiers and environmentalists. Sachs, Chernushenko, Hudson, and Weiss and his colleagues see skiing from an ecological modernization perspective, asserting that capitalism can be made sustainable through technological innovation and the transformation of organizational cultures that fail to account for the environment. This suggests the need for the "economization of ecology" and an "ecologisation of the economy," without radical structural transformation.[68] Skiing may be relatively sustainable compared with the extractive development of mountain environments through forestry or mining. Accounts that focus on the environmental impacts of the ski industry are important, however, because they illuminate that skiing is not *only* a non-consumptive relationship with mountainous nature. Skiing also requires the continuous *productive* appropriation of non-human nature. In this book, however, I am interested in how the slippery concept of sustainability is used by the ski industry, skiers, the mass media, and social movement groups. Analyzing how discourses of sustainability are mobilized, interpreted, and contested helps us understand how particular social groups become viewed as legitimate users and managers of mountain environments and to comprehend why certain social-environmental practices are deemed appropriate modes of interaction with mountainous nature, while the ecological and social legitimacy of other practices are questioned.

Methodological Overview

This analysis is grounded in a multi-method qualitative approach that combines discourse analysis, interviews, and field observation. I use discourse analysis to examine the cultural meanings of skiing. Building upon Michel Foucault's work, this approach uses qualitative techniques of textual analysis to examine the social uses of language by documenting recurring themes and systematic exclusions and asks who is entitled to speak through a particular discourse and who is marginalized from representation. It asks how discourse is used – and by whom – to sustain or challenge flows of power.[69] I adopt a broad definition of discourse that encompasses visual images, as well as printed text.

Interviews reveal how skiers interpret their experience. Using quota sampling, I interviewed forty-five skiers in the Vancouver to Whistler and the Nelson regions of British Columbia.[70] Interviewees included alpine (downhill) skiers, snowboarders, and telemark (downhill using a free-heel binding) skiers, but not cross-country skiers. There are three reasons for this. First, alpine skiers, snowboarders, and telemark skiers all use the same mountainous terrain in similar ways. At ski hills, they all ride chairlifts up the mountain and use gravity to move downhill. Cross-country skiers inhabit a completely different recreational landscape. Second, it is often difficult to draw sharp distinctions between ski resort and backcountry skiing in British Columbia. Several ski resorts provide chairlift access to adjacent backcountry touring areas or have a connection to nearby backcountry ski operations (cat-skiing or heli-skiing). Similarly, a significant number of alpine skiers, snowboarders, and telemarkers use both ski hills and the backcountry. Finally, several ski magazines cover both ski resorts and backcountry skiing.

To observe the places about which I write, I conducted eighteen days of unobtrusive field observation, split evenly between Whistler Black-comb and Whitewater ski resorts, between November 2006 and April 2007. Because of the distance between the resorts, I spent several consecutive weeks in each region and moved back and forth between the two resorts over the course of the ski season. This multi-faceted approach embraces the complexity of skiing as a discursively mediated sporting practice that draws together humans, mountains, technologies, weather, trees, and animals.

The Layout of the Book

The four core chapters of this book examine different dimensions of the ecopolitics of skiing. In Chapter 2, I examine how skiing landscapes are interpreted by diverse social actors: the ski industry, social movement groups, and the mass media. I also look at how these social constructions of the mountain landscape are interpreted by skiers. This analysis is grounded in the literature on the social construction of landscape, which focuses on the ways that distinct places are given meaning through social interaction.[71] The notion of discourse is important here.

Chapter 3 emphasizes that relations between skiers and mountain environments are not purely discursive by examining how skiing is a site of embodied interaction between humans and non-human nature, including mountains, weather, trees, and animals. These relationships are also mediated through myriad technologies. The work of Bruno Latour and Donna Haraway provides a conceptual tool kit for this analysis. Notions of cyborgs, collectives, and non-human actants (a term used by Latour to describe the active, but not necessarily intentional or conscious presence of non-humans within social life) emphasize that nature is not a tabula rasa that is constituted through human social action but rather is co-constructed by humans and non-humans. Instead of talking about skiing as a meeting point between society and nature as separate spheres, it makes sense to speak of skiing as a "natureculture" that is constituted by humans, non-humans, technologies, and discourse.[72]

Chapter 4 examines skiing as a site of ecopower relations among humans and non-humans. Drawing on Foucault's notion of biopower, I examine strategies used by the ski industry to present itself as a pro-environmental steward of mountain environments.[73] Similarly, skiers' narratives describe how skiing may act as a "technology of the self" that gives shape to environmental awareness and environmentally friendly behaviour.[74] Many skiers demonstrate high levels of environmental concern and commitment to environmentally friendly behaviour. They also engage in critical reflection about the ecological impacts of skiing's biopower relations with non-human nature and question the ecological legitimacy of new resort development.

Chapter 5 examines how skiing is shaped by the social dynamics of gender, class, and racialization. For example, skiing landscapes may be interpreted as spaces of "white culture," where First Nations are selectively visible through periodic outbursts of resistance to new resort development and expansion.[75] Similarly, an aggressive, risk-seeking guys' style of skiing is particularly valorized, which may devalue women's experience and reinforce the "gendered risk regime" of skiing.[76] Finally, skiing landscapes are constructed as places of rustic luxury, where skiing is linked to a West Coast lifestyle that requires economic and cultural capital.[77] This analysis suggests that power moves through the "capil-laries" of skiing, rather than through explicit acts of repression or exclusion.[78]

Just as each panel of a triptych is bound by its own frame, but all three frames are hinged together and lines within one panel bleed out into the adjoining panels, so the separate chapters of this book are inter-linked. We can focus our attention on one panel at a time to appreciate particular details. However, by stepping back and considering the work as a whole, we begin to see the larger picture. In the final chapter, I take such a backwards step to examine how the separate parts connect with each other. I also consider how this analysis may inform an ongoing political ecology of skiing, which recognizes and takes responsibility for the environmental ambiguities and tensions within the sport.

Skiing Naturecultures and the Mountainous Sublime

2

Skiing takes place on mountains and hills throughout North America, South America, Europe, and Asia. These places are made up of rock, soil, and trees and are inhabited by various animals. They exist separately from the skiers, resort corporations, and backcountry operations that use them. As mountain environments are altered for skiing, however, they become sportscapes that social actors invest with meaning.[1] Ski resort owners and managers, skiers, environmentalists, First Nations protesters, and the mass media articulate different meanings of these sportscapes. These divergent cultural constructions may conflict with each other, transforming mountain environments into "contested natures."[2] Cultural constructions of the environment matter because they define who may legitimately inhabit and use these places. They also identify which social actors deserve to be included in – and which may be excluded from – decision making about the use and management of mountain environments.

Discourse and the Construction of Landscapes

The Social Construction of Landscape

Social actors create landscapes, as they generate webs of cultural meaning that are laid over physical space. By being "interpreted, narrated, perceived, felt, understood, and imagined," social interaction imbues places with meaning.[3] Often a single place carries multiple meanings or interpretations. The version of a mountain landscape produced by a ski resort may be quite different from, even opposed to, versions of the same landscape articulated by environmentalists or First Nations protesters. Furthermore, the meanings attached to landscapes change historically and vary across cultures. As the historian E. John B. Allen documents, interactions with mountains and snow by Norwegian immigrants in American mining towns in the 1800s were tied to cultural norms of *idræt*, which promoted skiing as a means of personal development.[4] However, the spirit of *idræt* is harder to identify at modern ski resorts like Whistler Blackcomb, Aspen, or Vail, which define nature as a setting for leisure, tourism, and consumerism. The analytical task is to map out these constructions: how they come into being, how they are maintained, how they are challenged, and how they lose social currency and fade away.

Social constructions of landscape have often been dominated by the visual senses. The primacy of the gaze dates to the nineteenth century and the advent of British landscape painting, which reshaped the meaning of rural nature. As sociologists Phil Macnaghten and John Urry write, "The English countryside became the 'other' to the urban areas, full of landscaped estates, capitalist agriculture, concentrated wealth and rural leisure pursuits."[5] From this point onward, the invention and diffusion of photography, as well as train and car travel, have reinforced the primacy of the gaze. The camera lens or the window of a moving vehicle now typically frames our experience of nature.

Mountains provide a useful example of shifting cultural interpretations of landscape. For centuries before the romantic era, European mountains were viewed as inhospitable places. As historian Jim Ring writes, most people viewed mountains as "the habitation of gods, demons, witches and trolls; places to be feared and avoided at all costs." The geographer Yi-Fu Tuan similarly notes, "From Hellenistic to late medieval times mountains are shown as bare, sheer, and grotesque; remote, forbidding, and wrapt in mystery." While the Enlightenment made nature into an object for scientific investigation, Enlightenment aesthetic ideals continued to define mountains as unattractive.[6]

Romantic writers and artists – especially Byron, Shelley, and Ruskin – began to transform European and American perceptions of mountain environments by promoting the idea of the natural sublime, which focused on nature as simultaneously beautiful and awe-inspiring. Mountains increasingly became viewed as cathedrals – though cathedrals that inspired fear as well as devotion – begging for exploration. Early mountaineering stories often reflected this religious attitude toward mountains, combined with "a thirst for the awe-ful, the shivering pleasure of being half scared to death" that travelling into a rocky, icy, and barren landscape provided.[7] As mountaineering continued to develop, mountain landscapes became places to prove one's masculinity and national superiority. The work of writers and artists (and later, of photographers) transformed European mountain environments from inhospitable barriers to movement into valued sites of tourism travel. By the end of the nineteenth century, alpine skiing emerged as a means of experiencing the mountainous sublime of the European Alps during the winter.

Tourism has profound impacts on the places where it occurs. Locals and developers actively shape recreational and leisure landscapes to appeal to tourists. As tourists engage with these landscapes, they further shape their meaning. The concept of the tourist gaze describes how places are reconstructed so that they appeal to tourist consumption.[8] The tourist gaze highlights how tourists interact with landscapes primarily as culturally constructed images. Landscapes are places to look upon, rather than places to feel, smell, or hear. As objects of the tourist gaze, landscapes often become sights/sites to be recorded on film or video. Photo and video technologies have "constituted the very nature of tourist travel," as they determine "what is worth going to 'sightsee' and what images and memories should be brought back."[9] At Whistler Blackcomb, the tourist gaze is illustrated by the prevalence of people taking photos of themselves posed with the Coast Mountains as a backdrop, often at specifically demarcated viewpoints.

In his overview of the sociology of tourism, Adrian Franklin describes "tourisms of body and nature" – including sport tourism, food tourism, and sex tourism – that emphasize kinesthetic experience as a structuring force within tourist travel. Franklin writes, "Increasingly in recent years it is their own bodies that many tourists attend to, as tourists ... Tourists are increasingly doing things with their own bodies, with embodied objectives such as fitness, thrill, spirituality, risk, sensual connection, sexuality." Recently, Mimi Sheller and John Urry similarly describe tourism as a performance that joins together tourists, physical environments, and technological objects: "[Tourist] places consist of physical stuff, which is itself always in motion: new hotel developments, airports and roads, eroding beaches and erupting volcanoes, stinging mosquitoes and deadly viruses – a place can bite back." Even photography, a central component of the tourist gaze, is reconceptualized as an embodied performance by tourists. Through an examination of holiday photos in Denmark, Baerenholdt and his colleagues argue that "corporeal work, creativity and the other senses are involved in performing proper tourist photography – whether in front [of] or behind the camera. Touch, talking and body language are crucial to the production of holiday images."[10] Skiing tourism is also about more than gazing at the Coast Mountain landscape. It is an embodied practice that produces pleasure through the kinesthetic sensation of moving downhill through snow. The challenges of negotiating deep powder snow, weaving through moguls, or picking a line of descent through trees, rocks, or other skiers involve skiers' whole bodies in interaction with physical terrain.

Foucault, Discourse, and Power

Philosopher Michel Foucault's key concepts of discourse and power/ knowledge are useful tools for thinking about the social construction of sportscapes, as well as about the power effects of these constructions. Discourse is a central medium through which social actors create, reproduce, and challenge particular constructions of nature. Discourse is *"a system of communicative practices that are integrally related to wider social and cultural practices, and that help to construct specific frameworks of thinking."*[11] Discourse is not limited to printed text but encompasses the visual images found in magazines and on websites, which also create meaning. It is also present in the physical environment on billboards, signs, and clothing.

Discourses are systems of thought, or knowledge claims, that assume an existence independent of a particular speaker. We constantly draw upon them as resources for social interactions with others. In the context of ecopolitics, for example, governments often draw on the discourse of sustainable development to legitimize policy decisions. Conversely, the discourse of energy independence and security bolsters arguments for accelerating oil exploration and extraction. At Whistler Blackcomb, the landscape is dotted with signs that communicate discourses of environmental stewardship through animal habitat management, thereby connecting skiing and nature. As we engage with a multitude of discourses, our sense of self and our group identities take shape. Through engagement with pro-environmental discourse, for example, we might take on the label "environmentalist" as an identity. The discourses about skiing that circulate at ski hills, on ski websites, or in the mass media similarly shape what it means to be a skier.

Power is intimately bound up with discourse and knowledge. As Foucault writes, "Power and knowledge directly imply one another ... there is no power relation without the correlative constitution of a field of knowledge, nor any knowledge that does not presuppose and constitute at the same time power relations."[12] Discursive techniques of power change through time and should be analyzed at specific social-historical sites. At the same time, what is excluded from discourse is often as important as what is included. As Foucault notes, "Silence itself ... is less the absolute limit of discourse, the other side from which it is separated by a strict boundary, than an element that functions alongside the things said ... There is not one but many silences, and they are an integral part of the strategies that underlie and permeate discourses."[13] These patterned silences also create power effects as voices are marginalized or subordinated to dominant discourses.

Foucault's model of power is useful for understanding how skiing works as a recreational mode of interaction with non-human nature. Power is not only a macrosocial phenomenon that operates within the political and economic structures of states and markets. Power also operates throughout a multitude of social settings, such as the medical, psychiatric, and prison environments examined in Foucault's research. Inquiry into the political ecology of skiing extends this analysis and builds on prior research on how social power works through sport and leisure.

Relations of power often do not appear as large-scale acts of exclusion or repression. Rather, "capillary" flows of power operate in mundane, taken-for-granted ways.[14] While Foucault is attentive to the microphysics of power relations, he emphasizes the interplay between localized power relations, which involve individual subjects, and larger-scale operations of power on populations. Microsocial relations of power often cohere and produce "hegemonic effects" that link individuals to economic and political systems.[15] The ability to move between different levels of analysis is useful for understanding how the ecopolitics of skiing plays out among the economic structures of the ski industry, social movement campaigns, media discourses, individual skiers, and local mountain environments and their non-human inhabitants.

This model of power does not view it solely as a tool of control wielded by ruling elites, or a set of dominant social institutions, over everyone else. Power flows in multiple directions and is better conceptualized as a process of ongoing engagement and contestation, rather than a solid structure that, once established, is near-impossible to move. Just as power operates throughout a range of local sites, so do "points of resistance" appear "everywhere in the power network."[16] Foucault uses the term "agonism" to suggest that power relations resemble an ongoing wrestling match, with opponents reacting to each others' movements.[17] Within skiing, this process is illustrated when social movement campaigns question the ecological and social legitimacy of ski industry management of mountain environments. It is also illustrated as skiers draw on ski industry and social movement discourses when they discuss the political ecology of their sport.

Although Foucault is interested in how power is linked to discourse, his model of power is not reducible to immaterial cultural constructions. The body also works as a physical site of power relations. His writing on discourses and practices of imprisonment, for example, is concerned with historical shifts in the "political technology of the body."[18] Power relations produce "docile bodies," which are economically productive and useful but less inclined to political disobedience. Power is individualized through our bodies and is often organized through pleasure. As Foucault writes, "Pleasure and power do not cancel or turn back against one another; they seek out, overlap, and reinforce one another. They are linked together by complex mechanisms and devices of excitation and incitement."[19] This "sensualization of power" is an important consideration for understanding the political ecology of skiing, as the sport is premised upon exciting and pleasurable kinesthetic experiences of moving downhill through snow.

Ski Industry Constructions of the Mountain Landscape

Skiing, nature, and the mountainous sublime

Ski magazines and ski resort websites provide a useful starting point to examine discursive constructions of skiing landscapes. Magazines like *Powder* and *SBC Skier* repeatedly depict lone (typically young male) skiers, positioned against a largely uninhabited wilderness of giant, snow-covered mountains. This construction evokes the notion of the sublime, which Victorian-era mountaineers ascribed to mountains because they embodied a combination of "beauty, horror and immensity."[20] The sublime differs from the aesthetic of beauty, as it holds the promise of "both pleasure and pain."[21] The mountainous sublime of ski texts is certainly beautiful but also encompasses both awe and risk. This is suggested by recurrent photos of skiers arcing through the air and plummeting down steep chutes. These images illustrate how skiing contains elements of "edgework," wherein skiers' "failure to meet the challenge at hand will result in death or, at the very least, debilitating injury."[22] Sociologist Stephen Lyng emphasizes the psychological qualities of the "edge," though recurring images of risk-seeking skiers illustrate that the edge is also a physical place, made up of snow, rocks, and the vertical pitch of mountain environments. For example, the Kicking Horse Resort's website features a slideshow at the top of the home page. Photo after photo shows individual skiers going down steep, powdery slopes. These skiers are framed by a sublime wilderness of snow-covered mountains beneath clear blue skies. The Whitewater website also greets viewers with a photo of a male skier with snow spraying off his skis, leaning into a near-vertical slope. The Whitewater slogan "Pure, Simple and Real," described in Chapter 1, accompanies the image.[23]

Mountains provide settings for risk-taking and adventure, but they are not merely backdrops to the action. Individual mountain landscapes are unique: the experience of moving downhill in Utah is seen as fundamentally different from skiing in the Alberta Rockies. Exhortations for skiers to travel between different mountain landscapes accompany images of movement through snow. As mentioned, early mountaineering narratives described mountains as cathedrals. The following excerpt similarly likens skier-travellers to sages who follow a semi-mystical quest for connection with the mountainous sublime:

> Skiers wander, like a sage from any age, using the forces of nature to accomplish incredible deeds: making pilgrimages, seeking out the legendary and mystical from nature's most dramatic and dynamic landscapes. From Chamonix to Whistler, Tibet to Kluane, and to the Kootenays, ski bums are some of the few in modern society with the faith to follow their personal path.[24]

Skiing landscapes need to be experienced for their specificity because skiing is fundamentally an embodied athletic performance within a unique mountain environment. As Baerenholdt and his colleagues write about tourist places in general, "The human body engages with the natural world and hence produces spaces and places, rather than simply being located within them, or having them inscribed on its surface."[25] An editorial comment from *SBC Skier* provides a further illustration: "Especially for skiers, no visual stimulus of place or conditions is complete without the physical experience in that environment, regardless of whether it's the same physical experience we've had in other places."[26] Even though the physical actions of skiing may be similar, a unique connection is made between skiers and different mountain landscapes, whether in British Columbia, Alaska, or France. The quest to experience different skiing environments also builds on the presumption of a global market in skiing tourism. Unlike religious sages from prior historical periods, skiers' ability to experience new mountain landscapes is tied to their ability to traverse the globe using the infrastructure of contemporary "tourism mobilities."[27]

Dominant discourses of skiing position risk-seeking young, white male skiers as the natural inhabitants of the mountainous sublime. Female skiers also appear in photos, product ads, and interviews, though they typically remain at the margins of ski magazines' construction of mountain landscapes. As a result, the sublime mountain wilderness is defined as masculine space. This echoes accounts of how wilderness has historically been understood as a site for performing a particular variant of masculinity – the male adventure hero who is typically "white, heterosexual, bourgeois, athletic, courageous, risk taking, imperialist, and unmarked" – through sports like mountaineering.[28] The historian Susan Schrepfer describes this as a "masculine sublime," which is created through repeated images of male explorers travelling to new places. Within skiing, the object of exploration is the discovery of new snow and new lines down different mountains.[29]

Images of risk-taking and athletic heroism articulate a form of adventurous masculinity that makes (predominantly white) men appear to be the natural inhabitants of the mountainous sublime. This also recalls Dean MacCannell's discussion of "white culture" as a non-ethnicity that slips into the background and is generally taken for granted. He writes, "'White Culture,' as used here, is the structural ... pre-condition for the existence of 'ethnic' groups. White Culture is an enormous totalization which ... corresponds to the *being* of the third 'person' on the plane of language, and to 'white light' in physics."[30] According to the Canadian Ski Council, 14.1 percent of Canadian skiers do not identify as white.[31] Depicting skiing landscapes as places of white culture and excluding the increasing number of Canadian skiers of Chinese, South Asian, black, or First Nations ethnicity from media representations of skiing is a form of "symbolic violence."[32]

The physical spaces of ski resorts incorporate signs and objects that further imbue these places with meaning. At Whistler Blackcomb, signs, posters, architecture, and sculpture draw connections between skiing and nature. For example, signs point out the boundaries of Garibaldi Provincial Park, highlighting the connection between the Whistler skiing landscape and the protected wilderness next door. The Symphony area of Whistler Mountain provides access to slopes that were previously reserved for backcountry skiers. To draw from my field notes,

> The concept of the Symphony area is "bringing the backcountry inbounds" and trying to create a simulation of the backcountry

experience for Whistler Blackcomb skiers. The skiing here is good – there are large bowls that are not too difficult, as well as glade skiing, with narrow runs cut among the forest. The area also contains several signs about environmental stewardship and environmental education. Several of these focus on preserving animal habitat. Next to the chairlift, a large sign describes climate change as an environmental problem and details how creek-fed micro-hydro is being used to produce electricity used by the lift. Other signs tell skiers that the area has only had 5% of its trees cut for glading to create runs, instead of the 50% that is normal for ski run development.[33]

Whistler Blackcomb designed the Symphony area to feel less developed than the rest of the mountain, in order to give resort skiers a taste of a backcountry experience. However, snow grooming, ski patrols, chairlifts, and heated lodges minimize the risk and discomfort associated with actual backcountry travel. By blurring the boundaries between resort skiing and backcountry skiing, Whistler Blackcomb incorporates an approximation of backcountry nature and depicts the resort as a more natural space than it was before the Symphony expansion.

As animal geographies research illustrates, the meaning of particular places is frequently defined through associations with animals.[34] Animals are symbolically recruited into ski industry discourse to evoke the natural character of skiing landscapes. For example, Cypress Mountain, which is located just outside Vancouver, uses bears as symbols of mountainous nature on its website. The website contains several photos – taken during the summer – of a mother black bear and three cubs that inhabit the forests surrounding the ski hill. A photo gallery shows the bear and her cubs moving in and out of long grass along a hiking trail, eating and grooming themselves. In one photo, a cub stands on its hind legs and looks directly at the camera. These images establish the natural character of the skiing landscape, even though the resort is located at the edge of the Vancouver metropolis. The Kicking Horse Resort website similarly features photos of grizzly bears alongside images of snowboarders, skiers, and mountain bikers. Further connecting skiing, animals, and nature, Kicking Horse is home to a "grizzly refuge" that provides shelter for two orphaned cubs named Cari and Boo.[35]

Animals also inhabit the skiing landscape as ephemeral traces on the architecture of resort hotels and bars. At Big White, lodgings typically have animal names, for example, Black Bear, Grizzly Lodge, Eagles Resort, and Ptarmigan Inn Resort. Fernie similarly invokes animals in the architecture of skiing, where hotels are named Wolf's Den, Bear Paw, and Griz Inn. Both Sun Peaks and Big White also use bears as resort mascots, and their websites include photos of employees in bear costumes playfully interacting with visitors.[36]

Skiing discourse draws on animals as objects of environmental stewardship and management. The following statement comes from the Mount Washington website:

> We operate within a larger ecosystem and should strive to be stewards of fish and wildlife habitats ... There are measures we can take to better understand, minimize, and mitigate impacts to fish and wildlife, and in some cases, enhance habitat, particularly for species of concern. The benefits of these measures include promoting biodiversity and the natural systems that attract guests to the mountain landscape.

The Whistler Blackcomb website makes similar claims about wildlife stewardship and skiing, describing habitat management as part of the resort's environmental program. The Whitewater website also includes an environmental review that provides a virtual census of animals that populate this skiing landscape, including mule deer, white-tailed deer, black bears, grizzly bears, several bird species, and threatened mountain caribou. The environmental review examines soils, forests, waterways, plants, and animals in light of a proposed expansion to the resort. It documents concerns that resort managers plan to accommodate in order to expand in an environmentally sound manner. Throughout these websites, the symbolic presence of animals defines skiing landscapes as natural places and ski resort owners as responsible stewards of mountain environments.[37]

Images of bears, deer, and other animals appear throughout the Whistler Blackcomb landscape. For example, wooden carvings of bears and

Figure 2.1 The bear as a symbol of nature at Whistler Blackcomb

eagles dot the skiing landscape (see Figure 2.1). In contrast to website photos of black bears and grizzly bears, these sculptures make animals appear cute and safe rather than wild. Cute and cartoon-like simulations of bears also adorn Whistler souvenir shops, where they are dressed in Mountie uniforms, placed on T-shirts, postcards, boxer shorts, and stationery. These images parody the wildness of actual bears, but they also link skiing to an imagined version of Canadian nature. Along with magazine and website images of the mountainous sublime, the use of animals as symbols links skiing with nature and defines skiing as a pro-environmental practice within an attractive economy.

Skiing Naturecultures

An alternative discourse depicts skiing landscapes as simultaneously natural, social, and technological spaces, or naturecultures.[38] Stories about helicopter-accessed and snowcat skiing frequently appear in ski magazines, as do references to the chairlifts that carry skiers up mountains. An article on snowmobile-accessed backcountry skiing illustrates the ambiguous quality of the relationship between machines and nature within skiing:

> We are ready to leave, but starting the snowmobile seems a sacrilege. The juxtaposition is a difficult one – a wilderness experience made possible by a shrieking machine – and the price worth considering. Is it worth it to be in this place? We stand there looking at the machine for a moment, knowing the true significance of our experience. Then I pull the cord and we re-enter the industrial world with a two-stroke scream.[39]

The snowmobile is an unwelcome mediator between skiers and the mountain wilderness. Its presence is a reminder that being able to travel into the mountainous sublime depends on the artefacts of the "industrial world" that skiers return to at the end of the day. Although skiing landscapes may be defined as places to interact with nature, there is a tension between this interpretation and the acknowledgment that skiing landscapes are made up of a combination of non-human nature and technology.

Ski resort websites often depict mountain landscapes as naturecultures. For example, the Big White website does feature photos of lone skiers descending through deep powder, though much of its visual imagery shows groups of people posed near chairlifts, or in front of hotels and restaurants in the ski resort village. The website also includes a construction diary (complete with webcam broadcast) of the Snow Ghost Express chairlift, along with a photo gallery that documents the process of constructing the new lift.[40] Construction equipment flattens mountain vegetation and pours concrete to create space for loading and unloading areas. Machines clear a path through the forest to the top of the mountain. Helicopters, trucks, and cranes move large metal posts

Figure 2.2   Glacier Creek Lodge, Whistler Blackcomb

and flywheels into place. Ski resort websites generally emphasize the technologies of skiing – such as chairlifts and snow-making – more than ski magazines do. They also dedicate more space to promoting the built environment of ski resorts, such as hotels, restaurants, and lodges.

The blurring of the social and the natural into a skiing natureculture is further reflected in my field observation. For example, Glacier Creek Lodge is located two-thirds of the way up Blackcomb Mountain (see Figure 2.2):

> The space at Glacier Creek Lodge is meant to evoke a "rustic" feel, with lots of wood (tables, chairs, walls, ceiling, and exposed rafters) and exposed metal piping. Hanging from the ceiling are wooden sculptures made of laminated driftwood that is twisted together. The colour scheme is wood-brown and green, echoing the forest outside.[41]

At Whistler Blackcomb, lodges, restaurants, and other built spaces incorporate large windows that face the mountains, ample natural light, and exposed wood to create an aesthetic designed to blur the boundaries between mountainous nature and built architecture.

The lodge at Whitewater also integrates exposed unfinished wood and large wood beams to produce a rustic aesthetic. In contrast with the lodges at Whistler Blackcomb, here, fewer windows and less natural light create a sense of separation between this space and the mountain environment outside. The lodge walls are decorated with photos of the surrounding landscape, either uninhabited or featuring a single skier, which are reminiscent of the dominant imagery of ski magazines. However, the photos of the mountainous sublime that hang on the lodge walls contrast with ski run and chairlift names throughout the mountain that evoke the region's mining history, such as Sluice Box, Bonanza, Silver King, and Diamond Drill. Old mining equipment also hangs from the ceiling in the lodge pub. Throughout Whitewater, the skiing landscape is defined as not quite a wilderness but as a blend of the social and the natural.

Ski magazines and ski resort websites depict other versions of the ski landscape as well. Several articles and images focus on competition and racing, where the landscape recedes far into the background and the focus is on skiers as athletes. This landscape is characterized by well-groomed runs, rather than the deep, untracked powder of the sublime mountain wilderness. It is demarcated by fences and the presence of an audience. This contrasts with the wide open, uninhabited spaces of the mountainous sublime, where the only spectator is the reader outside the scene. Terrain parks and half-pipes are other versions of the skiing landscape. These are sections of ski hills designed so snowboarders and skiers can perform tricks and stunts, where the technological elements of skiing overwhelm any pretence of wild nature.

Ideas of skiing authenticity circulate through ski magazines. The more obviously human-constructed landscapes, like terrain parks or racing courses, seem to provide a less authentic skiing experience than more natural landscapes. The obituary of backcountry ski guide Hans Gmoser, who died in 2006 after a cycling accident, sums up this theme:

> In the end, to ski is to travel fast and free – over the untouched snow-covered country. To be bound to one slope, even to one mountain, by a lift may be convenient but it robs us of the greatest pleasure that skiing can give, that is, to travel through the wide wintry country; to follow the lure of the peaks which tempt on the horizon and to be alone for a few days, or even a few hours in, [sic] clear, mysterious surroundings.[42]

The emphasis on skiing within a sublime mountain wilderness valorizes a form of the sport that relatively few people experience. Most skiers keep to ski hills, which are characterized by the constant presence of other people rather than isolation, groomed runs or moguls rather than deep powder, and the presence of lodges, chairlifts, and restaurants rather than wilderness. The discourse of the mountainous sublime produces an object of desire. It does not reflect the resort naturecultures inhabited by most skiers.

Skiing and Tourism Networks

Ski magazines and websites connect skiing to global tourism networks. Recent work in the sociology of tourism and mobility emphasizes that "all places are tied into at least thin networks of connections that stretch beyond each such place and mean that nowhere can be an 'island.'"[43] Ski resorts are nodal points in tourism networks, involving the movement of people, money, machines, and greenhouse gas emissions from one place to another. The mountain environments where skiing takes place are never completely local but are simultaneously local and global places. Images of the mountainous sublime, or connections between skiing, nature, and pro-environmental values, coexist with tourism networks that produce significant greenhouse gas emissions and consumer waste. As a tourist practice, skiing contributes to environmental degradation at the same time that it relies on images of the mountainous sublime and presents itself as pro-environmental.

Magazine stories about seeking out new skiing experiences in places as far apart as Chile, Alaska, Finland, New Zealand, and China create connections between skiing and tourism. An article on skiing in Iran from *Backcountry* is noteworthy because it uses the typical skiing-travel format in an unusual manner. By turning a skier-tourist gaze on a place that is often negatively portrayed by the mass media, an alternative image of Iran is created that redefines the country as a site of outdoor recreation and nature tourism.[44] Another story about using skiing to empower young women in the Himalayas similarly makes skiing tourism political:

> Our next ski adventure is one of a different kind. We want to help Dolma in her quest to empower local girls – we want to share our skiing passion with them, and in the process learn more about their culture ... These mountain girls are natural skiers, sliding back and forth, faster and smoother with each lap ... 'This changed my life,' says Dyer. 'We're giving them a glimpse that there's more to life than just getting married.'[45]

These skiers' adventure in the Himalayas is not only about experiencing an exotic mountain landscape. Through the intervention of skier-tourists, young rural woman are taught that there is "more to life" than cultural tradition dictates. Mountain landscapes are often depicted as masculine sites of exploration and adventure. In this article, this theme is rewritten through the lens of Western liberal feminism. This recalls assertions that skiing-travel narratives offer an "imperialistic construction of freedom" for those with the economic capital to become skier-tourists, which is often imposed on local communities in these exotic locations.[46]

Narratives that politicize skiing tourism are a rarity. Skiing landscapes are most often defined as tourist places through a constant circulation of ads for ski resorts, hotels, travel agencies, and rental cars. Ski magazines and websites call on readers to envision themselves as skier-travellers. Ski resort websites also devote large amounts of cyberspace to real estate sales. These large, expensive homes are sold as family vacation retreats from everyday urban life. Terms like "rustic luxury" and "rustic elegance" describe the homes, suggesting that skiing mobility is often reserved for those with excess money and time.[47] The focus on second-home sales highlights the way that ski hill architecture is designed for tourist consumption rather than permanent residence within a community.

The automobile is an iconic symbol of mobility and tourism. Cultural theorist Roland Barthes notes that the car is "the supreme creation of an era ... a purely magical object." Elsewhere, sociologist John Urry uses the term "automobility" to describe "the networks of human activities, machines, roads, buildings, signs and cultures of mobility" that create car-driver hybrids.[48] The notion of automobility emphasizes that cars and drivers are individualized, but also that the shared use of space (highways, parkades) and shared cultural norms connect car-driver hybrids to each other. Symbolic connections between automobility, nature, and tourism are not new. Beginning in the early twentieth century, for example, Ford advertisements in *National Geographic* repeatedly told readers that the "freedom" of private car ownership enabled travel into recreational nature.[49]

Car ads similarly dot ski magazines, calling to readers as potential car buyers. These ads further define skiing landscapes as nodal points within mobility networks. Car ads reiterate themes of athleticism, exploration, adventure, outdoor recreation, and access to wilderness. One advertisement tells the reader how a Toyota SUV makes the "American Wild" accessible. A Honda Element ad shows the SUV, with its doors open, positioned against an urban backdrop. Illustrating how the car works as a "magical object," the viewer is positioned outside the vehicle, which is at ninety degrees to the camera, and looks through the open doors at a mountain wilderness. The copy asks the reader, "Where will it take you?" The car is sold as the means for urbanites to escape their everyday life and experience the mountainous sublime, allowing skiers to simultaneously inhabit the metropolis and nature. Skiing landscapes are depicted as natural environments, yet access to these places is based on automobility networks.

Photography also works to construct ski resorts as tourist places. As Baerenholdt and his colleagues observe, "Tourism and photography are modern twins. Vacationing is the single event where most snapshot images are made, and it is almost unthinkable to travel for pleasure without bringing the lightweight camera along and returning home with many snapshot memories."[50] Whistler Blackcomb, for example, demarcates places for visitors to take photos at the top of Whistler peak and at the top of the 7th Heaven chairlift. Signs direct skiers to the best views of

Figure 2.3   Skiers photographing Black Tusk from Whistler Mountain

the surrounding mountains so they can capture the landscape on film and bring it home as a souvenir (see Figure 2.3). Professional photographers are also available to take pictures of skier-tourists positioned against a mountain backdrop. Ski resort photography transforms the Coast Mountains environment into a site/sight for tourist consumption, thereby transforming local nature into a set of images that circulate within global mobility networks.

Skiers' Interpretations of the Landscape

Reading Skiing Media
Sport-specific media, such as ski magazines, help create a sense of community among sport participants and help socialize new members into sport subcultures. Outdoor sport magazines provide idealized images of recreational interactions with nature. Photos often outweigh texts in these magazines. As Douglas Booth notes in his analysis of surfing magazines, editors select photos to maximize affective response among

audiences.[51] Similarly, photos of skiers plunging through deep powder, jumping from high cliffs, or pausing on mountain peaks call for an emotional response from readers.

Interview participants, most of whom are familiar with ski magazines, support this interpretation of the affective work done by photos. As Shantel puts it, "I go for photos more than anything. If I look through a snowboard magazine, it's for the shots rather than the articles." Billy, a Nelson-area skier, further highlights the importance of visual imagery, saying, "The photos of the big mountain skiing in Alaska, and all of that, it's almost like looking at a *Playboy* sometimes." The analogy Billy draws between ski magazines and soft-core pornography illustrates the importance of the gaze for the affective work done by ski magazines. His observation also points to the implicitly masculine standpoint of ski magazine readers.[52] Whereas *Playboy* presents images of female bodies for male consumption, *Powder* (and other ski magazines) transforms mountains into sportscapes for a male skier's gaze.

When asked for their opinions about ski magazines, a majority of participants (thirty of forty-five) offered some form of critique. Several skiers find ski magazines' emphasis on consumerism and advertising for new gear unappealing. For example, Kristen says:

> And then, there are definitely some magazines that are really just about selling gear and looking good while skiing, and you know, throwing yourself off the highest cliffs possible [laughs]. And all of that, I don't really read those. Like, I'm kind of fascinated by them, in the same way that you're fascinated, you know, by a car crash that you're driving by [laughs] or something.

The routine combination of tourism, consumerism, wilderness, and risk is unrealistic and problematic for many skiers. A common response to questions about ski magazines is to dismiss them, as Gil does, by saying, "They're all ads."

Several participants are also critical of ski magazines' emphasis on risk-taking, arguing that ski magazines create a narrow depiction of the sport through repeated images of risk-seeking extreme skiing. This dominant media representation does not accurately reflect participants' experiences of the sport. For example, Roberta says,

> I do find that the ski magazines, most of them, even *Powder*, they don't ever talk about the more mellow kind of skiing that I feel like I participate in. I feel like it's very hardcore, extreme, and out of my league, and not really even a reality, you know, to most people. But I mean, it's neat, because it's almost like a freak show. You know, it's like, "Holy crap, they're crazy," you know [laughs], or whatever.

Roberta echoes sociologist Robert Stebbins's argument that focusing on risk as the defining characteristic of outdoor sport misses the point.[53] Although risk is present within skiing or snowboarding (and engaging in risk-taking can be enjoyable and rewarding), risk-seeking is often not the most important aspect of participants' personal experience.

A minority of participants respond that ski magazines are too male-oriented or reproduce troublesome images of women. For example, Kristen tells me that ski magazines "kind of interest" her, but she finds their portrayal of gender unappealing because they typically show "guys doing the fun stuff in them and then the girls are mostly looking pretty." Susan Frohlick's analysis of mountain film festivals documents how female viewers distance themselves from routine images of "versions of the hegemonic male adventure hero – white, heterosexual, bourgeois, athletic, courageous, risk taking, imperialist, and unmarked."[54] Interview participants similarly talk about how women often feature as decorations for a male gaze, not as competent skiers in their own right. Peg describes snowboard magazines as follows:

> Snowboarding magazines, a lot of the images of women are not something that I like. They're very derogatory, is that the word? They portray women as sexual objects ... Often a lot of pictures are guys doing tricks and women wearing bikinis.

This critical interpretation of gender and skiing media is consistent with Holly Thorpe's observation that female snowboarders often develop a critical awareness of media representations and challenge the idea that snowboarding is "a fulfilling activity to be engaged in by men and a 'cute' fashion to be consumed by women."[55] However, this critical discourse is not used very often, and it is usually invoked by women.

The dominant media representation of the mountain environment as a masculine sublime is not adopted without reflection by interview participants. Of course, not all skiers are critical of skiing media. When I asked Jason how he felt about ski magazines' portrayal of the sport, he replied, "They portray it not negative, totally positive. Adventurous, free. Exciting sport." Jake offers a similar assessment and reverses the notion that ski magazines glorify risk:

> Well, I like the extreme. I like looking at it. It's beautiful to see people flying in the air. The photography's awesome. It's just fantastic. Why should I look at a photo of some mundane run? So you have to go extreme to really make it interesting.

Participants demonstrate multiple ways of interpreting skiing media, characterized by appreciation as well as critique. As a particularly attentive audience, many skiers engage in "negotiated" reading of skiing media.[56] Skiers draw on their personal experience, as well as their engagement with media, to articulate their own meanings of the skiing landscape.

The Importance of Landscape

The Whistler Blackcomb landscape consists of two large mountains that provide skiers with unobstructed views of the Coast Mountains and the valley below. Whistler Village and the highway are visible from the ski hill, but few signs of extractive development, such as forestry or mining, are apparent. Whitewater, by contrast, is located in a mountain basin dominated by Ymir Mountain. Most Whitewater runs are named for the region's mining history, but that skiing landscape too has few markers of extractive development. Looking at and being within these mountain landscapes is integral to the skiing experience for many participants. For example, Malcolm tells me,

> Yeah, I really appreciate the mountains. The solitude and the scenery, and that feeling of isolation ... I'm a big fan of the landscape. Absolutely. I can stop on the hill and just, you know, stay there for fifteen minutes. Just quietly look around and enjoy the different species of trees, and the features of the landscape.

Donna articulates a similar theme and distinguishes between the skiing landscape and the urban landscape:

> I must have, I'm sure, a hundred pictures of Black Tusk [a prominent peak in the Coast Mountains] [laughs] in different conditions and varying light and clouds and things like that ... It's very rewarding, you know, on beautiful days. You sort of look around and go, "Ah." And I mean, I suppose it would be different if you were looking out, and looking at an urban environment, obviously, buildings ... Looking at the snow-capped peaks and the glaciers is, I mean, it's very enticing [laughs].

The importance of the landscape is often interpreted in visual terms, as the mountain environments of the Coast Mountains and the Kootenay region are valued as objects to gaze upon. This is consistent with the argument that a hegemony of vision dominates our sensual perceptions of nature.[57]

Vancouver and Whistler interview participants are particularly inclined to interpret the skiing landscape as a semi-wilderness, in contrast to the mundane urban environment. This is emphasized by Dennis, who states, "If I was looking at skyscrapers all around me and I was skiing, it wouldn't quite be the same. I'd probably go somewhere else. But, uh, being on the top of a mountain is fully– [there are] few feelings quite like being on top of a mountain." For Vancouver skiers, Whistler Blackcomb serves as a form of "metropolitan nature," which is easily accessible from the urban core and offers "what the visitors believe is an individualised experience of nature as the rejuvenating or refreshing antidote to the city."[58] Several participants interpret the skiing landscape as a refuge from everyday life in the city. This interpretation reproduces a nature-society dichotomy in which skiing is a means of entering into a natural – and more highly valued – space that is set apart from the urban space of Vancouver.

Several participants also describe forests as a particularly salient part of the landscape. Forests are valued as something to gaze upon but are also part of the landscape that skiers may interact with directly by skiing through glades – forested terrain where trees have been selectively cut to facilitate turning – instead of down cleared runs. Several interviewees assert that clear-cuts left over from logging mar the landscape and make it less appealing. Ana describes a backcountry ski day in Goat Range Provincial Park, near Nelson, saying, "Up Dennis Creek when we had a clear view and I could see all the clear-cuts around, it kind of makes me [sighs], and it's discouraging." Traces of industrial forestry are interpreted as a negative mark on the skiing landscape. Environmentalism often creates a dichotomy where relations with nature that involve recreation rather than productive labour appear to be more authentic. Skiers' talk about clear-cutting may reinforce this dichotomy, as skiing is positioned as a nature-oriented activity that is preferable to the forest industry's use of the BC landscape. Cultural boundary-work uses symbols and discourse to create social space and emphasize distinctions between different social groups. In this case, skiers' talk is a form of cultural boundary-work that differentiates recreation from extractive uses of mountain environments in a way that valorizes skiers' interactions with nature, while neglecting the ecological harms associated with the sport.

Most interviewees assert the importance of the skiing landscape, though several describe this as an add-on to their experience. For example, when I ask about the importance of landscape, Gil, a Nelson snowboarder, replies, "Well, it's not the number one factor [laughs]. You know? The ride's the number one factor. That's just a bonus." The pleasure derived from the visual gaze is often less important than good weather (deep snow or sunshine) or spending time with friends and family. The beauty of the landscape does not dictate where many people go skiing – access and cost have more to do with that – but the landscape is an important part of skiers' experience. A few respondents note they had not previously considered the importance of landscape but were coming to appreciate it. Sofia, for example, says she was not aware of how important the landscape was for her experience "until they started building condos in the view at Red [Mountain]. You know?" The importance of landscape may be latent, but when prior conceptions of the environment are disturbed, it comes to the surface.

Ski magazines and websites may construct skiing landscapes for a visual gaze, but skiers' interactions with mountain environments are not only visual. Skiing is ultimately about embodied interaction with the landscape. A recurrent theme in skiing media is that snow, air, rock, and mountains must be felt as well as seen for one to have a full experience of a particular skiing landscape. A magazine story about a heli-skiing trip emphasizes the tactile sensations of skiing:

> Then you ride. Alpine faces, perfectly spaced trees, rolling glaciers, all on snow that rolls at your waist and flies over your shoulders, stinging your cheeks and stirring your soul. You do this over and over until your legs start to quiver. Still the guide and the helicopter pilot have to drag you back to the lodge. Tomorrow, if you're lucky, you'll do it all again. A smile permanently etched on your face.[59]

In another example from *Powder* magazine, writer Mike England further highlights the embodied character of skiers' interactions with the landscape:

> Perhaps most importantly, we understand the inherent irony of our chosen sport – that bizarre combination of ambition and decadence, effort and indulgence, labor and leisure. The bitter cold of first chair leads to an infinite freedom, screaming down the fall line, a magnificent white wake billowing behind. Trudging up a steep, seemingly endless boot-pack, our burning lungs are exchanged for a buoyant glide through the heart of winter. Each run ends in exhaustion, beginning anew as we load the chair or strap on [climbing] skins for another round of tortured hedonism.[60]

Narratives of skiing as an embodied practice, involving the sensations of "stinging cheeks," "quivering legs," or "burning lungs," bring to mind geographer Yi-Fu Tuan's discussion of the limits of vision as a means of perceiving nature: "The person who just 'sees' is an onlooker, a sightseer ... The world perceived through the eyes is more abstract than that known to us through the other senses ... But the taste of lemon, the texture of warm skin, and the sound of rustling leaves reach us as just these sensations."[61]

   In their research on outdoor sport in France, Nancy Midol and Gerard Broyer similarly describe an "intimate dialogue" between skiers and mountains, through which skiers "blend with the environment, become one with it." They further observe that "the sensation of being at one with the environment, and the feeling of entering an altered state of consciousness have become familiar notions" for participants in sports like snowboarding, skiing, surfing, and windsurfing.[62] Skiers' interview talk supports this account and illustrates how interactions with mountain environments involve more than the visual gaze. "Euphoria," "adrenaline," "speed," "flow," and "rhythm" are keywords skiers use to describe embodied feelings of "taking advantage of gravity" (as Maurice puts it) to descend mountains through snow. Roberta describes the allure of the speed of skiing by saying, "I've always loved skiing, and I loved the speed at that age [eleven or twelve]. I was really into the speed. Now, I'm less so into the speed, but I remember the speed and the feeling of the wind, and the camaraderie." When asked what makes up a good ski day, Tim immediately describes the physical sensations of "getting ramped up on adrenalin. Like just getting that euphoria, that sense of joy. It's a drug high, you know?" Ana describes backcountry winter camping as a particularly "amazing" aspect of her skiing experience:

> To really get away and be snow caving out on a glacier and just to have that feeling of being in touch with the outside world and surviving in harsh elements and you're putting yourself even at more risk because you've been walking for two days ... so you're having to be that much more self-sufficient, which makes you that much more vulnerable. Which makes your feeling of [pauses] just the beauty and your feeling of exultedness – I don't know if that's the right word – but that [feeling is] even higher.

Ana's account suggests that the intimate dialogue between skiers and mountains can become more intimate and immediate in remote backcountry areas.

Embodied interactions with mountainous nature are not only euphoric or joyful. Ski magazine narratives balance pleasure and excitement with descriptions of discomfort and exhaustion. Alex, a Nelson-area skier, describes how the mountains affect skiers' bodies as he describes the first days of a new season:

> I mean, gosh, the first day skiing, or the second one after that, I can barely walk. I just feel like someone's beaten the crap out of me. So, it takes me a good week of skiing to get, you know, out of the soreness of just dealing with the vibration, and, you know, having my legs burn [laughs] when I'm cruising down the run.

Skiers also repeatedly talk about the positive value of exercise, exhaustion, and pushing physical boundaries. Kathlyn describes a good ski day by saying,

> I think [it's] getting in a good, solid, long day. And just feeling really exhausted by the end of the day. Um, I'd rather have not very good snow conditions, not very good visibility, and just push myself the whole day.

Several skiers describe feelings of satisfaction when they hike up a mountain to go backcountry skiing. Talk about the physicality of skiing suggests it might be thought of as a practice of "somatic selfhood," which Nikolas Rose defines as a range of practices used to achieve physical and psychological well-being.[63] Skiers' interview talk suggests that – at least in outdoor sport – practices of somatic selfhood are deeply intertwined with the natural environments in which they take place.

Skiers' talk about the exhaustion and the physical effort that skiing demands illustrates how nature "pushes back" on skiers' bodies or "observes and writes us" as skiers interact with the landscape.[64] Skiing-related injuries provide more extreme examples of how the landscape pushes back on skiers' bodies. For example, Natasha describes how she is working to recover from a knee injury received while skiing at Whistler. She says, "I was patrolling and caught an edge, and it was incredibly lame. I was on a groomed run at Whistler. And yeah, I just ruptured my ACL [a major ligament in the knee]. That was it." Natasha is an accomplished skier who is caught off guard when the snow on an intermediate run acts unpredictably, interrupts her ski, and throws her off balance. In his research on the ice storms that hit Quebec and Ontario in 1998, environmental sociologist Raymond Murphy uses the metaphor of a dance to describe the dynamic relationship between humans and non-humans. As he notes, this dance can be "adroitly or ineptly performed," with serious consequences.[65] When skiers misjudge the pitch of a slope or the texture of snow, the resulting injuries can leave material traces on skiers' bodies. Injuries serve as unpleasant reminders of how nature pushes back, emphasizing in stark terms that mountain landscape is not only something to gaze upon.

Backcountry and Resort Landscapes

Ski magazines and resort websites depict different types of skiing landscapes. Skiers also describe different versions of the skiing landscape. Several skiers distinguish between backcountry and ski resort landscapes as places that provide substantially different experiences of mountainous nature. Shantel, for example, contrasts skiing at Whitewater with backcountry skiing as follows:

> It's hard to compare them because, going up to Whitewater, you're surrounded by lots of other people generally. You're riding lifts, so you're not using your own power to climb to the top. You know, you're reliant on something else ... And I get the peacefulness of a backcountry experience over the kind of hectic feeling that ski hills sometimes provide.

Whitewater has only two chairlifts and one lodge building, but Shantel still describes it as a social, mechanized landscape. In contrast to Whitewater or Whistler Blackcomb, the backcountry is interpreted as a place where skiers can find solitude. Dean MacCannell describes the search for authenticity as a key element of tourist travel: "Reality and authenticity are thought to be elsewhere in other historical periods and other cultures, in purer, simpler lifestyles."[66] Ski resorts have become perceived as inauthentic places as they have evolved throughout the twentieth century. The "new Disney-World-full-service ski village" is the model for ski resorts to aspire to.[67] Backcountry skiing is one response for skiers who are disenchanted with the transformation of ski resorts, as the backcountry appears to be a more authentic mountain environment. Backcountry skiing takes place far from masses of people and the technological space of the resort, where chairlifts and lodge buildings are permanent fixtures. It also demands more physical effort from skiers.

Backcountry skiing brings participants closer to an experience with "wilderness," where the "absence of men and the presence of wild animals is assumed."[68] For Maurice, backcountry skiing embodies "the whole romantic notion of just being out in the middle of nowhere." Steve, a Vancouver participant, says, "The other big part of backcountry skiing is just getting out into the wilderness on my own, or with a group of people. It doesn't even have to be a great ski day. It doesn't have to be great conditions. It's just [the] getting out that I enjoy." Skiers list solitude, quiet, lack of mechanization, and the absence of people as reasons for preferring backcountry skiing. Cultural constructions of wilderness may be problematic because they idealize particular places and remove them from their socio-historical context. However, ideas of wilderness remain a powerful attractor for many backcountry skiers who search for environmentally authentic interactions with mountainous nature.

Several interview participants can be described as hybrid skiers who spend the bulk of their time at a resort and occasionally travel to the backcountry; others are primarily backcountry skiers who occasionally visit ski resorts. Despite the cultural boundary that demarcates ski resort and backcountry skiing landscapes, there is not a firm divide within the practices of many skiers, who move back and forth between these different places. Furthermore, backcountry skiing, though not dependent on chairlift infrastructure, is often accessed through snowcats, helicopters, or snowmobiles, all of which consume fuel and emit greenhouse gases, air pollution, and noise pollution. Even where skiers hike into the backcountry, they remain dependent on ecologically troublesome cars and highways to reach backcountry access points. As skiers define the backcountry as wilderness, in contrast to the social space of the ski resort, the environmental impacts of backcountry skiing disappear from view.

Social Movement Accounts of Skiing Landscapes

Environmentalist Challenges to Ski Development

By challenging new ski development on environmental or social justice grounds, social movement groups articulate their own meanings of skiing landscapes. Environmentalists describe how ski development transforms "wilderness" landscapes, inhabited by grizzly bears, caribou, and other animals, into human-centred recreational landscapes. Protests over the proposed Jumbo Glacier Resort illustrate how skiing enters our political ecology. The development would put a new resort in the Purcell range of southeastern British Columbia. Since it was proposed in 1991, the resort has been the object of numerous letter-writing campaigns, petitions, and public demonstrations organized by environmental groups in the nearby communities of Nelson and Invermere, as well as by provincial environmental organizations. When the resort developer began temporary roadwork in August 2008, protesters blockaded the construction site, claiming victory when construction halted. Although the provincial Environmental Assessment Certificate for the project was renewed in January 2009, on-the-ground work on the resort has not begun.

Wilderness is a central theme in environmentalist resistance to the project. Jumbo Wild – a local environmental campaign founded in opposition to the Jumbo Glacier Resort development – incorporates wildness into its name. The website is produced by the Jumbo Creek Conservation Society and Wildsight, environmental organizations based in the Kootenays. The website asserts that "the Jumbo Valley is a rare treasure, ecologically viable despite past and present recreation and industry activity ... In all, JGR [Jumbo Glacier Resort] would absorb 6,000 hectares of public land for redevelopment into a European resort replica." West Coast Environmental Law similarly draws on notions of wilderness as a "healthy refuge" for bears and caribou in its opposition to the resort:

The development calls for two gondolas, an aerial tram, and 25 ski lifts – infrastructure that would take in an estimated 6,000 hectares of critical grizzly and caribou habitat. It is adjacent to the Purcell Wilderness Conservancy and threatens to undermine the Conservancy's value as a healthy refuge to protect biodiversity.[69]

Environmentalists' use of wilderness and wildlife discourse is ironically similar to the mountainous sublime produced by ski magazines and resort websites. Ideas about wilderness environments, including mountains and forests, are socially constructed and historically variable. Ski resorts circulate images of mountain wilderness as they assert their power to manage non-human nature, while environmental groups use similar images to challenge skiing's environmental legitimacy. This illustrates how ideas of wilderness can be linked to divergent ecopolitical standpoints. One discourse links skiing, nature, animals, and environmental values. The other uses wilderness to redefine skiing as an environmental problem, wherein the sport is linked to technology, society, and mass tourism in opposition to wildlife, nature, and environmental values.

Ski resort texts use animals as symbols to link skiing with nature and environmental values. Environmental groups also draw on animals as they describe natural landscapes under threat from ski development. Much of the Jumbo Wild campaign centres on grizzly bears as symbols of threatened wilderness. The Sierra Club similarly attempts to speak on behalf of grizzly bears, wolverines, and mountain goats as non-humans in need of protection from ski development:

> Jumbo Pass has been logged and mined in the past, but is still home to one of BC's most significant grizzly bear populations. Biologists estimate there are 64 grizzly bears – a significant number considering BC's grizzly bears could number as few as 1,000. Other threatened species such as wolverine[s] and mountain goats also inhabit the area.[70]

Jumbo Wild is not the only campaign against ski development wherein environmentalists attempt to speak on behalf of animals. Mountain caribou have also become a focal point in environmentalist campaigns against the expansion of heli-skiing in southeastern British Columbia, where the caribou are endangered. Wildsight opposes provincial government plans to increase the number of heli-ski tenures in the province, which may accelerate human encroachment on caribou habitat. Claiming that it is not opposed to tourism development, Wildsight attempts to speak on behalf of the caribou as it demands "responsible motorized recreation."[71] According to its website, "Wildsight continues to educate the tourism sector and the government about the contradiction between their marketing of 'Super, Natural British Columbia,' [a provincial slogan] and their simultaneous sacrifice of wilderness and wildlife." Wildsight highlights the discrepancy between the discourse of British Columbia as a "natural" place and the risk of increased stress to caribou herds from heli-skiing. This rhetorical strategy embodies what Bronislaw Szerszynski calls an ironic environmental politics, which includes "the rhetorical tactics that are used by environmental protest movements in order to draw attention to that disconnection – when they highlight the gap between 'is' and 'ought,' or between appearance and reality."[72]

Environmental movement attempts to speak on behalf of the grizzly bears, caribou, and wolverines that inhabit the mountains of British Columbia illustrate the plasticity of animals within ecopolitics. As symbols of nature, animals are both aligned with skiing (by the ski industry) and described as threatened by skiing (by environmentalists). As Michael Woods notes in his study of conflicts over fox hunting in the United Kingdom, "While animals are by nature barred from physical participation in the political process, their representations are frequently evoked in political discourse."[73] The question of which human social actors become authoritative spokespeople for non-human animals has important ecopolitical implications. The symbolic constructions of animals that are accepted as legitimate help determine the future of the "flesh and blood creatures [that] do not always live up to their representations" in tourist industry, government, or social movement discourse.[74]

First Nations Challenges to Ski Development
In places like Sun Peaks and Melvin Creek, First Nations groups articulate another version of the skiing landscape. Sun Peaks Resort is located near

Kamloops, northeast of Vancouver. Secwepemc protesters began organizing roadblocks and protest camps against a planned expansion to the resort in 2000. Between 2001 and 2004, media coverage of the conflict over the expansion described recurrent blockades, public demonstrations, and the arrests of protesters by the RCMP. The following excerpt is from the Skwelkwek'welt Protection Centre website:

> It appears that the people of the Neskonlith Indian [Nation] have physically re-established ourselves in the financially wealthy section of Sun Peaks. I know it has primarily been the place of ReMax Real Estate Agents and wealthy home buyers. Did you know that condos go [for] approximately $300,000 and a single family home for $1 million ... What do we get out of those deals, absolutely nothing.[75]

Ski development is defined as an illegitimate intrusion onto unceded First Nations territory. By permitting the resort expansion, the provincial government is ignoring Aboriginal title to unceded – or "stolen" – lands.[76] For protesters, ski resort expansion risks disrupting traditional relationships with the landscape and its inhabitants and should be opposed on those grounds.

The proposed Cayoosh ski resort is another site where First Nations protesters, as well as environmentalists, question the social and environmental legitimacy of ski development. The resort would be located in the Melvin Creek area, near the town of Lillooet, north of Whistler. St'at'imc protesters began using camps and blockades against the project in 2000. Although media coverage of this conflict was not as prevalent as it was for Sun Peaks, news articles published between 2001 and 2005 chronicle the protests and the arrests of protesters. An Assembly of First Nations resolution in opposition to the development invokes St'at'imc claims that they are "the rightful owners of [their] traditional territory and everything pertaining thereto."[77] Like the Sun Peaks protesters, St'at'imc protesters see ski development as an illegitimate intrusion on unceded First Nations lands.

Several environmental organizations, including the Western Canada Wilderness Committee (commonly referred to as the Wilderness

Committee), Sierra Club, and British Columbia Environmental Network, support St'at'imc efforts to claim Aboriginal title over Melvin Creek. The Wilderness Committee website links First Nations political objectives to its own ecopolitical interests in wilderness conservation as follows: "The entire St'at'imc Nation has rejected the industrial tourism ski-city proposed for Melvin Creek as being too destructive to environmental and cultural values." Environmentalists warn that "pristine mountains," an "untouched watershed," and the "wilderness" traditionally occupied by the St'at'imc risks transformation into a "ski city."[78] Environmentalists attempt to construct an ecopolitics that is attuned to ecological concerns and First Nations political claims. By defining St'at'imc territory as pristine and untouched, however, this discourse risks marginalizing the St'at'imc as contemporary political actors by placing them on the natural side of a nature-culture dichotomy. This illustrates how environmentalist discourse, even when supportive of First Nations political claims, risks mistranslating First Nations' constructions of place into an environmentalist framework for understanding mountain environments.

Media Coverage of Social Movements and Skiing

Newspaper coverage of social movement protest further demonstrates how skiing landscapes become contested places. Social movements depend on the mass media to circulate their claims among the public and to gain political leverage. Media coverage circulates environmentalist claims about skiing's impacts on wildlife landscapes. For example, a 2004 article from the *Trail Daily Times* reports on the environmental assessment approval granted to the Jumbo Glacier Resort by the provincial government. The article notes that opinion on the resort is polarized and provides an outlet for environmental discourse that rejects the project:

> Proponents [of Jumbo Glacier Resort] point to the ability to offer accessible year-round skiing on the glaciers surrounding the valley, an opportunity available nowhere else in North America. But critics complain the development will threaten grizzlies and other wildlife, swamp a wilderness area and wreck established businesses that offer other outdoor activities, including heli-skiing.[79]

Environmental critics gain access to the news to shape media representations of the skiing landscape, serving as a voice for grizzly bears and wilderness. News media similarly report claims about the intrusion of skiing into First Nations landscapes. For example, a 2003 article from the *Kamloops Daily News* describes a public protest at Sun Peaks: "Signs reading 'Tourism or terrorism' and 'Sun Peaks kills' greeted skiers at Sun Peaks Resort Sunday as a group protested land claims issues at the village."[80] Another article reports on a protest rally held at a Delta Hotel in Calgary in support of the Sun Peaks protesters. The article gives voice to activist claims that ski development intrudes on First Nations rights and environmental values: "Protesters argued that the expansion [at Sun Peaks] will destroy several ecosystems and is proposed to be on territory that the natives have never ceded."[81]

News stories about skiing and protest do not simply reproduce the ski industry's presentation of itself, as circulated through ski magazines and resort websites. Instead, skiing is linked to tourism and economic development, and environmentalists appear as authoritative speakers on behalf of non-human nature. In 2004, a local Cranbrook paper, the *Daily Townsman*, published an overview of the conflict over Jumbo Pass in which readers are told that the resort "has been at the centre of a long-running storm pitting environmentalists, public opponents and a Panorama-based heli-ski resort against tourism and economic development supporters."[82] A *Globe and Mail* article on the Jumbo conflict similarly positions wilderness values against economic development:

> In an economically depressed area like the Kootenays, it is hard to understand why anyone would be against a project that promises to create 800 full-time jobs, and 1,000 person years of construction work. Could it be that in the vast wilderness around them, the people of the Kootenays see something more important than economic opportunity?[83]

Rather than mediating between competing claims to environmental sustainability in relation to skiing, newspapers often frame social movement protest in terms of environmental values versus economic well-being. When animals enter media texts, they typically appear within the environmentalist discourse of threatened wilderness. Echoing environmentalist websites, newspaper articles adopt the grizzly bear as an emblem of the Jumbo Pass conflict, or use the mountain caribou as a symbol of threatened wilderness in the BC backcountry. Environmentalists often succeed in their attempts to position themselves as authoritative news sources acting on behalf of wildlife.

Through their selection of news sources, the news media create a "hierarchy of credibility," which informs readers who are the knowledgeable and legitimate voices on particular social issues.[84] Media access is essential for social movements because, in our media-saturated social environment, "outside the sphere of the media there is only political marginality."[85] Environmentalists and First Nations protesters are incorporated into the hierarchy of credibility of media coverage of skiing in British Columbia. Prior research on social movements and the mass media suggests that media accounts of protest provide visibility to social movement actors but simplify their messages. By emphasizing the drama of protest, conflict, and arrests, media narratives often neglect the substantive issues social movements attempt to raise. In conflict over skiing, environmentalist and First Nations protesters use newspaper coverage to articulate their own constructions of the BC landscape and to challenge the ski industry's construction of the landscape. This is consistent with Simon Cottle's optimistic assessment that we are witnessing increasingly "variable, shifting and sometimes more progressive alignments of the news media's reporting of demonstrations and protests than in the past."[86]

Conclusion: The Contested Meaning of Skiing Landscapes

Several different social actors invest skiing sportscapes with meaning, including the ski industry, skiers, social movement groups, and the media. Cultural constructions of skiing sportscapes are not politically neutral. They produce ecopolitical power effects, as they define what mountain environments should be used for and who may legitimately access and manage them. As different social groups assert conflicting interpretations of skiing landscapes, these places become contested natures.[87] Discourses circulate through ski magazines and websites, as well as within the physical landscape of ski resorts, which draw upon

images of the mountainous sublime to naturalize the ski industry's occupation and management of mountain environments. This discourse
gives skiing the appearance of being a pro-environmental mode of attractive development that draws tourists to British Columbia without
damaging non-human nature.[88] Social movements similarly draw upon
images of nature as they raise questions about the ecological and social
legitimacy of skiing. These conceptions of skiing and nature influence
skiers' interpretations of the environmental implications of their recreational interactions with nature. If skiers accept the ski industry's dominant discourse, they may fail to notice the environmental incongruities
of their sport. Conversely, exposure to the counter-discourses of environmental and First Nations groups may cause skiers to be more self-reflexive
about their use of mountain environments.

Ski magazines articulate a dominant discourse that links skiing, risk,
and masculinity through repeated images of lone (typically white) male
skiers descending steep slopes within an uninhabited mountain landscape. This discourse creates a gendered version of the skiing landscape
and recalls observations that mountain environments have traditionally
served as sites for performing adventurous acts of white masculinity.
This discourse represents skiing's particular version of hegemonic masculinity. As gender sociologist R.W. Connell writes, "At any given time,
one form of masculinity rather than others is culturally exalted.
Hegemonic masculinity can be defined as the configuration of gender
practice which embodies the currently accepted answer to the problem
of the legitimacy of patriarchy." As Connell and James Messerschmidt
are careful to point out, forms of hegemonic masculinity emerge and
gain cultural currency within distinct social and historical contexts.[89]
Furthermore, valorized forms of hegemonic masculinity often act as
ideals to aspire toward, rather than descriptions of average male behaviour or appearance. Ski texts position adventurous – typically white – men
as the natural inhabitants of the mountainous sublime. This illustrates
how "capillary" flows of power operate within the everyday, taken-for-
granted circulation of skiing discourse.[90] This discourse does not exclude
others from the actual practice of skiing, but it does define who is most
welcome within recreational mountain environments. Risk-seeking

masculinity is the privileged position for interacting with mountain environments, while other modes of interaction with nature through skiing are marginalized and devalued.

Animals are often used symbolically to construct the meaning of particular places. The ski industry uses images of bears, deer, and other animals to define skiing as an environmentally benevolent practice. Environmentalists also draw on images of bears and mountain caribou as symbols of nature, but in a decidedly different way. Grizzly bears and mountain caribou become symbols of wilderness under threat of transformation into tourist places through ski development. This illustrates how animals, as symbols of nature, can be adapted to fit opposing ecopolitical positions. Symbolic representations of animals carry power effects, as they shape policies that affect the lives of the "flesh and blood creatures" that often do not "live up to their representations."[91] The question of who is granted the authority to speak on behalf of non-human animals – government employees, scientific experts, ski industry representatives, or environmental activists? – is integral to the political ecology of skiing. Accepting the notion that ski resort managers are stewards of local wildlife populations suggests a different strategy for managing mountain environments than environmentalist claims that ski resort and heli-skiing expansion risks displacing sensitive species from their habitat.

The creation of cultural meanings of the environment is a process that incorporates a broad range of objects that we interact with. Outside the textual worlds of ski magazines and resort websites, resort owners and managers at Whistler Blackcomb and Whitewater construct the meaning of skiing landscapes through signs, posters, and artwork that appears in ski lodges, near chairlifts, or in gift shops. The Whitewater website includes material on the resort's pro-environmental stance, yet symbolic connections between skiing and nature are rarely made explicit within the physical space of the resort. Whistler Blackcomb, by contrast, expends a great deal of effort creating symbolic links between skiing and nature using several different techniques. Signs point to the connections between the ski resort and neighbouring Garibaldi Provincial Park. The Symphony Amphitheatre area is designed as a simulation of backcountry skiing, with its aura of environmental authenticity. Images of bears, deer, eagles, and other animals are used as symbols of nature on signs scattered throughout the landscape. On-hill lodges are designed to blur the boundaries between architecture and nature. These strategies define skiing as an ecologically sound mode of interaction with mountain environments, while the ecological impacts of skiing become a patterned silence. By conveying the message that skiers' presence is ecologically benign, these discourses work against the formation of environmental self-reflexivity about the environmental costs of the sport.

The construction of Whistler Blackcomb as a tourist landscape is accomplished through the demarcation of viewpoints and photo spots, as well as the presence of on-hill photographers. By contrast, attempts to construct Whitewater as a site for the tourist gaze are less obvious. Attempts to link skiing and nature are also less explicit at Whitewater than at Whistler Blackcomb. These differences in how the two resorts present themselves to the public may be linked. As Whitewater is relatively peripheral to global networks of skiing tourism, perhaps its managers feel less obligated to expend effort forging links between skiing and nature. By contrast, the owners and managers of Whistler Blackcomb may be more concerned with linking skiing and nature because they are self-conscious of their status as a tourist destination. Compared with Whitewater, Whistler Blackcomb is a more developed version of the ski resort as a rural mountainous version of the fantasy city.[92] Efforts to link skiing and nature work to naturalize the Whistler Blackcomb sportscape in a way that is less necessary at Whitewater.

This chapter approaches skiing through social constructionism and Foucauldian discourse theory. This approach can be limited by its tendency to overemphasize the visual and the symbolic. Environmental knowledge may be socially constructed, but it is constructed through interaction with non-humans. Nature and society constantly interact in an ongoing "dance of human agents with nature's actants."[93] Skiers repeatedly describe the beauty of the skiing landscape as a fundamental part of their recreational experience. While the landscape is valued as something to gaze upon, it is also valued as a physical place to engage with through embodied action. Nature repeatedly pushes back on skiers' bodies through exertion, exhaustion, or the discomfort of bad weather.[94]

In extreme cases, skiers' interactions with the landscape produce injury, or even death in the case of avalanche mortality. This illustrates the utility of a materialist constructionism that emphasizes the importance of machines, animals, weather systems, and plants as relevant participants in the political ecology of skiing.

Cyborg Skiers and Snowy Collectives   **3**

It is increasingly difficult to speak of the environment and society as separate entities. As environmental sociologist Raymond Murphy observes, contemporary societies have not detached themselves from nature (as many social science narratives suggest) but rather are "characterized by a uniquely intense interaction between human social constructions and nature's constructions."[1] Murphy uses dance as a metaphor to describe the complex, dynamic relationship between humans and non-humans who are "entangled and affected by the other's movements yet independently making moves that may be either in harmony or out of step."[2] Discourse is an integral component of skiing, as it shapes how participants interpret their interactions with mountain environments and defines who may legitimately manage and use these places. It is also important to understand how humans physically interact with nature through skiing, as these interactions impact directly on the ecological well-being of mountain environments and their non-human inhabitants.

Tracing out the material connections within skiing moves the analysis forward by highlighting the role of skiing technologies and mobility networks in extending skiers' capacities to interact with mountains and snow across a variety of locations. This analysis also highlights how mobility networks and skiing technologies produce negative consequences for mountain environments in terms of energy use, wildlife impacts, and greenhouse gas emissions. The political ecology of skiing is shaped by discourses circulated by the ski industry, mass media, and social movement organizations. It is also shaped by skiers' recognition – or their denial – of skiing as a "cyborg" practice that links people, machines, and nature in ways that are pleasurable but not always ecologically benign.[3]

Collectives and Cyborgs

Skiing forms naturecultures by bringing together humans, non-human nature, and technologies.[4] Skiers and ski resort companies enrol ski gear, specialized clothing, chairlifts, trees, and snow into skiing as a recreational use of mountain environments. The work of science studies researchers Bruno Latour and Donna Haraway provokes a reconsideration of assumptions about environment and society that are inherited through the social sciences.

Bruno Latour's actor-network theory challenges the "modern constitution" that treats society and nature as separate spheres and that works to suppress and "purify" connections between these spheres.[5] The modern constitution produces a myth of nature as a "Neutral Tool under complete human control," where non-humans exist primarily for our exploitation and consumption.[6] However, the non-human world is not as passive as this dominant narrative suggests. Humans continuously interact with non-human nature to achieve our own ends, but humans are not the only active participants in this process. Humans may find, when using mountains for skiing, that snow can behave in unruly, unpredictable ways, as in the case of avalanches, often resulting in fatalities. Taking a less extreme example, variable snowfall from year to year makes a difference in the number of skiers who visit a particular ski resort, thereby impacting the resort's profitability and ability to continue operating. To describe the active character of nature in co-creating the world, Latour refers to nature's non-human "actants," which join human actors as part of a collective. The term "actants" does not attempt to answer questions of intentionality or agency among non-humans. The intentions of snow, trees, or grizzly bears do not have to be gauged in order to appreciate the ways in which non-humans appear as interveners in the social and "make a difference" in our lives.[7]

The concept of collectives is useful for thinking about the complex interactions among humans and non-humans that overflow the boundaries between environment and society. The emphasis is on relationships, surprising and contingent connections, and the active qualities of non-human nature. Relationships between humans and non-humans forge new connections "that did not exist before and that to some degree modifies the original" human actors and non-human actants.[8] Non-humans fill our social worlds, but their presence is often obscured from view in social science narratives. Accounts of *social* facts, *social* structures, or *social* processes create black boxes that make "the joint production of [human] actors and [non-human] artifacts entirely opaque."[9] Just like the black box in an airplane, as long as things run smoothly, no one worries about what is going on inside, but when things go wrong, the black box is opened up and closely examined. The irrelevance of non-human actants has been taken for granted in much sociological research, even though "non-humans proliferate below the bottom line of social theory."[10]

Machines also enter our collectives as actants. From providing us with food or shelter to writing novels or playing music, we constantly recruit machines to achieve our goals. The result is that we become dependent upon – and to a degree inseparable from – the machines that facilitate interaction with the environment and with each other. Latour refers to these relationships as "socio-technical imbroglios" of humans and non-humans.[11] Technological objects, through their ubiquitous presence, "lend their 'steely' quality to the hapless 'society.'"[12] Skiing, for example, requires the presence of ski lodges, chairlifts, skis, and other steely objects, which mediate between skiers and mountain environments.

An actor-network approach is useful because it draws attention to the constant presence of machines and non-human nature within skiing. Cultural representations of nature shape the meaning of skiing, but so does the physical presence of mountains, weather systems, and resort infrastructure. The imagery of ski magazines or websites often obscures the ecological impacts of relationships between humans and non-humans. Opening up the black boxes created by skiing discourse reveals how non-human members of skiing collectives may be harmed through their associations with skiers and the skiing industry.

Haraway uses the metaphor of the cyborg to describe the increasingly blurred boundaries between humans and non-humans produced by modern technoscience.[13] These include the barriers between humans and animals, as well as between the natural, the social, and the technological. Cyborg social worlds are co-created by humans and non-humans. "If the world exists for us as 'nature,' this designates a kind of relationship, an achievement among many actors, not all of them human, not all of them organic, not all of them technological ... nature is made, but not entirely by humans," Haraway writes.[14] To take on the role and identity of a skier, for example, individual humans enter cyborg relationships with skis, boots, poles, and a whole array of other gear and outdoor clothing.

The cyborg is an iconic figure of science fiction literature and film. It is partly organic and partly mechanical but fully neither. The cyborg is often a villainous figure, such as Darth Vader from *Star Wars* or the Borg from *Star Trek*. Haraway's choice of this particular metaphor suggests that the outcomes of blurring society, nature, and technology are not always appealing or benevolent. However, we collectively create and inherit cyborg configurations, so we must take responsibility for them. Haraway suggests this as she writes of "inhabiting the cyborg," which is a figure of domination and a figure that "opens up radical possibilities at the same time."[15] The technological mediations of skiing as a cyborg practice filter skiers' experiences of mountain environments. Michel Foucault stresses the connections between the microphysics of power and the larger-scale hegemonic effects that tie individuals to economic or political structures.[16] The figure of the cyborg skier similarly illustrates how individual skiers physically embody capitalism through their pleasurable interactions with mountain environments. The cyborg skier is inseparable from consumer capitalism and its attendant ecological impacts, which move ski gear and clothing from production centres around the world to ski shops and mountain slopes in Vancouver, Whistler, and Nelson.

Skiers as Cyborg Figures

A range of different technologies shapes skiers' experiences of mountain environments. Mike Michael distinguishes between "epochal" and "mundane" technologies. Epochal technologies effect a profound social change. Examples include the printing press, automobile, personal computer, and Internet. Mundane technologies, by contrast, appear less important, as they are "unnoticed, everyday, always present."[17] For example, Michael describes hiking boots as a mundane technology that enables hikers to seek out and experience the natural sublime. He writes, "Walking boots are, ideally, meant to be invisible, or, rather, intangible ... boots are simple tools that quietly expand the capacities of the body, and thus the affordances of nature."[18] Mundane technologies are prolific within skiing, as skiers use them as extensions of the skiing body. These technologies include skis, boots, bindings, and poles. They also include goggles and specialized ski clothing such as insulated and water-resistant pants, jackets, and gloves; long underwear; sweaters; and helmets or toques.

The history of the mundane technologies of skiing traces back to simple wooden skis used for winter travel in Scandinavia and Siberia four to six thousand years ago. In an early example of the connection between skiing and mobility, skis – then referred to as "Norwegian snowshoes" – were brought to North America through nineteenth-century Scandinavian migration. Skiers used wooden skis with leather bindings and boots to transport mail between small gold-rush towns in Colorado and California, which were otherwise inaccessible during the winter. Skiing was similarly introduced to British Columbia through Scandinavian migration to logging and mining communities. By the twentieth century, recreational and competitive skiing displaced utilitarian, work-oriented forms of skiing. Through changing manufacturing technologies, wood skis and leather boots were replaced by fibreglass skis with metal edges and plastic boots. Leather and wooden ski gear made the sport uncomfortable and difficult to master. As ski historian John Fry notes, "Leather boots were without interior padding or insulation, and toe frostbite was common. Skiers spent hours screwing and gluing steel edges back onto their wooden skis to replace the sections that had been torn off when they hit rocks."[19] Technological shifts to fibreglass and plastic made skiing safer and more comfortable, thereby broadening its appeal. Technological changes in ski gear accompanied changes in skiing technique that also made the sport easier to learn. The traditional telemark turn – named for the Telemark region of Norway – relies on free-heel bindings that hold the front of the foot tight to the ski while allowing the back of the foot to move up and down. Skiers alternately drop each knee to create a curve that guides their turns. Alpine turns, by contrast, use fixed-heel bindings that allow skiers to keep their skis parallel and rotate their knees to initiate and control their turns. The alpine turn is easier to learn and requires less physical effort. While modern variations of telemark skiing persist, alpine skiing has dominated the sport since the 1930s.

Skiers can be separated from the technologies of skiing. Skiers take off their gear at the end of the day and store it until they need it again. The skiing body is not cybernetic in the sense that it is tied up with "bio-medical and chemical methods ... for re-structuring, modifying, enhancing" the body.[20] However, skiers and their gear exist as cyborg entities within skiing discourse and practice. As Iain Borden observes of the connections between skateboards and their riders, "The more proficient skateboarder quickly reconceives of the skateboard as at once separate to, and part of her or his body, and so integral to their relation to the external world."[21] The skiing body similarly depends on the technologies of skiing to engage with mountain landscapes. Skis, snowboards, boots, and poles extend the capacities of skiers' bodies to interact with mountainous nature.

Specific cyborg arrangements between skiers and ski gear produce different ways of interacting with mountain environments. The wooden skis and leather bindings used by early skiers made skiing technically difficult, physically demanding, and risky. Technological improvement in the sport has been a process of making skiing safer, easier to learn, and more comfortable. Instead of viewing mountains as inhospitable and dangerous places, skiers approach mountains as playgrounds or outdoor gymnasiums. Over the past two decades, skis have become shorter and wider, with a more exaggerated inward curve at the waist (the centre of the ski beneath the boot), which facilitates turning. These design features are now standard at Whistler Blackcomb and Whitewater. On the occasions when I observed a skier with older gear, the long, straight skis stood out dramatically, thereby emphasizing how wider, shorter skis have become the norm. Most skiers incorporate the latest technological developments in skiing, opting to take advantage of the increased comfort and safety of the sport.

A dominant discourse circulates through ski magazines that fetishizes relationships between skiers and their gear. A large portion of each magazine issue is dedicated to advertisements and reviews for skis, poles, bindings, and boots, as well as goggles, gloves, and clothing. Ski magazines routinely link high-profile skiers, images of sublime mountain landscapes, and the latest products available for skier-consumers. Ski magazines repeatedly call to skiers as buyers of the latest gear, tempting them with promises of being able to ski with greater skill and speed. As social theorist Zygmunt Bauman writes, "Consumerism is ... an economics of deception, excess and waste ... [For] expectations to be kept alive and for new hopes to promptly fill the void left by hopes already discredited and discarded, the road from shop to garbage bin needs to be short and the passage swift."[22] Ski gear manufacturers and ski magazines call upon skiers to physically embody an ecologically problematic consumer capitalism. Planned obsolescence and disposability are built into the figure of the cyborg skier. For example, an ad for Atomic Sweet Mamas – a ski designed specifically for women – shows a young woman working at Burger World, a fictional fast-food restaurant. The accompanying caption is written in the woman's voice and reads, "You think I like working nights at Burger World? Supersize this pal. I work here because I have to. How else can I afford my season pass? How else do I catch first tracks? I'll admit it. I'm obsessed."[23] The tag line for the ad tells the reader that the skis "won't solve your career problems but will make you a better skier." Even if you work at an uninspiring, poorly paid job in order to afford your skis and pass (and one doubts whether working at Burger World provides the economic means for new skis and a season pass), a new pair of skis will make those first tracks better.

A narrative of technological evolution works through these texts. Ski gear is continuously improving, and skiers need the latest gear to participate in the evolution of the sport. This narrative was picked up and promoted by the ski industry early on. As Fry notes, "The notion that gear was primarily responsible for how well people skied gained traction, particularly after plastic boots leveraged the mechanical power of the lower leg to make the ski's edge carve. Marketers and ski magazines encouraged the notion."[24] In cyborg manner, becoming a better skier is not just a matter of practice and hard work but happens through buying the newest skis or boots. An editorial from *Powder* invokes this narrative of technological progress: "That's the beauty of skiing. It never gets old, never ceases to evolve. Just when you think you have it dialed, something happens – equipment changes, technique is innovated, and just like that a new frontier opens up."[25] The skiing cyborg is positioned as a skier-consumer, linked not only to mundane technologies but also to ski gear corporations. The interplay between microsocial and macrosocial flows of power is suggested in the ways that skiers are tied to globalized flows of cultural and economic capital through gear production and consumption. Michael makes a similar point in his analysis of hiking. He writes, "The pure relation is not simply localized between human individual body and immediate environment – it incorporates the global: boots mediate between distributed heterogeneous networks that encompass globalized systems and the global environment."[26] Flows of ski gear and money connect centres of production and consumption located in the United States, France, Austria, Italy, the United Kingdom, Japan, and Canada.

I asked interview participants how often they buy new gear and asked about the importance of having new gear. One of the dominant interview themes is that new gear is unimportant as long as the old gear continues to work, which diverges sharply from ski magazine discourse. For example, Rosana says,

> I don't really think gear matters at all, actually. And I've been trying to also instill that in [my son]. Like, you see people with gear, you know, they're gear heads. They've got everything, and they're all dressed up. And they kind of walk out of the lodge and that's pretty much it. And I've been teaching for years, you know. I've had pretty good gear ... But it's not at all about the gear, as long as you're warm and comfortable.

Kristen provides another example of this theme, emphasizing that she buys her ski gear used in order to save money:

> Well, I'm only on my second set [of gear] ... And I've never bought
> anything brand new. Everything is from the gear swap. And it's all
> as cheap as possible. For me it's not about having the latest, greatest
> technology.

Skiers who invoke this theme have a utilitarian relationship to their gear.
Several also mention the financial costs of new gear as a barrier to up-
grading as often as they would like. This is illustrated in Malcolm's
comment:

> I try to milk my gear to the bitter end, man. But recently, I invested
> a lot of money in very good gear, because I've never had very good
> gear before [laughs]. Those boots, for example, I'll probably have
> them for the rest of my life, unless something seriously wrong hap-
> pens with them. My skis I've had five years. I'm very happy with them.
> I will probably ski them until they break, basically. You know, there's
> an economic reality there, too.

This discourse challenges ski magazine narratives of technological
progress and illustrates how skiers negotiate the media discourses of
their sport. Even if skiers are called on by magazines and websites to
imagine themselves as skier-consumers, this process is often unsuccess-
ful. For these skiers, the human body is more important than its technological counterparts, and the technological mediations between skiers
and nature are downplayed rather than valorized.

Another theme from the interviews resonates with the ski magazine
discourse of technological evolution. Having current gear is important
because technological change produces improved cyborg skiers. For
example, Donna says,

> I want to be able to perform well. And if having something newer,
> like obviously when the shaped skis first came in, with some side-cut,
> that obviously– and the shorter length now, of course. And they still
> seem to be getting shorter. If that's going to make me ski better, then
> of course I'm going to be interested in something like that.

Donna interprets changes to ski gear as creating more rewarding interactions with mountain environments. Jake provides another example of this theme:

> Every time I get a pair of skis, they're better, and they work better. And now these that I have here were $1,150, but I got them for three and a quarter. They're Atomics ... they're fantastic. They get wider, and they carve better. These things weigh a ton. Must be fifteen pounds. They sit in that snow, boy, you know, boom, they're awesome.

If the previous discourse, of new gear as unimportant, is human-centred in its attitude toward skiing technologies, the discourse articulated by Donna, Jake, and other skiers embraces skiing as a cyborg practice. Rather than creating a barrier between skiers and mountainous nature, new technologies enhance skiers' abilities to connect with non-human nature. This perspective neglects the ecological impacts of the economy of excess and waste integral to the cycle of continually producing, marketing, and disposing of new skiing technologies.[27]

Machines and the Nature of Skiing

Shaping and Moving through Skiing Sportscapes

Ski resorts use a range of technologies to reshape mountain environments and facilitate skiers' movement through these places. Snow-grooming machines smooth out snow and create a more even surface for skiers to navigate. Avalanche-control explosives are used to remove dangerous loads of snow and ice and reduce skiers' risk. Mountain forests are logged and gladed (selectively logged rather than clear-cut) to create skiable terrain. Unlike Whitewater, Whistler Blackcomb employs snow-making machines, especially at lower elevations, to shape the skiing landscape so lower portions of the mountains can stay open beyond the season permitted by weather. Snow-making also provides snow when weather is non-cooperative throughout the regular season. Much of the "techno-natural" creation of the skiing landscape occurs off-stage, so that skiers arrive at a mountain that is preformed for their recreation.[28] Trees are cut outside the ski season; snow grooming takes place during the night. The process of transformation is black-boxed, so the skiing landscape appears natural, rather than the result of active construction by ski resort companies.

Another set of machines, including gondolas, chairlifts, and T-bars, provides movement through the skiing landscape. Chairlifts are the most prevalent of these technologies of mobility. They have bench seats and are suspended above the ground by a cable, which is moved by large flywheels at each end of the lift. They carry between two and six skiers per chair. Gondolas, enclosed cabins suspended from cables above the ground, are generally larger and hold more skiers than chairlifts. They are used for longer ascents at large mountains. T-bars, which are increasingly rare at North American resorts, move skiers along the ground over shorter distances than those covered by chairlifts or gondolas. Each bar pulls two skiers, standing upright on skis or snowboards, up a slope.

At Whistler Blackcomb, thirty-eight lifts provide access to over 3,000 hectares of skiable terrain. To go from the village to the top of either Whistler (an elevation gain of 1,530 metres) or Blackcomb (an elevation gain of 1,609 metres) takes at least two, if not three or four, lifts. Most of these are newer, high-speed quad (four-person) chairlifts (see Figure 3.1). The mountain has a few older, slower chairlifts, as well as T-bars that provide access to glacier terrain. Whitewater, by contrast, has two older, relatively slow chairlifts, as well as a short rope tow for beginning skiers (see Figure 3.2). These lifts give Whitewater an archaic feel and embody the slow pace of this resort compared with the busy environment of Whistler. At both mountains, skiers can see chairlifts from most of the skiable terrain. This contrasts with images of uninhabited mountains that circulate through ski magazines and websites. The techno-natural reality of skiing is that skiers' ability to engage with mountain environments depends on lift infrastructure, resort labour, and a continuous flow of energy.

Chairlifts remove the need to climb up mountains before skiing down. Other technologies of mobility include the snowmobiles used by resort workers, particularly when carrying equipment like bamboo poles and

Figure 3.1   The chairlift as a technology of mobility, Whistler Blackcomb

Figure 3.2   The chairlift as a technology of mobility, Whitewater

plastic fencing used to mark off closed terrain or racing areas. Ski patrollers and first aid attendants also use snowmobiles to reach injured skiers and take them down the mountain for medical attention. In extreme situations, helicopters are used to search for skiers who have become lost (e.g., by travelling out of bounds) or to evacuate injured skiers from terrain that is too steep or precarious for snowmobiles. Outside the boundaries of ski resorts, many skiers use snowmobiles to access backcountry terrain. Most professional backcountry guiding operations similarly rely on snowcats and helicopters to access their tenure areas.

During my interviews with skiers, participants repeatedly talked about the chairlifts that enable them to access terrain at ski resorts. They also discuss the snowmobiles, helicopters, and snowcats that provide backcountry access. Skiers often invoke these technologies of mobility when talking about skiing's negative environmental impacts. A recurrent theme focuses on the energy required to power these machines and the pollution they produce. For example, Maurice is a skier in the Nelson region who prefers backcountry skiing because of the opportunities it offers beyond the boundaries of the ski resort. Early in our conversation, he tells me, "Right from age sixteen, I knew I wanted to backcountry ski. Because then you have limitless terrain. I really felt that Whitewater, even though there was lots of places to hike to [outside ski hill boundaries], I felt like it was pretty small. And I got pretty tired of it." He acknowledges the environmental impact of his snowmobile, which allows him to extend his experience beyond the resort sportscape:

> It's become a very hip thing to do. Backcountry ski. To own a sled. And it's an issue in terms of noise pollution, air pollution. So yeah, currently I have this gas-spewing machine that I probably fill up the tank six times a winter. Maybe eight times a winter. So, thirty litres about per tank, you know. That's a fair [amount] of fossil fuel. And there's the side of it that's guilty. Guilty pleasure kind of thing.

Later, when I ask if he would describe himself as an environmentalist, Maurice replies, "I have environmentalist tendencies, and I make a lot of choices that would reflect that. But not all my choices. If I was truly an environmentalist, would I own a Ski-Doo?" This response illustrates a tension between espousing a pro-environmental standpoint and simultaneously relying on a "gas-spewing machine" to access the backcountry. Maurice illustrates how skiers may embody a "disconnection between private belief and public behaviour" that characterizes ecological irony.[29]

When I ask Jason, a Whistler Blackcomb skier with limited backcountry experience, whether skiing is an environmentally friendly activity, he immediately turns to the impacts of snowmobiles used for backcountry access:

> *Interviewer:* So do you think of skiing as an environmentally friendly activity?
> *Participant:* If it doesn't include snowmobiling, yeah. Like snowmobile access would kind of defeat that.
> *Interviewer:* Right. So why is that?
> *Participant:* Oh, snowmobiles pollute like hell. They're awful polluters. A lot of people want to use snowmobiles to get access. But skiing on its own? Uh, the big issue is using a chairlift. It's diesel powered. Or electrical powered. But besides that, it's probably one of the more pure sports you can do.

Although Jason cites both snowmobiles and chairlifts for their energy consumption, he defines snowmobiles as worse for the environment than chairlifts. By distancing skiing from the issue of energy use, he asserts that it is "one of the more pure sports" that can be done to interact with nature. In order to define the sport as ecologically benign, he first has to "purify" the necessary connections between human skiers and the technologies of mobility that provide access to mountainous nature.[30] Jason alludes to the ecological irony inherent in skiing but, unlike Maurice, he does not implicate himself in his account of skiing's negative environmental impacts.

Another recurring theme focuses on the impact that snowmobiles and helicopters have on wildlife in the backcountry. Peg voices her frustration with the expansion of heli-skiing because of its impact on endangered mountain caribou:

But here, especially, the helicopter skiing, and the fact that Canadian Mountain Holidays has, basically, practically free rights to Crown land while we have a species, the mountain caribou, that's on the brink of extinction – like, how those can be happening at the same time is infuriating.

Peg's comments draw out a point of tension between skiing and environmental values. The same technologies that facilitate skiers' interactions with nature create environmental problems, as they risk expelling sensitive animal species from skiing collectives.

Skiing technologies, like many technologies, often produce unintended ecological consequences. Snowmobiles, chairlifts, helicopters, and snowcats enable skiers to enter mountain environments, but they depend on environmental withdrawals of fossil fuel or hydroelectric power, as well as environmental additions of greenhouse gas emissions and noise pollution.[31] This environmental ambiguity passes largely unacknowledged by ski magazines and resort websites, or even by environmental organization websites. However, this ambiguity is recognized and articulated by many skiers as they reflect on the political ecology of their sport.

Cellphones and Cameras as Technologies of Skiing

Although not essential to the sport, cellphones and cameras are incorporated as technologies of skiing by many skiers. Like ski gear or clothing, these are personal technologies that extend the capacities of skiers' bodies and mediate their perceptions of mountain environments. Skiers use cellphones and short-distance radios to communicate with each other across the mountain landscape. While riding chairlifts or in lodges, skiers talk with friends and family members about where they have skied, where they should meet, which runs are in good shape, and which chairlifts are more or less crowded. These communication technologies shape skiers' use of their environment by effectively shrinking the mountain sportscape and making it easier to navigate from one place to another. Cellphones and radios may also cause skiers to disengage from their immediate surroundings. At Whistler Blackcomb, for example, I watched from a chairlift as a young woman attempted to carry on a phone conversation while she slowly skied down a run, holding her cellphone in one hand and both poles in the other. In his examination of tourism in Wales, Mike Michael claims that the "cellphone-in-the-countryside" produces ironic spatialities that blur the boundaries between rural/natural and urban/technological. He writes, "On one level it is claimed that 'the cellphone-in-the-countryside' disrupts the countryside by importing urban values; on another level, tourists from the city are a source of revenue that makes such a countryside 'sustainable.'"[32] Particularly among skiers from Vancouver and Whistler, cultural boundary-work separates the skiing landscape from the urban spaces of Vancouver. However, the presence of cellphones and radios within the skiing landscape works against the idea that skiing offers a respite from urban lifestyles. Cellphones, which are particularly visible at Whistler Blackcomb, alter skiers' perception of mountain environments. As skiers expect the same ability to communicate with friends or family they take for granted in the city, any sense of the mountains as sublime nature becomes elusive.

Cameras also appear as technologies of skiing, particularly at Whistler Blackcomb. According to John Urry and Jonas Larsen, photography is central to the transformation of physical environments into sights/sites for the tourist gaze.[33] Skiers routinely take photos of themselves and each other, with the Coast Mountains landscape in the background. This is particularly evident at the top of the Peak Chair on Whistler, where skiers can look out at Black Tusk peak in Garibaldi Provincial Park, or at the top of the 7th Heaven chairlift on Blackcomb. Skiers also have their photos taken next to the Experts Only signs positioned at the top of double-diamond runs (the most advanced terrain). The technological mediations of photography alter our relationships with non-human nature. Through photography, "nature has been transformed into diverse and collectable spectacles. Nature thus comes to be divided up and collected by the sightseer as a set of discrete, atomised sights."[34] Skiing is not reducible to the visual consumption of nature, as its appeal is based on embodied interaction with mountains and snow. The prevalence of cameras, however, illustrates how mountain environments become objects for the skiers' gaze. At Whistler Blackcomb, cameras reframe the Coast Mountains and freeze them as mementos that skiers circulate through tourism mobility networks.

Automobility Networks

Car ads in ski magazines link skiing, tourism, and mobility by promising access to mountainous nature. Skiing also depends on physical networks of automobility, which are made up of vehicles, drivers, roads, and parking lots that come together as a socio-technical system.[35] Automobility permits the movement of people from place to place, for work or leisure, but it is also "interconnected with other mobile systems that organise flows of information, population, petroleum oil, risks and disasters, images and dreams."[36]

In the first half of the twentieth century, skiers typically relied on train travel to reach ski resorts from urban areas. The rapid spread of highways and car ownership in the second half of the twentieth century encouraged increasing numbers of North Americans to leave cities to get back to nature through camping, fishing, hiking, and other forms of outdoor recreation. The growth of automobility also facilitated the expansion of ski resort infrastructure throughout western North America. Automobility networks continue to provide the primary means of access to ski resorts. They connect local mountain environments to nearby towns and cities (Vancouver and Squamish near Whistler; Nelson near Whitewater) and to the world beyond. As "magic objects," cars transport skiers between mundane urban places of work and rural places of recreation.[37] Cars also work as signifiers of the economic capital necessary to participate in skiing. Lexus, Porsche, and Mercedes cars and SUVs bearing British Columbia, Washington, or Alberta licence plates regularly travel the highway between Vancouver and Whistler Blackcomb. Limousines modelled after SUVs also transport wealthier tourists from Vancouver International Airport to the mountains.

A large amount of space at Whitewater and Whistler Blackcomb is dedicated to parking lots (see Figure 3.3). A series of unpaved lots, used primarily by day visitors, surrounds Whistler Village, and underground parking is available for hotel guests. Another set of parking lots is located near the Excalibur Gondola at the base of Blackcomb Mountain. A

Figure 3.3   Skiing and automobility, Whitewater

covered parkade serves the Creekside Gondola, a few kilometres south of Whistler Village. Whitewater resort has three parking lots, two of which are close to the Silver King chairlift and lodge building. The third, an overflow lot for busy days, is close to the cross-country ski trails adjacent to the resort. Although school buses and charter buses are visible at both places, private cars dominate the parking lots that flank the ski resorts. These parking lots are nodal points in automobility networks, where movement comes to a pause for several hours.

Parking lots at Whistler Blackcomb are located at the edges of the skiing landscape or beneath hotels in order to maintain the pedestrian-oriented design of Whistler Village. Despite the skiing landscape being made accessible through automobility, this connection is black-boxed at Whistler, where cars are kept to the margins of the village. This recalls

William Philpott's history of Vail, Colorado, where resort development was premised on the ability to build new highway infrastructure to provide easier access to tourists.[38] At the same time, cars were limited to the margins of the resort to give visitors the impression of a European alpine village. The layout of parking lots at Whistler Blackcomb purifies the pedestrian-oriented village from the reality of skiers' reliance on cars, highways, and their associated ecological impacts.

Cars and highways link local ski resorts to broader tourism networks. The Sea to Sky Highway connects Whistler Blackcomb to Vancouver and its international airport. The highway is an important part of the experience of skiing at Whistler Blackcomb. As historian Doreen Armitage notes, the highway has "been labelled everything from one of the great scenic highways of the world to British Columbia's Killer Highway, infamous for its rockfalls, floods, debris torrents and car accidents."[39] Highway 3 similarly connects Whitewater to the nearby community of Nelson and the regional airport in Castlegar. Through these cities and their associated airports, local mountain environments join global systems of aeromobility that bring tourists from the United States, the United Kingdom, Japan, and Australia.[40]

Skiers often describe their car use as a point of tension between their identity as skiers and their environmental values. Automobility networks permit skiers to interact with non-human nature, as they connect skiers who live in Vancouver or Nelson to Whistler Blackcomb or Whitewater, or to backcountry access points in the Coast Mountains or the West Kootenay region. The car is, for most, an essential technology of skiing. Donna describes this connection with reference to the Sea to Sky Highway:

> In a way, it's almost the people coming up [to Whistler] here in the vehicles [that's the biggest environmental impact]. I mean, on weekends it's like a snake of traffic of people accessing the area.

Several participants view these connections with automobility as environmentally troublesome because of the role automobility plays in global climate change. Allison says,

> Well, we drive [laughs] to get there. And we drive far distances. And that's not environmentally sustainable at all. Like, there's no way we're within our footprint if we're doing that. Like, if we wanted to be environmentally sustainable, we'd take the bus and go skiing at Grouse [instead of driving to Whistler].

A self-identified environmentalist, Allison highlights how skiers' choices to ski a bigger mountain with more terrain are linked to active decisions to participate in automobility. Her self-conscious laughter highlights the irony inherent in her response, in Szerszynski's sense, as she demonstrates an awareness of the contradictions between espousing pro-environmental beliefs and engaging in environmentally harmful behaviour.[41] As Allison notes, the North Shore ski resorts, including Grouse Mountain, Mount Seymour, and Cypress Mountain, are close to Vancouver and are accessible by public transit. These mountains do not, however, offer the amount and variety of terrain found at Whistler Blackcomb. Cypress Mountain, the largest of the North Shore ski hills, has fifty-two runs, a 610-metre vertical rise (the distance from the base of the chairlift to the peak), and nearly 250 hectares of skiable terrain. Whistler Blackcomb, by contrast, has over two hundred runs (on two separate mountains), a 1,530-metre vertical rise on Whistler Mountain and a 1,609-metre vertical rise on Blackcomb Mountain, and almost 2,000 hectares of skiable terrain. For many skiers, the attraction of a larger mountain with more terrain accentuates the ecological ironies already inherent in the sport.

Several interview participants try to mitigate the impacts of their reliance on cars by adjusting their everyday behaviour. Strategies for doing this include carpooling, car sharing, or buying a more fuel-efficient vehicle. For example, Frank describes his strategy for reducing the harmful effects of his car use:

> I car-share. I don't own a vehicle. Like, I car-share with another friend and [clears throat] we hardly use it. It's just to get out of town. But the ironic thing is, the one time I am driving, it is to go skiing [laughs], right? In the winter. And it's an SUV. It's a big vehicle, so we can fit lots of gear and lots of people. Um, you know, and it's been sitting

for two weeks; I haven't used it. But if I want to go skiing this weekend, we're going to use it.

Frank uses the word "ironic" to describe his car use, which is limited to
travelling out of the city to go skiing. While he describes car sharing as
a pro-environmental strategy, his laughter suggests an awareness of the
contradictions inherent in his standpoint as a skier who relies on automobility networks and who defines himself as someone who tries to
"lead my life in a way that has [as] minimal [an] ecological impact as
possible." Jeffrey provides another example of attempting to mitigate
the relationship between skiing and automobility, saying, "I bought a
Smart car because of the environment. And it's about the minimum
amount of fuel I can burn. So I'm willing to put my money into that ...
I'm quite aware of the environment and willing to put some effort into
maintaining it."

Skiing depends on technologies of mobility, as they provide skiers
with access to mountain environments. Automobility networks require
large-scale natural resource use for cars, roads, and other infrastructure,
while producing air pollution and greenhouse gases that contribute to
global climate change. The relationship between skiing and automobility
results in an environmental ambiguity that skiers notice, though it is
typically ignored in the ski industry's presentation of itself as a pro-
environmental manager of mountain environments. Although some
skiers manage the negative environmental impacts of their car use
through car sharing or carpooling, these individual responses are constrained by the path dependence of established automobility networks.[42]

Nature's Actants: Weather Talk and Animal Encounters

Weather Talk

In British Columbia, Pacific and Arctic weather systems provide the
snow that is essential to skiing, as well as wind and rain. Weather shapes
skiers' interactions with mountain environments in profound ways. Soft,
fresh snow makes it easier to turn skis or a snowboard and get down the
hill. When the snow is deep and light (with a relatively low moisture

content), as it often is after a storm at Whitewater, it gives one the sensation of floating. Deep snow also presents challenges, as it requires that skiers put their weight further back in the heels of their boots to keep the tips of the skis out of the snow. When snow is deep and heavy (with a relatively high moisture content), which is often the case in coastal regions like that of Whistler Blackcomb, it takes more leg strength to turn the skis. After several days without fresh snow, slopes can become compacted and icy, demanding more effort to dig in the edges of skis to make turns. Rain or freezing rain can soak through outerwear, making it difficult to see through goggles or making chairlift rides miserable. Weather conditions also dictate what terrain is skiable. For example, the steep, avalanche-prone slopes of Powder Keg Bowl or Ymir Peak at Whitewater become dangerously unskiable immediately after a large snowfall.

Ski magazines and websites circulate idealized images of mountains covered in deep blankets of snow beneath blue skies and sunshine. Weather talk permeates chairlift, ski lodge, and pub conversations among skiers. Weather talk turns on how much snow the mountain has and whether it is dry, wet, light, heavy, crusty, or chunky. Skiers lament prolonged absences of snow or describe how wonderful it feels to be in the mountains on a sunny day. My field notes illustrate the force of snow, wind, and rain on a March day at Whistler Blackcomb:

> There was 15 centimetres of snow overnight, which brought out a large crowd early in the day. By early morning, however, the freezing level (where snow gives way to rain) had almost reached the top of the mountain. It rained off and on, heavy at times, and was mixed with occasional freezing rain and snow as well. Because of warm temperatures and rain, the snow was wet and sticky, making it quite difficult to control turns. Due to high wind, the alpine T-bars never opened, nor did access to Blackcomb Glacier or Spanky's Ladder. During the last couple of runs of the day, I saw almost no one else on the mountain, which was a sharp contrast to the busy lift lines at the beginning of the day. Weather was the major subject of skiers' talk on the lifts, at the lodge, and at Merlins Bar and Grill, at the base

of Blackcomb, after skiing. Most of the discussion I overheard focused on how bad the conditions and weather were.[43]

Overnight snowfall draws skiers out to the mountains. However, on this particular day, new snow was followed by rain, giving Whistler Blackcomb the feeling of a ghost town. At the same time, high winds were a particularly unruly actant and prevented lifts from operating. This field note excerpt highlights how skiers' experience of nature is shaped not only by cultural representations of the sport, which typically depict skiing landscapes as sunny and coated with deep snow. Embodied interactions with non-human nature, which do not always conform to cultural representations, also influence skiers' knowledge of mountain environments.

Weather is a central element of skiers' narratives of their sport. Most skiers describe new snow as their ideal conditions, though sunshine can make up for a lack of fresh snowfall. There is a palpable sense of excitement in chairlift lines early in the morning after a large snowfall. At Whitewater, I heard this referred to as powder panic (see Figure 3.4). When there is lots of new snow, the soundscape of the hill is punctuated by shouts of joy. When it has not snowed for several days, however, the landscape can feel strangely silent.

When asked what makes for a good skiing day, Rosana's reply is brief and to the point: "Powder [laughs]. Deep, lots of powder. Light." Answering the same question, Lou echoes the discourse of deep snow and clear skies found in ski magazines and on ski websites. "Well, a great ski day would be deep, light powder, on a bright sunny day. That would be the best thing." The ideal for most participants is sunshine and good snow, a phrase invoked repeatedly. When prompted to define good snow, skiers' answers are remarkably consistent. Kristen says, "Good snow? ... I would describe it as soft and fluffy, like a pillow. But not too deep, so that if you fall it doesn't hurt but it's still easy to get back up. And yeah, just snow that kind of flies around you as you ski down it." Frank invokes Whistler Blackcomb advertisements as a resource most people around Vancouver can use to understand its meaning:

Figure 3.4   Powder panic at Whitewater

Interviewer: So now, in general, can you describe what makes up a good ski day for you?

Participant: Snow. Period.

Interviewer: And how would you describe that for somebody who wasn't a skier?

Participant: Well, most people, at least in Vancouver, have had pretty good exposure to, you know, at least Whistler Blackcomb commercials, or something like that. So most people would understand that, you know, when [I say] powder, or lots of snow, that that's a good thing.

Good snow is about quantity as well as quality. It should be deep, but also light, fresh, and untracked. Using environmental sociologist

Raymond Murphy's metaphor of a dance between human actors and non-human actants, good snow is skiers' shorthand for the ideal dance partner.[44]

The inverse of this ideal is rain, fog, cloud, or whiteouts that cause poor visibility. Jason answers my question about good skiing by referring to what it is not: "A good ski day? Almost every day is a good ski day. Unless it's raining. It's always good unless it's raining." Similarly, Billy observes that heavy cloud or fog creates problems for backcountry skiing. "If it's a whiteout, it's really troublesome [laughs]. I've had a couple trips where you can't see anything. You don't know where you are." Interview participants repeatedly emphasize the importance of snow, rain, wind, and sun for mediating their relationships with mountain environments. Weather is the foundation of good skiing but creates serious challenges when it is unruly. The ideal weather described by interview participants – good snow and sunshine – echoes dominant visual representation of skiing found in magazines and on resort websites. What is ideal for skiers is made to seem typical in these texts. Based on field notes and interviews, this combination of big powder days, sunshine, and blue skies is rare. Fresh snow is often accompanied by overcast skies and poor visibility. When the weather is warm, heavy snow makes turning difficult. Weather, as an actant, frequently diverges from the idealized representations found in ski magazines and on resort websites.

Stories of bad weather, including rain and fog, or prolonged snow droughts illustrate that weather can be an unruly actant, not behaving the way skiers would like. Kathlyn talks about how she had to get used to conditions of poor visibility, which often prevail at Whistler Blackcomb, after she moved from Ontario to Vancouver:

> The visibility, it was definitely something you have to adapt to. But I did get used to it. I think my balance was improved a lot from that. And my family came and visited me, and it was really, um, cloudy and got really bad visibility, hard to see. And I could remember the feeling of when I first felt like that, and how I think I've become more comfortable with it.

As environmental sociologist Raymond Murphy observes in his analysis of the 1998 ice storms that knocked out power in Quebec, Ontario, and the northeastern United States, "The freezing rain produced by primal nature crushed not only electrical transmission lines but also discourse which claimed that it would not happen."[45] There is often a gap between cultural representations of nature, which reinforce our expectations about how the non-human world should behave, and its insistent materiality.

Avalanches represent an extreme example of how weather can become an unruly actant. Through heavy snow loading or high winds, mountain slopes become unstable. At Whistler or Whitewater, access to terrain is shut off until conditions have stabilized. Resort employees often accomplish this by using explosives to trigger controlled slides. In these instances, machines are enrolled to actively reconstruct skiing landscapes and manage them for skiers' safety. For backcountry skiers, this kind of unruly weather means waiting until terrain has stabilized on its own or else seeking out safer terrain on forested slopes where risk is lower. Interview participants who prefer backcountry skiing talk about avalanche risk and their strategies for managing or avoiding it. Jenny describes cancelling a planned trip because of avalanche conditions. As a response to the weather, she turns to the more controlled environment of the ski hill:

> And then this year, I guess we just did [a multi-day backcountry trip at] Christmas, and not spring break, because the conditions were getting a bit dodgy here. Like, I remember there was just a lot of – tons of snow at early season, but then the avalanche thing was a bit, I don't know, [I] wasn't super-comfortable with it ... There were a few weekends, or a few times, we said, "Okay, well, let's not go [backcountry skiing], and let's go to Whistler instead."

Many skiers engage in cultural boundary-work that distinguishes natural and environmentally authentic backcountry places from the social landscapes of ski resorts. Avalanche talk further reinforces this nature-culture binary within skiing, which can be expressed in the following form: backcountry-natural-risky versus resort-cultural-safe. The greater environmental authenticity offered by backcountry skiing carries with it the increased risk of encountering unruly nature.

The introduction and diffusion of the Internet created widespread cultural change. The Internet also alters interactions with nature, as illustrated in skiers' talk about their Web use. A few interviewees use the Internet to research new gear or participate in social networking sites devoted to skiing, but these applications are not widely used. Most skiers, however, use websites on an ongoing basis to monitor weather and avalanche conditions at ski hills and in the backcountry. When asked about Internet use and skiing, Rosana answers, "I go on ski hill websites. Check out their conditions [laughs]. Check out how much snow they have, what the temperatures are." Heather's answer to the same question is in a similar vein: "I go on the avalanche website a lot throughout the winter. I'm trying to think of anything else. I definitely go on the Whistler Blackcomb website to check out snow conditions. Um, but that would be about it." Ski resort websites and the Canadian Avalanche Association website were repeatedly cited as resources for weather monitoring. The Internet allows skiers to avoid mountain environments during bad weather or during periods of high avalanche risk. It is a technology that is routinely enrolled by skiers so they can adapt to the movements of weather systems, thereby making their interactions with nature more predictable.

Animals as Significant Others

Images of animals link skiing and nature within ski websites and at ski resorts, while environmentalists use bears and mountain caribou as symbols of wilderness under threat from ski development. Animals are not only present in skiing as cultural symbols but also appear as actants. Through her recent work on dog-human relations through practices like dog breeding, training, competitions, and pet keeping, Donna Haraway argues that "companion species" is a more useful metaphor than the cyborg for understanding human/non-human relationships.[46] This notion recognizes the social significance of animals. They inhabit our homes and make up a meaningful part of our lives. Relationships of significant otherness, however, are "partial connections" marked by gaps of language and physiology, "within which the players are neither wholes nor parts."[47] Haraway argues against overly symbolic interpretations of human-animal relations, where animals enter the social only insofar as people invest them with cultural meaning. Writing about dogs, Haraway notes, "They are not a projection, nor the realization of an intention ... They are dogs; i.e., a species in ... relationship with human beings. The relationship is not especially nice; it is full of waste, cruelty, indifference, ignorance, and loss, as well as of joy, invention, labor, intelligence, and play."[48] Beyond the symbolic bears or caribou that enter skiing discourse, embodied animals inhabit skiing landscapes and may be impacted by human activity. As environmental groups point out, political decisions to develop new ski resorts or expand existing resorts alter animals' lives. Reshaping mountain environments into places for skiing risks expelling sensitive animals like grizzly bears or wolverines from these leisure and tourism places.

Many skiers note that animals are not a big part of their skiing experience. A few comment that many animals hibernate during the ski season. Ana says, "Yeah, it's winter, so a lot of things are hibernating ... Not lots of huge wildlife images come into my head, aside from birds." Animals are at the edges of many skiers' interpretations of their interactions with mountain environments, though they are certainly present. Most interview participants could recall encountering animals through skiing. Predominantly these are birds, such as whisky jacks, ravens, ptarmigans, or grouse. Sofia, a Nelson participant, talks about how she enjoys watching ravens while skiing. She says, "It's interesting to see the birds. I always watch the birds. The ravens are fascinating, the way they do their big rolls when they're happy." Kathlyn provides another example of this, describing regular interactions between birds and skiers at Whistler Blackcomb:

Well, birds are around all the time. At Whistler, the birds are kind of [laughs] interesting. Because there'll be these huge lift lines, and they have these cheeky little birds that will come up and land on your finger. And it's become more of like entertainment sort of value. People feeding them and stuff.

Several interviewees attend to birds as inhabitants of a shared environment. As Mike states when asked about animals and skiing, "Birds are the most common, but never, uh ... never unnoticed or taken for granted." For many interview participants, however, birds do seem to be taken for granted. Their presence is less noteworthy than the occasional encounter with a large animal, such as a bear or cougar.

Skiers' narratives about animal encounters produce a long list of significant others that occupy skiing landscapes. These include rabbits, deer, squirrels, bears, large cats (bobcats, cougars, and lynx), porcupines, moose, mountain goats, bighorn sheep, and coyotes. For example, Lou tells me what animals he has seen:

> *Participant:* Lots of chipmunks and squirrels, but ... I see tracks. Tracks of rabbits, weasels. But, um, not anything any bigger than that. Although I did see a lynx once. A long time ago.
> *Interviewer:* Can you tell me a bit about that?
> *Participant:* I was heading up Silver King. It's called Toad Mountain now, but we used to call it Silver King hill. And, uh, we were just trekking up to ski down and just came across him. Just for a moment saw him sitting on the snow ahead of us in the trail and taking off through the woods. Yeah, it's quite an experience.

Evangelina, a Vancouver skier, tells a similar story about a memorable encounter with a bear during a backcountry trip:

> I was on a ski traverse a whole bunch of years ago and we actually were coming up to a col and there was a bear coming out of her den, with her cubs, which was one of the most incredible things I've ever witnessed. Just having to reroute my ski route because there was a bear there [laughs]. So that was really neat.

These stories illustrate how encounters with larger animals take on more meaning than regular contact with smaller animals like birds or squirrels. Bear encounters, in particular, evoke the natural sublime, with its combination of beauty, awe, and an element of fear.

If animals are significant others, as Haraway suggests, skiers' narratives indicate that some animals (bears, lynx) assume greater significance as skiers interpret and narrate their experiences of mountainous nature. Similarly, the physical presence of birds within skiing landscapes contrasts with the symbolic use of larger animals like bears or wolves to link skiing and nature. Animals that embody the natural sublime, such as grizzly bears or mountain caribou, are also more likely to enter ecopolitics through environmental movement claims-making. This highlights an asymmetry between cultural representations of skiing landscapes and skiers' embodied experience of mountainous nature.

Tourism Networks and Powder Nomads
Mountains like Whistler Blackcomb or Whitewater are local places, made up of rocks, soil, glaciers, trees, animals, buildings, and chairlifts. However, ski resorts are not closed systems with firm boundaries. These local environments connect to large-scale flows of humans and non-humans. As warm Pacific Ocean air meets the Coast Mountains, snow falls at Whistler Blackcomb. Whitewater receives snow as Pacific storm systems move inland and rise over the Columbia Mountains. Chairlifts connect local mountain environments to production centres in Utah and Colorado (where the two largest chairlift manufacturers, Doppelmayr CTEC and Leitner-Poma, are headquartered) and to flows of capital from Europe. Ski hills are embedded within global flows of skiers and ski hill workers through tourism and migration. Ski magazines and resort websites represent skiing landscapes for a tourist gaze by circulating travel information, links to travel agencies, and advertisements for hotels, airlines, and car rental companies. The system of automobility – comprising cars, highways, and parking lots – connects local skiing landscapes to nearby cities and airports, which serve as nodal points in global tourist networks. These global networks allow skiers to travel and experience different places but also involve harmful ecological impacts through oil and gas consumption, which contribute to greenhouse gas emissions and global climate change.

Skiers' interview talk illustrates how skiing is not limited to interaction with local mountain landscapes. Several participants describe travelling to ski at least once a year and consider ski travel an important part of their experience. Dominique, who is primarily a Whitewater skier, tells me, "I try to get to Red as much as I can. Red Mountain. Otherwise, like, I'll go wherever. I try to go to Whistler at least once a year. I've been to Big White, Kicking Horse in the past couple of years, a couple of times. And I used to ski Sunshine Village in Banff for a year." Skiing tourism allows participants to experience different landscapes, which are valued for their specific qualities. When I ask Dominique why she travels to Red and Whistler, she replies, "I like Red Mountain just because it's different. There's lots of easily accessible terrain. There's a bit steeper runs. There's more to do there, compared to Whitewater ... And then Whistler, I think it's for the novelty." When talking about the appeal of skiing at Whistler, Mason draws on his experiences of other places:

> When I lived in Toronto, we skied in Europe a lot. And even though I skied in Lake Louise and Sunshine, Whistler was the first place that reminded me of the Alps, where you could see peak after peak. Lake Louise is nice, but you're basically looking into a big valley. Whistler, you see peaks way into the horizon.

Mason participates in global networks of skier-tourist travel. By contrast, the majority of interviewees focus on travel within western Canada and the United States, rather than exotic locations featured in ski magazine travel narratives, such as France, Japan, Chile, and Iran.

Sociologist Adrian Franklin describes tourism as a process of "ordering" places, people, and objects. He writes, "Tourism is a social activity, yes, but, it cannot be reduced to the social because it is relationally linked to a wide variety of objects, machines, systems, texts, non-humans, bureaucracies, times and so on, without which it would not happen and could not have become what it has."[49] Weather systems, for example, shape skiers' interactions with local mountain environments, but they also order global skiing-tourism networks. During February 2007, I repeatedly observed skier-tourists talking about the high level of hotel bookings at Whistler Village because of the lack of snow in Europe and eastern North America. The mountains of coastal British Columbia received heavy snowfall throughout November and December. As skier-tourists learned about these global weather patterns, ski trips initially planned for Austria, Quebec, or New Hampshire were redirected to Whistler Blackcomb. Snowfall, or the lack of it, shapes travel on a large scale, directing skier-tourists' attention to one mountainous region or another.

Whistler Blackcomb, more than Whitewater, is a nodal point within global tourism networks. Lift lines and gondolas fill with travel talk about arriving at Whistler from elsewhere, orienting to the mountain and the village, and comparing the area with ski resorts in the United States and Europe. While sharing lifts with strangers, I frequently heard about annual ski vacations to Whistler from the United Kingdom, the United States, or elsewhere in Canada. Although accents and languages are often inaccurate signifiers, the Whistler soundscape is punctuated by American, British, and Australian accents, and by skiers speaking French, German, Spanish, and Japanese. A series of national flags frame the entrance to the Whistler gondola, visually marking out a point where tourism flows converge. The nations represented include New Zealand, Australia, France, Italy, Germany, Greece, Korea, Japan, China, Canada, the United States, and Mexico. Finally, souvenir shops scattered throughout Whistler Blackcomb sell T-shirts, stuffed animals, and postcards that incorporate iconic images of Canadiana, such as the national flag, wildlife, and mountain vistas. As important tourist objects, these souvenirs join together nature, skiing, and the Canadian nation and define the meaning of the BC landscape for skier-tourists.[50]

Whistler Blackcomb is also a nodal point for flows of migration. Ski hill workers wear name tags that indicate where they are from. A significant number of resort employees are from Australia or elsewhere in Canada, though migrants from Europe also work at the hill. Ian Verchere's memoir of growing up in Whistler includes a two-page photo of these name tags, which identify workers from New Zealand, Australia, the United Kingdom, Japan, and South Korea.[51] Talking with skiers on chairlifts led to stories about moving to Whistler from Ontario, Australia, and the United Kingdom in order to live there for a ski season or longer. These skiers may be thought of as powder nomads, a more geographically diffuse version of the traditional ski bum, which better reflects the ability to "travel lightly" across contemporary societies.[52]

Young, predominantly male North Americans have long sought personal freedom through skiing by moving to towns like Aspen, Colorado. By taking on menial jobs, ski bums inhabit mountain environments as members of a community of skiers rather than as short-term tourists. Writing about the figure of the ski bum, Coleman notes, "The term – coined in the late 1940s – referred to college-aged people who put their regular lives on hold, moved to resort towns, and took whatever jobs they could in order to ski."[53] In recent years, large North American resorts have increasingly turned to low-waged migrant labour from the global south to fill service jobs. Whistler Blackcomb, however, continues to attract skiers from around the world, who come to fill service jobs and immerse themselves in skiing as a lifestyle, often while struggling to find affordable housing or living in overcrowded conditions in nearby communities. Powder nomads are a more serious class of skier-tourist who migrate to British Columbia because of the pull of the skiing landscape. Skiing and snowboarding is the focal point of their lives for the duration of the winter, providing the opportunity for longer-lasting and deeper interactions with mountain environments than are available to short-term skier tourists.

Powder nomadism sometimes turns into long-term residency in Whistler or Nelson, a process historian Hal Rothman calls becoming a "neo-native" of tourism-oriented communities.[54] A few interview participants initially moved to Whistler or Nelson because of skiing and decided to become permanent residents. Edward is a Nelson-based skier originally from Ontario. He tells me about seeking out a ski town in the BC Interior:

> *Interviewer:* So is [skiing] part of what drew you to this area?
> *Participant:* Yeah, absolutely. We came out west looking for a town that had a ski hill within twenty minutes that had really good snow
> ...
> *Interviewer:* Right. So somewhere like here or Fernie?
> *Respondent:* Here, Red [Rossland], Fernie were about the three that we were considering, yeah.

In Edward's narrative, really good snow, as well as large mountains and backcountry touring possibilities, pulled him away from his home in central Canada and toward British Columbia. His story of moving west illustrates the role played by non-human nature, including mountains and weather systems, in shaping mobility networks. Jason offers another story of powder nomadism, describing his route from Ontario to Whistler this way:

> *Participant:* I'm an Ontario transplant.
> *Interviewer:* Okay. And how many seasons have you been here?
> *Participant:* This will be my fifth winter. But I moved here seven years ago ...
> *Interviewer:* And so was the landscape here part of the draw, or what brought you here?
> *Participant:* I lived in Banff before this, and that's ... The west is always a draw. [I didn't have a plan for] Whistler, but it was always a draw back in Ontario. So yeah, the landscape here definitely helps. It's always been in my imagination, here.

These narratives demonstrate that skiers are mobile rather than attached to a single environment. As imagined landscapes draw powder nomads to the mountains of British Columbia, lines of migration are drawn in snow.

Whitewater and Whistler Blackcomb embody different types of connections between skiing and tourism. Whitewater is inhabited by locals more than by tourists, which contributes to the small, tight-knit feeling that is absent at Whistler Blackcomb. Friends and acquaintances regularly run into each other in chairlift lines, the cafeteria, or the pub and stop to talk or share a few runs. This kind of interaction is much less visible among the larger crowds of visitors at Whistler Blackcomb. Whitewater has a small clothing and ski gear shop, selling souvenir clothing with the ski resort logo, as well as copies of the Whitewater cookbook. Compared with Whistler Blackcomb, however, there is a notable absence of shops selling Canadiana tourist objects.

Skiing tourism and powder nomadism illustrate how skiers, like many people, are becoming increasingly accustomed to "travelling lightly" across national boundaries. Ski resorts serve as nodal points in tourism networks, connected by cars, highways, airplanes, and airports, to the rest of the world. Skiing-tourism networks, however, are only partially global. Whistler Blackcomb, a key nodal point in the global skiing-tourism network, is strongly tied to flows of people from North America, Europe, Australia, and Japan. By contrast, skiers from Central and South America, Africa, eastern Europe, and much of Asia are marginal to this skiing-tourism network. Immobility and coerced mobility (for example, as refugees rather than as tourists) remain the reality for large numbers of people worldwide, who are denied the privileges associated with what Zygmunt Bauman terms "liquid life."[55] Access to highly valued recreational environments, including famous ski resorts at St. Moritz, Chamonix, Vail, Aspen, or Whistler Blackcomb remains a form of "environmental privilege" reserved primarily for people in the global north, as well as the wealthy throughout the world.[56]

Conclusion: Skiing as a Collective of Humans and Non-Humans

Skiing joins together human actors and mountain environments made up of rocks, soil, weather systems, vegetation, and animals. It is not only a social practice, where nature serves as the backdrop for human action. Analyses of the cultural discourses that circulate through skiing are enriched by attempts to understand the materiality of skiers' interactions with nature. Skiers' abilities to interact with mountain environments depend upon an array of technologies, including boots, bindings, skis, snowboards, and specialized ski clothing. To speak of skiers is always to speak of human-technology hybrids that engage with mountainous nature. Ski resort companies employ other technologies to physically reshape skiing landscapes. Media images of skiing often evoke an uninhabited mountainous sublime. In contrast to these media images, accounting for the presence of chairlifts, lodge buildings, snow-grooming machines, and other technologies within the analysis demonstrates that skiing produces sportscapes that are better understood as naturecultures or as technonatures.[57] This approach draws out much of what is black-boxed within skiing discourse and creates a more complex account of the ecopolitical dimensions of the sport.

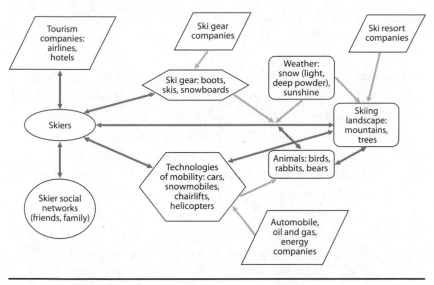

Figure 3.5   Mapping the skiing collective

Figure 3.5 draws upon skiers' interview talk, skiing texts, and field notes to visualize the connections between groups of actors and actants within skiing collectives. Members of the collective include humans (skiers and their social networks), economic structures (ski gear companies, ski resort companies, car manufacturers, and tourism networks), machines (ski gear, cars, and chairlifts), and non-human nature (animals, weather, and mountains). Modelling skiing as a collective of humans and non-humans addresses a gap within much of the existing research on outdoor sport. When sociologists of sport examine activities like snowboarding, skateboarding, or windsurfing, the non-human environment is often bracketed out of the analysis. Instead, the focus is typically on gender, sexuality, class, ethnicity, and other forms of social power that shape sport participation. Mapping connections between sporting bodies, machines, animals, and environments highlights how nature matters within outdoor sport in two related ways. The specific qualities of skiing environments have important effects on participants, producing unique skiing experiences in one place that will not be repeated elsewhere. The relationships among sport participants, technologies, and non-human nature also produce negative ecological impacts through consumerism, fossil fuel consumption and carbon emissions, or wildlife disturbance.

Comparisons between Whistler Blackcomb and Whitewater demonstrate how "particular nuances and unique flavours" characterize different skiing collectives.[58] Skiers at both resorts range in age from grade school to those in their sixties and older, though the average age at Whitewater seems younger (twenties and thirties) than at Whistler (thirties to fifties). Whistler also seems to be characterized by more of a gender balance than Whitewater, which feels more male-dominated. Although both resorts are marked by dominant whiteness, there is more of a multi-ethnic presence at Whistler. Taking these observations together, in some respects Whistler Blackcomb is a more socially inclusive recreational environment than Whitewater.

Whistler Village is a place of rustic luxury patterned on an idealized Canadian mountain village. It is a mountainous, rural version of a fantasy city dedicated to consumerism and riskless risk.[59] Whitewater is more rustic than luxurious. It lacks Whistler's collection of high-end hotels, chic cafés, sports clothing stores, and nightclubs. Although versions of these amenities are available nearby in Nelson, the ski hill itself has only one lodge building, which is dwarfed by the surrounding mountains. Whistler Blackcomb might be more socially inclusive in some respects, but it requires greater economic capital to participate in this recreational landscape than is necessary at Whitewater.

Technological mediations also distinguish the two skiing collectives. Whistler Blackcomb is crossed by thirty-eight lifts, most of which are newer, high-speed, high-capacity chairlifts. This is a sharp contrast from the two old two-seat chairlifts that slowly move skiers up the mountain at Whitewater. Cellphones, personal radios, cameras, and video cameras are also more visible at Whistler than at Whitewater. The socio-technical relationships at Whistler Blackcomb are more obvious than those at Whitewater. Ski industry and environmentalist representations of skiing landscapes use images of uninhabited, sublime mountain environments. Images of wilderness that rely upon "the absence of men and the presence of wild animals" have been subject to sustained criticism because they are ahistoric and they reproduce an ecologically harmful nature-culture binary.[60] Ski resort landscapes cannot be considered wilderness in any meaningful sense, but the different technological mediations at Whistler Blackcomb and Whitewater recall Roderick Frazier Nash's argument that wilderness is a relative value ascribed to a place, or a point on a "spectrum of conditions or environments ranging ... from the primeval to the paved."[61] The significant technological differences between the two resorts suggest that small regional resorts like Whitewater give skiers a closer approximation of mountain wilderness than can be found at large tourism destinations like Whistler Blackcomb.

These comparisons illustrate that even though there are many similarities across skiing collectives, unique qualities distinguish them from each other. The two ski resorts construct substantially different versions of mountainous nature. At Whistler Blackcomb, the meaning of mountains is firmly attached to social practices of consumerism and global tourist travel, with the environmental impacts associated with excess, waste, and fossil fuel use. Although the search for "authenticity" in tourist travel is illusory, Whitewater is less of a rural, mountainous version of the fantasy city than is Whistler Blackcomb.[62] Assessments of the ecological impacts of skiing should remain attentive to the significant differences between the types of interaction with human nature that specific ski resorts cultivate.

An actor-network approach is useful for moving beyond an analysis of cultural constructions of skiing to account for embodied interactions between skiers and nature, but it is less attuned to the variety of "mobilities" within and beyond these networks.[63] On a microsocial scale, this includes the mobility enabled by skis, snowboards, chairlifts, T-bars, helicopters, snowmobiles, and snowcats. On a macrosocial scale, automobility and aeromobility networks connect local mountain environments to cities and airports around the world.[64] Attention to mobility highlights the non-local ecological impacts of skiing. Environmental groups raise questions about skiing's impacts on local wildlife populations, but they direct less attention to skiing's close connections with automobility and aeromobility networks. These networks involve significant environmental withdrawals of fossil fuels and other natural resources to build cars, planes, and transportation infrastructure. They also involve environmental additions of carbon emissions, which are altering the global climate, along with other air pollutants.[65] Accounting for these non-local impacts and how they might be mitigated is also an important task for a political ecology of skiing.

Environmental Subjectivity and the Ecopolitics of Skiing

4

Is skiing an environmentally sustainable way to interact with nature? I posed this question to skiers during interviews in homes, cafés, and ski hill pubs. Sustainability is a contested concept. It is invoked in programs for substantial environmental change but is also easily repackaged into consumer capitalism. Despite the slippery nature of sustainability, it is useful for orienting discussions about skiing and mountain environments. Ski resorts boast of their environmental awards and habitat management practices, giving the impression that skiing is ecologically benign. This discourse positions skiing as a form of attractive development, where the product sold is experience, rather than timber or minerals. Environmental groups occasionally challenge skiing over the ecological legitimacy of new development projects. The most extreme example of this was the Earth Liberation Front's arson at Vail Resort, Colorado, in the 1990s, in protest against the resort's planned expansion into threatened lynx habitat. Skiers' interview talk provides insight into these divergent ideas of skiing and sustainability.

Power relations between humans and non-human nature work through skiing at microsocial and macrosocial scales. Skiing is a way to get to know and appreciate nature, and it may shape participants' environmental values, behaviours, and identities. Skiing is also the site of larger-scale biopower relations between human ski resort managers and non-human animals and vegetation. The ski industry defines these biopower relations in the productive language of habitat stewardship, whereas social movement groups raise questions about the ecological and social legitimacy of relationships between skiing and non-human nature. These different scales of ecopower overlap and intersect. Skiers' understanding of large-scale biopower relations between the ski industry and nature shape their environmental subjectivities. Conversely, skiers' interpretations of their sport as environmentally sustainable or problematic may influence the strategies and behaviours of the ski industry and environmental groups.

Environmental Subjectivity and Biopower

Subjectivity and Technologies of the Self

In "The Subject and Power," Michel Foucault sets out a useful definition of subjectivity and its double meaning. "There are two meanings of the word 'subject': subject to someone else by control and dependence, and tied to his own identity by conscience or self-knowledge. Both meanings suggest a form of power that subjugates and makes subject to."[1] Our sense of ourselves as the central actors in our own lives is coupled with a process that subjects us to outside forces through discourse and power. The formation of subjectivity is a process that both constrains and enables social action.

The question of subjectivity is central to Foucault's later work. Focusing on ancient Greece and Rome, he explores how "technologies of the self" come into play around sexuality within and outside marriage, or within love relations among men. These technologies of the self consist of a repertoire of physical and mental practices that individuals use "to transform themselves in order to attain a certain state of happiness, purity, wisdom, perfection, or immortality."[2] These practices include rituals of withdrawal, purification, endurance, and daily meditation. These are all distinct "actions on the self by the self ... by which one changes, purifies, transforms, and transfigures oneself."[3] These practices create a personal "intensification of the relation to oneself" but also involve taking up discourse as "an attitude, a mode of behavior" and transforming it into "ways of living."[4] Technologies of the self are also social practices, as they connect participants to "relationships between individuals, to exchanges and communications, and at times even to institutions."[5] Skiing may work as an individual technology of the self, yet it also involves environmental withdrawals and additions to mountain environments, communications of discourses about environmental sustainability or degradation, and institutions like ski resorts or ski gear corporations.

In his lectures published as *The Hermeneutics of the Subject,* Foucault draws out the political dimensions of subjectivity. In ancient Greek and Roman texts, the care of the self is explicitly related to the care of others. Plato's writing, for example, ties subjectivity to political citizenship within the city-state. As Foucault sums up, "I must take care of myself ... to have a proper knowledge of the political *tekhnē* that will allow me to take care of others."[6] Turning to the nineteenth century, Foucault notes that revolutionary subjectivities form through a process akin to religious conversion as political consciousness is developed and through practices of the self. This discussion of political subjectivity is salient for thinking about how subjectivities form in relation to environmental politics as different scales of ecopower connect individual behaviour and beliefs to large-scale relationships between social institutions and non-human nature.

The notion of subjectivity is used in sport sociology to examine how sport constructs subjectivities related to gender and sexuality. For example, Pirkko Markula and Richard Pringle describe how male rugby players adopt dominant models of masculinity and individualize them. They also describe how women's "hybrid" fitness programs, which draw on tai chi, yoga, and strength training, transform participants' sense of self. Barbara Ravel and Geneviève Rail explore understandings of sexuality among lesbian and bisexual women in all-women sports teams in Quebec. Holly Thorpe examines snowboarding, media discourse, and subjectivity among female boarders. Mainstream representations of snowboarding "promote snowboarding as a fulfilling activity to be engaged in by men and a 'cute' fashion to be consumed by women."[7] However, a minority of female boarders speak back against this dominant discourse through niche magazines and women-only snowboard videos. These counter-discourses offer possibilities for alternative forms of female snowboarding subjectivity.

Sport can act as a technology of the self, as snowboarding, hybrid fitness programs, and rugby recall earlier practices of purification, gymnastics, or endurance that shape participants' subjectivities. Through sport, participants internalize, negotiate, and sometimes resist dominant discourses about gender and sexuality. However, this body of research pays little attention to the physical environments where sport is located. In snowboarding, mountaineering, or surfing, participants construct their subjectivities through embodied experiences of snow, rock, and water respectively. Geographer Nigel Thrift rejects a human-centred model of subjectivity and argues that "space, understood as an ensemble of animate beings in interaction with each other ... has its own push."[8] Our sense of self is discursively mediated but also develops through interaction with physical environments and their non-human inhabitants. If we build upon Thrift's work, "environmental subjectivity" refers to the formation of identities, beliefs, and practices in relation to non-human nature and environmental politics. Environmental subjectivity embodies attitudinal characteristics like environmental values and concerns, as well as everyday behaviours like recycling, buying organic, or reducing consumption. If we extend Foucault's discussion of care of the self and political citizenship, it also embodies participation in pro-environmental citizenship through green voting, environmental group membership, attending protests, or writing letters. These different dimensions of environmentalism are often bound together as part of being an environmentally concerned consumer and citizen.

Biopower and Ecopolitics

According to Foucault, power over a group of people or a territory was traditionally characterized by the right of rulers to take the lives of their subordinates. Biopower, by contrast, is oriented toward monitoring and managing populations in the interests of health and productivity. It is "continuous, scientific, and it is the power to make live."[9] Biopower is the macrosocial partner of disciplinary forms of power that function at the level of individual bodies. If disciplinary power works "on the body as a machine ... [to increase its] usefulness and its docility," then biopower works on the "species body," through research and planning, to make it productive.[10] The emergence of biopower and the population as a distinct object of government is integral to the operation of capitalism, as this requires "the controlled insertion of bodies into the machinery of production and the adjustment of the phenomena of population to economic processes."[11]

The concept of biopower highlights the intersection of discourse and modern systems of governance. It is also useful for drawing Foucault's work into the environmental social sciences. *Society Must Be Defended* collects Foucault's lectures at the College de France from 1975 to 1976. In the closing lecture, Foucault alludes to the ecological dimension of biopower as he describes how it operates on physical environments as well as human populations. He writes, "This includes the direct effects of the geographical, climatic, or hydrographic environment ... And also the problem of the environment to the extent that it is not a natural environment, that it has been created by the population and therefore has effects on that population."[12] Foucault describes how social groups denaturalize the environment as it is broken up into populations or natural resources and fit into management regimes oriented toward productivity.

Extending this insight, Paul Rutherford argues that scientific expertise produces systems of environmental power and knowledge that define non-human populations and make them manageable. Ski resort strategies of habitat management for the health and productivity of deer, fish, black bears, or grizzly bears may be viewed as examples of this form of biopower. Timothy Luke similarly draws on the notion of biopower to describe eco-managerialist approaches to society-nature interaction that work toward "redefining and then administering the earth as 'natural resources'" that can be appropriated for capitalist production.[13] Within skiing, mountains are subject to biopower as they are logged, groomed, and fitted with chairlifts and lodges to make them more productive for the ski industry. A Foucauldian approach to skiing highlights connections between microsocial and macrosocial dimensions of ecopolitics through a parallel focus on environmental subjectivity and biopower.

Skiers and Environmental Subjectivity

A substantial body of research focuses on environmental values and levels of environmental concern.[14] This research examines how attitudes toward nature, environmental issues, and environmental policy vary across social groups (i.e., by gender or economic class) or through time. The Human Exceptionalism Paradigm (HEP) and New Environmental Paradigm (NEP) scale is one measure widely used for this purpose. Whereas the HEP emphasizes faith in technology and human control over nature, the NEP sees humanity as embedded within and dependent upon natural systems and processes.[15] David Tindall, Scott Davies, and Céline Mauboulès measure commitment to environmentalism by asking movement participants about pro-environmental political actions, such as writing letters, supporting boycotts, or joining protests. They also examine participation in environmentally friendly behaviour, which includes things that can be done in everyday life, like carpooling or using public transit, buying organic food, conserving energy or water, and recycling.[16]

I asked skiers about several dimensions of environmental attitudes and behaviour that can be brought together through the concept of environmental subjectivity. Environmental subjectivity incorporates values, environmentally friendly behaviour, and participation in environmental citizenship through green voting or environmental group membership. Figure 4.1 uses network analysis techniques to map skiers' talk

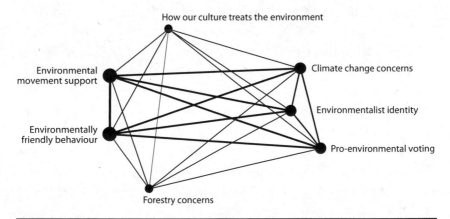

Figure 4.1   Connections among dimensions of environmental subjectivity

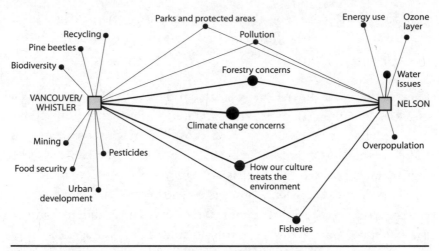

Figure 4.2 Skiers' environmental concerns by region (Vancouver/Whistler and Nelson)

about these different dimensions of environmental subjectivity. Node size reflects the relative number of skiers who talk about each theme (concern about climate change, environmentalist identity, and so on).[17] Line thickness reflects how frequently pairs of themes appear together. This figure illustrates the connection between different dimensions of environmental subjectivity, including concern with climate change, environmentally friendly behaviour, and environmental movement support.

Interview participants generally demonstrate high levels of environmental concern and describe a broad range of environmental issues. Figure 4.2 treats skiers' environmental concerns as nodes in a two-mode discourse network in which environmental issues (circular nodes) are linked to the region where interviews were conducted (square nodes). When asked about their environmental concerns, climate change came up repeatedly for skiers in Vancouver, Whistler, and Nelson. This could reflect the high media profile of the issue, both in the news and in films like *The Day After Tomorrow* and *An Inconvenient Truth*. Luciana invokes climate change in reference to her experience as a skier in Nelson:

> The global warming's always a big thing. 'Cause the snow, some years are getting worse and worse and worse. I was talking with friends

about how much snow there used to be when I was a kid here. And so far, we seem okay this year, but the last few years haven't been that great.

Luciana thinks of climate change through the prism of her experience as a skier. Her interactions with the mountains allow her to connect this global environmental issue to memories of "how much snow there used to be" in the Nelson area. One barrier to action on climate change is that many people feel the issue is far removed from everyday life. As Rachel Slocum notes, "One obstacle to getting people to care about climate change is the fact that it is technically complex and, for most of the 1990s, was portrayed as scientifically uncertain."[18] Greenpeace uses the polar bear as a symbol of nature to mobilize local action and support for climate change policy. "The polar bear is a boundary object that attempts to translate the immensity and distance of climate change ... It is a temporary bridge that allows communication and understanding among the constituencies of scientists, policymakers, and citizens."[19] Luciana draws on her standpoint as a skier to personalize and localize the abstract concept of climate change. Like the polar bears invoked by Greenpeace, the mountains of Whitewater or Whistler Blackcomb may help translate the abstract issue of global climate change into a personal environmental concern for many skiers.

Sofia, who has been involved in several environmental groups and identifies herself as an environmentalist, also talks about climate change. She begins by demonstrating her knowledge of climate change by referencing a 1987 government document on the issue. When asked about her environmental concerns, she briefly mentions that "deforestation is dreadful, of course," then continues,

> I mean global warming. We were told in '87, in a government standing committee on the environment, chapter two said global warming is real and serious. And ski areas are going to get affected by it. But that's pretty, sort of like, my backyard. There's much more about it than that.

Sofia links her concerns to her experience as a skier, but she is quick to emphasize that it is a broader issue, one not limited to impacts on her recreational environment. She uses her standpoint as a skier when talking about environmental issues, but her concern with climate change links to a broader sense of environmental subjectivity.

Concerns about climate change connect to skiing because it may alter the future of the sport but also because skiing contributes to climate change through energy use for chairlifts and car transportation. Steve is ambiguous about the ecopolitics of skiing. He describes skiing as a "sustainable activity" that is good because it "gets people out. It gets people exercising. It gets people into the mountains." However, while talking about his concerns with climate change, he describes ski resort energy use as ecologically troublesome:

> I think the ski industry, the resorts, will hopefully start picking up on sustainable energy ideas and trying to look for alternative power sources to run the lifts. 'Cause, I mean, you're riding these diesel-generated, diesel I guess, or electric. But diesel is probably the [general] option, which is not sustainable in the long run. I hope that ski areas will start looking at that.

Steve highlights a key environmental ambiguity within skiing. It "gets people into the mountains" and gives skiers the opportunity to interact with nature, but the use of diesel engines to power chairlifts releases greenhouse gases to the atmosphere and contributes to global climate change. The ski industry relies on images of nature to advertise the sport, while also depending on environmental withdrawals of fossil fuels and additions of greenhouse gases.[20]

Skiers talk about a wide range of other environmental concerns, including forestry practices, protected areas, pollution, water quality, fisheries, and fish farming. In addition, several participants say that it is hard to isolate particular issues of concern. Rather, they are concerned about several environmental problems that result from a broader culture of disrespect for the environment. As Kathlyn puts it, "I'm definitely concerned about the environment ... And it's like, the whole lifestyle that Western culture has is not made to coexist with the environment, pretty much ... I think it's just a general lack of respect." Similarly, Peg says, "I'm generally a strong environmental advocate ... Top of my mind is climate change. And just generally the way that our culture treats the environment." There is a notable regional difference in skiers' expressions of environmental concern (recall Figure 4.2). Participants across both regions talk about the environmental impacts of climate change. Although Vancouver-Whistler participants cite a range of issues, climate change dominates talk about environmental concern. Nelson-area skiers, by contrast, often raise concerns about natural resource use, focusing on water, fisheries, and forestry.

Most participants also talk about engaging in environmentally friendly behaviour in their homes and day-to-day lives. This often focuses on food choices (organic, local) or buying non-toxic and biodegradable cleaning products. Frank tells me, "If I had the choice between farmed salmon or fresh [wild] salmon, I'll pay more for the fresh or the wild salmon." Sadie provides another example of commitment to environmentally friendly behaviour:

> We buy lots of organic stuff. All of our cleaning products are not tested on animals and are phosphate-free and, you know, whatever we can do. And that's everything from ... dish soap to laundry soap to actual cleaning products ... Absolutely, that [environmental concern] factors into everything that we purchase.

Skiers' engagement in environmentally friendly behaviour often focuses on consumer choices about food and cleaning products. Gert Spaargaren and Arthur Mol assert the importance of individual acts of political consumerism and ecological citizenship, which are hybrid concepts that blur distinctions between citizens and consumers. These practices are useful for "organising de-territorialised, non-state forms of (trans)national environmental authority which can help realise the ambitious goal of greening global consumption."[21] Skiers' talk about trying to adhere to environmental values illustrates how, as Spaargaren and Mol put it, "by living their daily lives, individuals are confronted with the impacts of globalisation in a direct and concrete manner. The food we eat, the clothes we wear and the cars we drive come from [a] system of provisions that by now have global reach."[22]

Kenneth Gould, David Pellow, and Allan Schnaiberg express skepticism about consumer action as a force for ecopolitical transformation, arguing, "The question of how much we are consuming (i.e., growth) is rarely challenged. The focus is on changing only what goods we are consuming." Andrew Szasz similarly argues that green consumerism works as an "inverted quarantine" to insulate individuals from environmental pollution, rather than to challenge the social structures causing ecological degradation.[23] Political consumerism is not an alternative to other forms of ecopolitical engagement, as it often fails to disrupt the logic of "deception, excess and waste" inherent in capitalist consumerism.[24] For many people, however, it is a key component of being a pro-environmental subject that is often linked to environmental movement support or green voting.

Several participants describe transportation as an area where they focus their environmentally friendly behaviour. The intimate connection between skiing and automobility is another key example of the environmental ambiguity of skiing. Although skiers espouse pro-environmental values and act on their environmental concerns, most rely on cars and highways to reach the mountains. Through their participation in automobility, skiers contribute to the same environmental problems that they are concerned about, such as climate change. Car sharing, carpooling, owning a Smart car, using biodiesel, or cycling instead of driving are alternative transportation choices some participants make in order to mitigate this ecological irony. For example, Kristen says, "I've actively chosen not to own a vehicle or to drive a vehicle. And when I did have a vehicle, it ran on vegetable oil, so I wasn't using fossil fuel ... I ride my bike everywhere." Edward similarly talks about hitchhiking to Whitewater instead of driving as a form of carpooling:

> One of the big things I do is I try not to drive to the hill. I hitch[hike] all the time, to carpool with people. My wife takes the car because of

our son. But even if she didn't, I'd still walk down and grab a ride [rather than drive myself], just to save the pollution going up there, the CO_2.

Vancouver-Whistler skiers talk about trying to address the impacts of their car use more often than Nelson participants do. This is likely related to differences between living in an urban area and a small town. In a large centre, alternatives to private car use, such as infrastructure for transit and cycling, may be more visible or accessible. Where people live closer together, coordinating carpooling or car sharing is relatively easier. In rural areas, lower population density and lack of transit infrastructure produce greater path dependence on ecologically harmful automobility networks.[25] Path dependence on established systems limits the range of options available to rural skiers to engage in political consumerism and ecological citizenship.

A large proportion of interview participants have current or prior connections to environmental organizations. For many participants, this is limited to financial donations rather than to direct involvement in environmental group campaigns or protests. For example, when asked if he's been involved in the environmental movement, Tim replies,

> I've paid the guys for Greenpeace, you know, when the guy's standing outside the store. But not a real active member, or anything like that ... I like what Sierra Club does. I think they're a good organization. But I'm not really environmentally active, aside from philosophically, and then through my political views, or whatever. I mean, I voted for Green [the Green Party] in the last few elections.

This casual and sporadic connection to the environmental movement is typical of many skiers. It is what David Tindall refers to as low-cost activism, which does not demand a great deal of time, organizational commitment, or personal risk.[26] Several participants list the Wilderness Committee (the largest regional organization in British Columbia), Sierra Club, and Greenpeace as recipients of their financial support.

Some skiers also engage in medium- or high-cost activism that involves direct participation in environmental groups. Roberta says, "I was involved with saving the Carmanah [an area of old-growth forest on Vancouver

Island], so I was a protester and I stood on the logging road for weeks." Roberta is one of a few participants that attended protests or blockades during conflicts over forestry practices and old-growth forests. Other participants have been directly involved in university-based environmental groups or have taken part in community-based environmental campaigns. Several participants also talk about voting for the New Democratic Party or Green Party because of these parties' environmental values.

The majority of interview participants espouse pro-environmental values, engage in environmentally friendly behaviour, and support the environmental movement. However, when asked whether they think of themselves as environmentalists, there is often discomfort about this label. For example, when I ask Dennis about environmental concerns, he answers "all of them." Similarly, when I ask about environmentally friendly behaviour, he replies, "You know, that's huge. Everything I purchase, I try to think about it." A few minutes later, when asked if he would call himself an environmentalist, he says, "You know, I'd love to one day be able to call myself that. I don't know how it would happen. I don't know what I can do ... I don't know. I don't know where to start." Dennis illustrates the complexity of the relationship between environmental values, actions, and environmentalist identity.

Interview participants are almost evenly divided between those who call themselves environmentalists and those who would not. Many skiers feel that although they are environmentally concerned, they are not active enough in the formal environmental movement to adopt this identity. Judith provides an example of this:

> *Interviewer:* So, would you tend to call yourself an environmentalist?
> *Participant:* [pause] I would like to, but I don't think I could.
> *Interviewer:* Yeah, why is that?
> *Participant:* I don't feel like I do enough. Like, I feel like I try to live, you know, I compost, I recycle, I do kind of – all the things which I think everyone should do. But I don't feel like yet in my life I've gone beyond that ... And I feel like to call yourself an environmentalist that ... you've kind of taken a step beyond the norm. And I feel like I'm the normal person who is aware of the environment and tries to be conscious of my actions and the impact they're having.

Comparing self-identified environmentalists with non-environmentalists, however, reveals only marginal differences in environmental concern, movement participation, and environmentally friendly behaviour. The main issue is ambiguity about the term "environmentalist" as a label and whether respondents wish to adopt it as an identity. Sociologist Manuel Castells notes, "For a given individual ... there may be a plurality of identities. Yet, such a plurality is a source of stress and contradiction in both self-representation and social action."[27] Even though skiers take on some of the elements associated with an environmentalist political identity, they may not feel willing to adopt the label "environmentalist" as a form of self-representation. Castells further argues that environmentalism has become a central "project identity" for individual and collective actors in contemporary societies. Project identities redefine our "position in society and, by so doing, seek the transformation of overall social structure."[28] Few skiers, however, take on an environmentalist identity to this extent. Rather, drawing on interviewees' own language, "environmentally aware" and "environmentally conscious" are more accurate terms to describe many of those skiers who distance themselves from environmental movement social networks and an environmentalist project identity.

Interview participants generally demonstrate high levels of environmental awareness and concern. Most engage in practices of environmentally friendly behaviour, and many have also been involved with the environmental movement. These skiers demonstrate how different dimensions of ecopolitics – values, identity, consumer behaviour, and social movement participation – join together as elements of environmental subjectivity. This account of skiers as ecological citizens and political consumers is consistent with prior survey research, which finds that skiers tend to rank at least as high as the general public on environmental values scales.[29] Skiers' interview talk resonates with cultural representations of skiing that link skiing with nature and a pro-environmental standpoint. Skiers' participation in ecological citizenship and political consumerism also suggests they would be an attentive audience for environmental movement claims about the negative ecological impacts of their sport.

Skiing as an Environmentalist Practice

Ski Resorts and Pro-Environmental Discourse

The main function of ski resort websites is to appeal to users as skier-tourists, yet most also espouse a pro-environmental standpoint. For example, the Whistler Blackcomb website has this to say about its Habitat Improvement Team, an environmental restoration initiative:

> The Whistler Blackcomb Habitat Improvement Team (HIT) was created in 1998 to provide the opportunity for local residents and WB employees to participate in hands-on projects benefiting the local environment. WB coordinates the volunteers for this program, providing the tools, equipment and transportation needed and hosting après activities after each session. HIT meets every second Tuesday evening from June to September to embark on tree planting, mountain bike trail maintenance, erosion control, stream and wetland stewardship and cleanup activities.[30]

Whistler Blackcomb also adopted the Whistler: It's Our Nature sustainability initiative and the Natural Step Framework for environmental planning, which is described as a systems-based approach to sustainability that is used by municipalities, corporations, and other organizations. In the section on sustainability planning for the resort, the website reads,

> Whistler Blackcomb is one of six "early adopter" organizations to partner in the Whistler: It's Our Nature sustainability initiative. Whistler: It's Our Nature is a community program to promote and support a sustainable Whistler. This program encourages businesses, households and other organizations to practice sustainability, including using the Natural Step Framework as their "sustainability compass." Within Whistler Blackcomb, we are working with our staff through departmental training and the development of issue-specific working groups to educate our staff about the Natural Step Framework and how it can be used to improve sustainability in our operations.[31]

Ski resorts – at Whistler Blackcomb and elsewhere – express their commitments to environmentalism through reduced power usage, waste reduction programs, wildlife habitat management, or the creation of pedestrian-friendly built environments.

The use of sustainability discourse by companies like Intrawest may reflect the legitimate desire of ski industry owners and managers to move toward a less ecologically harmful version of capitalism. From a more cynical perspective, it may be a strategy to distract environmentally concerned customers from the ecological harms associated with resort development. It undoubtedly mirrors the remarkable diffusion of pro-environmental discourse from social movements to broader social arenas. As Castells observes, "If we are to appraise social movements by their historical productivity ... by their impact on cultural values and society's institutions, the environmental movement has earned a distinctive place in the landscape of human adventure."[32] Setting aside the motivation of resort owners and managers, the ski industry's incorporation of sustainability measures like Natural Step recalls Mol and Spaargaren's ecological modernization theory (EMT).[33] This theoretical perspective asserts that neither technological industrialization nor capitalist social relations are inherently unsustainable. The central idea of EMT is that fundamental transformations must occur within modern institutions to correct the structural design faults that produce environmental damage. However, these fundamental transformations do not require dismantling the social structures of modern consumer capitalism. Instead, Mol and Spaargaren argue that capitalism constantly adapts to new conditions, that environmental degradation appears within alternative economic systems, and that there are no viable alternatives to current economic structures. In a similar vein, David Chernushenko and Bob Sachs each emphasize steps ski resorts can take to improve their environmental practices, such as conserving resources, enhancing wildlife habitat, and adopting green technologies.[34]

Ski resort environmentalism also involves leading others, including the public and resort employees, through environmental education. This is one way in which biopower relations between the ski industry and mountain environments translate into the microsocial scale of eco-politics. The Mount Washington website provides an example of this:

> Because of our setting in an outdoor, natural environment and the clear connection between that natural environment and the guest experience, we have an excellent opportunity to take a leadership role in environmental education and in enhancing the environmental awareness of our guests, surrounding communities, and employees.[35]

Ski corporations claim to contribute to enhancing environmental awareness among employees and clientele as environmental subjectivities take shape through skiers' embodied experiences of an "outdoor, natural environment." This discourse is reminiscent of Foucault's notion of pastoral power, which is "entirely defined by its beneficence; its only *raison d'être* is doing good, and in order to do good."[36] Pastoral power originates from the Christian exercise of power to promote the well-being of individuals under its auspices. As Foucault notes, "The pastorate is connected to salvation ... This is true both for individuals and for the community. The pastorate therefore guides individuals and the community on the way to salvation."[37] Much as environmental groups work to promote environmental values, Mount Washington asserts that it helps guide skiers to ecological salvation. Ski resort environmental education may inspire individual acts of environmental consumerism, but it differs from environmental movement discourse in its silence on the negative environmental impacts of skiing.

Pro-environmental discourse appears throughout the physical landscape of Whistler Blackcomb. Signs about animal stewardship are placed around the Crystal Chair area on Blackcomb Mountain. These signs assert that glading – selective logging to create space for skiers to move through the forest – creates habitat and new food sources for bears and deer, thereby benefiting animal inhabitants of skiing landscapes (see Figure 4.3). Similar signs about environmentally sensitive ski run design are located in the Symphony area of Whistler Mountain. These signs inform skiers that "tree islands" in the area provide for the well-being of local bear and deer populations. Where the long, gentle run out from the Blackcomb Glacier crosses Horstman Creek, another sign tells skiers that the bridge was rebuilt to protect the creek and enhance downstream habitat for rainbow, kokanee, and Dolly Varden trout as part of the resort's Operation Green-Up. Glacier Lodge, a large restaurant midway up

Blackcomb Mountain, also includes a large sign about environmental stewardship that features several photos of black bears, meant to represent the local bears whose well-being is ensured by Whistler Blackcomb's habitat stewardship.

As environmental historian Tina Loo observes, attempts to systematize wildlife management through the twentieth century are a key part of the ongoing "rationalization of people's relationship to the natural world."[38] This process is visible within skiing, as bears, deer, or fish become objects of environmental management through ski resort environmentalism. These practices may be categorized as examples of the productive dimensions of biopower, oriented toward managing the well-being and productivity of the local environment and its non-human populations. Despite wildlife stewardship practices being framed as commitments to sustainability, Jack Turner expresses skepticism about productive biopower relations between humans and animals. He argues, "Ecological management is Foucault's normalization and disciplinary control projected from social institutions onto ecosystems ... the new doctors of nature go about their mission ... the preservation of biodiversity."[39] Stewardship of bears, deer, fish, and other animals might be reinterpreted as a form of species-colonization that social organizations work upon nature.

Signs positioned around Whistler Blackcomb incorporate a range of other pro-environmental discourses. Posters in Whistler Village promote an educational event about climate change titled Global Cooling, with the tag line Save Our Snow. The Symphony area on Whistler Mountain, which offers a simulated backcountry experience with the safety and convenience of the ski resort, is rife with environmentally oriented texts. This includes a large educational sign about climate change that is prominently displayed near the Symphony chairlift. The sign introduces and explains the issue, then tells skiers about the microhydro project being used to produce electricity for the chairlift from a nearby creek. Other signs inform readers that the Symphony area has only had 5 percent of its trees cut through glading, in comparison with the 50 percent that is normal for ski run creation. At recycling stations throughout Whistler Blackcomb, skiers are called upon to "help us conserve the environment." These signs echo the environmental discourse of ski resort

Figure 4.3   Managing bear and deer habitat, Whistler Blackcomb

websites and further define ski resort companies as pro-environmental managers of British Columbia's mountain environments. This discourse symbolizes moves toward attractive development in the province and ecological modernization within the ski industry. However, it removes from sight environmentalist questions about the ecological legitimacy of skiing's biopower relationships with nature.

The recurrent use of pro-environmental discourse at Whistler Blackcomb is rarely seen at Whitewater. In Last Run at Coal Oil Johnny's Pub there is a recycling sign above the garbage can that reads Be Aware, Save with Care, asking skiers not to throw out recyclables. Compared with the numerous pro-environmental signs at Whistler Blackcomb, this is a subtle – almost unnoticeable – nod to environmental values. Other than the presence of recycling bins, there is little attempt by Whitewater to "educate" skiers about environmentally friendly behaviour. Environmental discourse is a patterned silence within the physical landscape of Whitewater, in contrast to its website, which contains material on its environmental stewardship practices. The differences between how

Whistler Blackcomb and Whitewater use environmental discourse likely relates to other differences between the resorts. Whistler Blackcomb is a large resort that is central to international tourism networks. It resembles a rural, mountainous version of a themed fantasy city of consumerism and riskless risk.[40] The promotion of a pro-environmental mythology of skiing at Whistler Blackcomb masks the ecologically problematic dimensions of skiing's relationship with consumerism and global mobility.[41] Whitewater, by contrast, is a peripheral space within skiing-tourism networks and is less oriented toward creating an experience of rustic luxury. As a result, perhaps Whitewater managers feel less pressure than those at Whistler Blackcomb to display their pro-environmental credentials.

Pro-Environmental Representations of Skiing in the Mass Media

BC ski resorts often present themselves as pro-environmental stewards of mountain landscapes, but this position is often disputed by environmentalists. Political conflict over the meaning of these landscapes plays out in the mass media. A dominant news media discourse links skiing to tourism and economic development, rather than to environmentalism. Attempts by ski industry news sources to define themselves as pro-environmental also appear, though to a lesser extent, in media texts.

The Jumbo Pass conflict provides a useful example of this. Jumbo Pass is located in the Purcell Mountains of southeastern British Columbia. The nearest cities are Invermere to the east and Nelson to the southwest. Hikers and backcountry skiers use the area, and environmentalists value it as wildlife habitat. Jumbo Glacier Resort is a planned year-round ski resort that has been the object of social movement mobilization since it was proposed more than twenty years ago. In media coverage of the conflict, representatives of the development define themselves as pro-environmental by stating that they have responded to concerns raised by provincial environmental assessments of the project. An article from the *Cranbrook Daily Townsman*, a local newspaper that provides regular coverage of the Jumbo dispute, illustrates this. Grant Costello, a vice-president with the development company, invokes the provincial government's environmental assessment approval to assert the company's ecological legitimacy:

"It's been very satisfying to have received primary approval through the environmental certificate issued last year and now to be in the final stages of the provincial review process."

Costello says critics of the resort proposal are not as numerous as it often appears and he welcomes any meaningful input from them. "If they have information other than saying they don't want development of any kind in the Jumbo Valley, we will respond to that information. That's what a public open house is for."

The mammoth resort has already been scaled down from its original size and several changes made, including a state-of-the-art effluent disposal system to deal with environmental and wildlife concerns, he says.[42]

Resort proponents frame environmentalist opposition as anti-development absolutism because the provincial government's environmental review approved the project. It is worth observing, as David Boyd does in his review of Canadian environmental policy, that every project that has undergone provincial environmental assessment in British Columbia has been approved.[43] Costello uses environmental assessment approval as a strategy to claim environmental legitimacy for the project. By doing so, he is able to portray environmentalists as unreasonable and unwilling to offer "meaningful input," which is limited to deliberative discussion about *how* the resort will be built to minimize its ecological impact. It does not include questions about *whether* an existing collective of wildlife (including sensitive species like grizzly bears and wolverines) and recreational users should be transformed and reconstituted as a new ski resort collective.[44]

Another media discourse describes how ski hills adopt technological improvements to lessen their impact on the environment and move skiing further toward sustainability. This is often linked to descriptions of skiing as a canary in the coal mine for the impacts of climate change, much like the world's low-lying cities (such as Venice or New Orleans), or melting ice caps in the Arctic or Antarctica. Several articles discuss attempts by the ski industry to adapt to the uncertainties of climate change by enrolling machines into projects for increased snow-making and glacier preservation. For example, a 2003 article from the *Nanaimo Daily News* states,

Whistler itself is aware of the looming problem of global warming. The municipality has recently adopted standards to make itself more environmentally sustainable. And Intrawest Resorts, the operators of Whistler Blackcomb, is expecting to invest millions of dollars in new snow-making equipment over the coming years.[45]

Ski resorts' attempts to address climate change go beyond increased snow-making and glacier preservation. Another article on climate change and skiing tells readers that Whistler Blackcomb is improving its environmental practices through technological innovation:

> Whistler Blackcomb is trying to grow back the glaciers by adding artificial snow and by building snow fences to protect them from wind erosion, DeJong [Whistler Blackcomb's environmental resource manager] says.
>
> The resort is also trying to set a good example by using fuel-efficient snow-grooming machines and the hill is even researching the viability of putting wind turbines on their mountains to produce clean energy.[46]

Media accounts of alternative energy and energy efficiency measures link skiing to an environmentalist standpoint. As in ski resort websites, ski industry environmentalism echoes ecological modernization theory's assertion that environmental sustainability is achievable within existing economic and political structures through technological change and more efficient use of resources.[47]

In these mass media texts, as in ski industry discourse, skiing's own contribution to climate change becomes a "patterned silence."[48] Representations of the sport as pro-environmental neglect its intimate connections to automobility networks and global tourist travel, which produce significant amounts of greenhouse gases and contribute to global climate change. There is a circular relationship between skiing, mobility, and climate change. Skiers depend on automobility and aeromobility networks to access mountainous nature. These networks contribute to global climate change, which disproportionately affects the alpine environments skiers value. By focusing only on skiing's vulnerability and adaptation to climate change, media accounts can frame skiing as a pro-environmental mode of interaction with mountainous nature. A complete account would acknowledge the ecological irony inherent in the gap between pro-environmental representations of skiing and skiers' reliance on environmentally problematic mobility networks.[49]

Skiing as an Environmental Problem

Ski companies position themselves as pro-environmental stewards of mountain landscapes. By challenging ski development at places like Jumbo Pass, Sun Peaks, and Melvin Creek, environmentalists and First Nations protesters question the ecological and social legitimacy of skiing. Environmental groups claim that new ski development transforms existing natural landscapes into social spaces for recreation and mass tourism, as deforestation for ski runs and resort infrastructure risk displacing sensitive animal species such as grizzly bears, mountain caribou, and wolverines. Other negative ecological impacts from skiing include soil erosion, damage to vegetation, stress to local animal populations, power use for chairlifts, water pollution from resort waste, and water and energy consumption for artificial snow-making.[50] Skiing might be interpreted as relatively sustainable when compared with extractive uses of mountain environments like logging or mining, but it does produce its own negative environmental effects.

Environmental Reflexivity within Skiing Texts

Interpretations of skiing as an environmental problem rarely appear in ski magazines or on ski resort websites. Most resort websites include sections on pro-environmental behaviour, though only a couple acknowledge the negative environmental consequences produced by skiing. Discussions of these impacts are typically only a prelude to claims that they are being addressed. For example, Mount Washington highlights the problematic connections between skiing and private car use in the context of attempts to improve transit links with local communities.[51] This theme, which appears only on the Mount Washington website, highlights how the ecologically troublesome relationship between skiing and automobility normally fades into the background of skiing discourse.

Ski magazines offer a few more examples of environmental self-reflexivity than do resort websites. In particular, magazine articles occasionally raise questions about the environmental ethics of using helicopters and snowmobiles for backcountry access. The following excerpt is from a *Backcountry* article by Emily Stifler on heli-skiing, which focuses on British Columbia, Alaska, and the Himalayas as prime destinations:

> It remains to be seen if this market will take off at all. In the meantime ethical dilemmas surrounding helis in the backcountry abound. HeliCat Canada ... claims heli-accessed skiing "exerts minimal environmental impact." This statement, self-propelled touring proponents argue, doesn't entirely hold water: a six-passenger helicopter can use over 60 gallons of petroleum per hour, and increasing human presence in remote wilderness certainly impacts natural habitat.[52]

The text is accompanied by website listings and contact information for several heli-ski companies in British Columbia, thereby appealing to magazine readers as potential skier-tourists. The magazine neglects to provide links to sites where readers may find additional information on the environmental questions raised in the article. Wildsight, for example, is a BC environmental group that has actively campaigned to restrict mechanized backcountry access because of concerns over wildlife impacts.[53] The *Backcountry* article suggests that skier-tourists should be environmentally aware – but not to such a degree that it stops them from participating in heli-skiing or other forms of skiing tourism.

Although self-reflection on mechanized backcountry access is valuable, this accounts for a small part of the ski industry. Ski magazines give little attention to the mundane impacts of ski resorts, which involve energy and water consumption, changes to alpine vegetation patterns, and stress to local wildlife. In a rare example, environmental reflexivity enters *Powder* magazine's coverage of the conflict over the proposed Jumbo Glacier Resort. The author, Mitchell Scott, is sympathetic to environmentalist claims that the resort is unnecessary and undesirable. In spite of his misgivings, however, he concludes that the resort will be too alluring for skiers to resist:

From the all-important skier's point of view, seeing resorts like Whistler go the way of crowds and high-speed lifts, maybe a new resort [Jumbo Pass] tucked away in the wilderness isn't such a bad idea. "None of us want it, nor do we think we need it," says Byron Grey, a long-time Invermere local who ski tours Jumbo Pass on a weekly basis. "But make no mistake, I'll be up there for first chair every big day." This seems to sum up the sentiments of many BC skiers. No one thinks the province needs a Jumbo, but once the bull wheels go in and the snow starts to fall, rest assured they'll be there, unwrapping their winter gifts.[54]

As in Stifler's *Backcountry* article on heli-skiing, environmental reflexivity enters Scott's text in a manner that is constrained and subsumed to an "all important skier's point of view." Scott raises environmental questions about the proposal but does not mention the specific environmental groups that mobilized in opposition to the resort. A "skier's point of view" includes occasional attention to the environmental impacts of the sport, but environmental reflexivity is not a barrier to "unwrapping [the] winter gifts" of new ski resort development.

Environmental Reflexivity among Skiers

Skiers make up an attentive audience for ski industry and social movement discourse about the sport. Skiers' reflections on their sport offer insight into how these discourses are interpreted and put into practice. A recurrent narrative among skiers, which resonates with ski industry discourse of skiing and the environment, describes how skiing may inspire care for nature through interaction with the mountains. As such, skiing may work as an environmental technology of the self, a physical practice used to shape participants' subjectivities.[55] This theme illustrates how subjectivities are formed through bodily encounters with non-human environments and their inhabitants.

Edward describes the connections between skiing and environmental subjectivity by saying, "I think if it gets people out into the mountains, they'll appreciate the beauty, and hopefully that'll sink in and they'll think about their impact on the environment by seeing it." Heather similarly links her skiing experience with her own environmental values:

"Well, I feel like ... [skiing has] given me kind of a love for the wilderness. And I know that a lot of the choices I make probably stem from that experience. And I want that to always be part of my life. So I want to try to contribute in some way, so that that can always be there." The choices she mentions include commitments to environmentally friendly behaviour (she talks about using a travel mug, using less packaging, and reducing car use) and financial support for environmental organizations. Nicola similarly talks about how skiing with her family exposed her two children – a son and a daughter – to nature as teenagers. She describes their later involvement in environmentalism as a legacy of their early skiing experience: "And later on, how they got into the environment, and so on, through their skiing and their outdoor pursuits. But also, that as teenagers they did something worthwhile, something active, and so on, which has really given them a legacy for their later life." In these narratives, skiing helps participants develop their environmental subjectivities and interest in ecopolitics. Similar connections between outdoor sport and environmentalism have been noted among surfers whose interaction with ocean environments leads them to engage with environmentalism.[56]

Despite valuing skiing as a mode of interaction with mountainous nature, most interviewees also articulate environmental critiques of skiing. A common theme is that skiing impacts wildlife, both through habitat displacement on ski hills and through the noise pollution of backcountry snowmobile and helicopter use. For example, Shantel responds to a question about Jumbo Glacier Resort by saying,

> It's always good that industry is thinking more, and they're pressured to do so, to think more toward lower environmental impact. But lower environmental impact means nothing when it comes to– we've got a pristine wilderness that has grizzlies and wildlife that will be impacted. And there's no amount of environmental sensitivity in building a resort that can prevent that. You know, our bears and wildlife are being displaced as it is as communities expand ... We're already pushing them so far away from their original habitats that, you know, I'm very much opposed to Jumbo.

Shantel's comment illustrates how relations of biopower within skiing are not oriented only toward managing wildlife for population health, as suggested by ski resort claims about habitat stewardship. In asserting that pristine wilderness needs protection from ski development, Shantel echoes environmental movement discourse that ski industry expansion involves the expulsion of species that are less well equipped to cohabit as members of skiing collectives. This illustrates that there is tension, as well as harmony, between large-scale operations of biopower and the formation of environmental subjectivity through skiing.

Nicola, a Vancouver-area skier, offers a similar critique of the Jumbo Resort development. She also describes helicopter and car use as ways in which wildlife is affected by skiing:

> I'm against that development there. That is grizzly habitat, and it has shrunk so much that we cannot afford to take any more away. And I've also read studies that, you know, the impact on wildlife, their winter survival is so precarious, if they're disturbed again and again with helicopters, or cars, or whatever. And they have to use up so much energy for flying away and flying up, that they don't use for food collection and survival, that ... puts them at risk, too.

Nicola tells me that she has read studies about the impact of skiing on wildlife habitat, thereby reinforcing her authority to speak on this issue. She also invokes the grizzly bear as a key symbol of threatened wilderness. This echoes environmentalist discourse that positions skiing against animals like grizzly bears, whose coexistence within skiing collectives would be "precarious." Nicola attempts to move beyond the "all-important skiers' standpoint" and instead adopts a wildlife standpoint, much as environmentalists attempt to do.[57]

Skiers also hone in on the energy required to run chairlifts, drive to ski areas, or power snowmobiles and helicopters for backcountry skiing access. Jess argues that backcountry skiing can be environmentally sustainable but that ski resorts are less sustainable "because there's a lot of energy going into powering those lifts. You know, that's not human-powered energy. Whereas in the backcountry it is." Energy use is also cited by Jenny as evidence of the unsustainability of skiing:

> Lots of people think of skiing as going to their Whistler condo in
> their Hummer3 or whatever. And, you know, having the newest gear
> and the newest outfit, and going up and down lifts all day which are
> powered by some sort of electricity, and some sort of energy.

Jenny's comment implies that environmentally aware skiers (a category
she identifies with) represent a minority. She asserts that, instead, many
skiers engage in the sport as a consumerist practice, which is closely
bound up with energy use and automobility networks. Her invocation
of the Hummer3, an iconic symbol of conspicuous consumption, provides a vivid image of the ecological ambiguity within skiing. Jenny's
response locates skiing within an economy of consumerism and waste.
As Zygmunt Bauman writes, "In a world filled with consumers and the
objects of their consumption, life is hovering uneasily between the joys
of consumption and the horrors of the rubbish heap."[58]
Interview participants repeatedly describe skiing's intimate ties to
automobility as one of the main environmental tensions within skiing.
Several skiers acknowledge that their pro-environmental values do not
mesh well with their reliance on cars to access mountain environments.
Interview talk about skiing and automobility contrasts with the invisibility of this discourse within ski magazines, resort websites, newspaper
articles, and environmentalist websites. Besides talking about the impacts
of their own car use, several participants also refer to ties with automobility when discussing the 2010 Winter Olympics. For example, Peg views
the choice to upgrade the highway instead of revitalizing rail service as
a wasted opportunity:

> I think it's absolutely ridiculous that they're upgrading the Sea to Sky
> Highway and not building a train to go up there. That was such an
> opportunity to meet that mission [of a "sustainable" Olympics]. That
> would have been a great example that they really meant it. And I
> think that was a controversial issue. And I think they made the wrong
> decision.

Several skiers see a disconnect between government and Olympic organizers' claims to sustainability, while Olympic-inspired highway expansion

proceeds between Vancouver and Whistler. The decision not to use the Olympics to revitalize rail service further entrenches the path dependence of Whistler-bound skiers on existing automobility networks.[59]

The highway expansion also met with environmental protest over impacts to bird habitat at Eagleridge Bluffs, near the affluent suburb of West Vancouver. Olympics critic Helen Lenskyj summarizes the dispute, writing, "As protesters pointed out, despite the Olympic bid's promises of 'multi-modal' approaches to transportation, the highway represented yet another environmental sacrifice to the automobile."[60] As in environmentalist discourse, which circulated in provincial media coverage of the protests, several skiers invoke the choice to upgrade the highway to bolster their skepticism about VANOC (Vancouver Organizing Committee for the 2010 Olympic and Paralympic Winter Games) and the provincial government's professed commitment to environmental values. Skiers' talk about 2010 Olympics highway construction provides another example of the tensions between the different scales at which ecopolitics operates through skiing. It also demonstrates that skiers' interpretations of their sport may be influenced by social movement discourse, as well as by ski industry discourse.

Skiers' interview talk describes environmental ambiguities at the heart of skiing. Skiing is valued because it brings skiers into embodied relationships with mountainous nature. Many skiers also demonstrate awareness of their sport's negative impacts through wildlife disruption and energy use. These different interpretations of skiing's relationship with the environment are not mutually exclusive. For many skiers, such as Roberta, they coexist in tension with each other:

> I find myself in personal conflict being a skier. As an environmentalist and, you know, loving skiing. So I'm always walking that line and trying to find a way to have as little impact as I can. But I think it's possible.

Skiers' reflections on the sustainability of skiing echo ski industry discourse that links skiing, nature, and a pro-environmental standpoint. Skiers also evoke environmentalist discourse about skiing's negative impacts. Skiers' interview talk highlights the ecological ambiguities inherent in skiing, which rarely appear in ski magazines or on ski websites. Meaningful action by the ski industry to mitigate tensions between pro-environmental discourse and ecologically harmful impacts on mountain environments would likely be welcomed by many skiers.

Conclusion: Skiing, Biopower, and Ecopolitics

As a form of attractive development, skiing does not transform the BC landscape into natural resources.[61] Instead, skiing appears as a relatively benign use of the landscape, based on the non-consumptive experience of mountainous nature. A common discourse focuses on how the ski industry engages in something akin to ecological modernization.[62] The industry strives to improve its environmental practices without disturbing existing economic or political social structures. Technological innovation is part of this, as is stewardship of wildlife habitat. This interpretation of skiing is echoed in interviews with skiers, who often speak of skiing as a valuable mode of interacting with – and coming to care for – mountain environments.

Environmental sustainability is a slippery and contested concept, as illustrated in environmentalist mobilization against new ski development. Skiing is arguably less ecologically harmful than extractive industries like forestry or mining, which have traditionally dominated the political economy of British Columbia. Narratives that celebrate the increased prominence of attractive development ignore the ways in which such development produces its own ecological impacts. The production of skiing as a consumer experience requires the deforestation of ski runs, as well as energy use for transportation and snow-making. These processes involve significant withdrawals from non-human nature in the form of trees cut and energy used. These processes also produce additions to non-human nature in the form of water pollution or greenhouse gas emissions.[63]

Shifts toward attractive development do not remove mountain environments from biopower relations between humans and non-humans. Biopower is oriented toward the rational surveillance and management of populations in the interests of health and productivity. The concept of biopower may be extended to the non-human world, as wildlife populations or forests are defined as populations or resources that are managed for productivity. Through skiing, mountains, forests, and the animals that inhabit them are incorporated into different sets of biopower relations than those inherent in extractive industries. These biopower relations reconstruct mountainous nature as sportscapes that attract skiers and tourists.[64]

Animal habitat management programs connect skiing to a pro-environmental standpoint, while obscuring the ways in which associations between skiers and animals may have harmful effects. Biopower relations between the ski industry and wildlife populations are not only productive. As mountain environments are transformed for recreational use, animals may be harmed or pushed out of their habitat. Writing against the ski industry's pro-environmental representation of itself, Hal Clifford argues that the expansion of modern ski resorts resulted in a decline in animal populations: "Wildlife habitat is fragmented by roads, trails, and ski slopes ... Sensitive species ... unable to tolerate increased human presence, flee not only the disturbed areas, but also much larger regions around them."[65] This assessment brings to mind Foucault's discussion of the Middle Ages leper colony as the embodiment of the exercise of power based on categorization and "a rigorous division, a distancing, a rule of no contact between one individual (or group of individuals) and another." As skiing collectives take shape, some animals are incorporated through productive forms of biopower, while those that cannot cohabit with skiers, hotels, lodges, and chairlifts are pushed out. As in the case of the leper colony, animals that do not fit into our vision for the landscape move out "into a vague, external world beyond the town's walls, beyond the limits of the community."[66]

Many skiers describe how skiing enables them to come into contact with and care about nature. This theme is similar to Nancy Midol and Gerard Broyer's observation that skiers among the "whiz sports" movement in France use sport to create new relationships with nature, through "dropping one's defenses, feeling the harmony, becoming the snowfield, becoming one with the scenery." This is also consistent with Susan Schrepfer's historical account of how participation in recreational mountaineering influenced many key members of the early American environmental movement.[67] It further echoes research on connections between surfing and environmental activism that form through surfers' embodied experiences of water pollution.[68] As skiing helps participants form a more pro-environmental sense of themselves, we might think of it as an environmental technology of the self.[69] Despite ski industry attempts to link skiing and nature, skiers may be a particularly attentive audience for environmentalist claims about the negative impacts of the sport.

Most interview participants also articulate environmental critiques of their sport, as they repeatedly demonstrate awareness of the contradictions inherent in skiing's relationship with nature. Skiing is valued because it allows participants to interact with mountainous nature, but the sport also contributes to environmental degradation through wildlife displacement and energy consumption. Similarly, skiers describe how the sport is bound up with automobility and aeromobility networks that enable skiers to access mountainous nature but also contribute to greenhouse gas emissions and exacerbate global climate change.[70] Skiers' reflections on the political ecology of their sport complicates pro-environmental narratives of skiing and the attractive economy more broadly. The political ecology of skiing is marked by several ecological ironies, or gaps between professed pro-environmental values and active engagement in ecologically harmful practices.[71] Many skiers would welcome meaningful steps by the ski industry toward mitigating these ecological ironies.

Skiing and Social Power   **5**

An examination of the ways in which gender, class, race, and ethnicity inflect skiers' interactions with mountainous nature provides a more complex picture of the political ecology of skiing. Skiing landscapes work as sites of normalized whiteness and the selective visibility of First Nations. Similarly, skiing culture often privileges a "guys' style" of skiing that may discourage female participation in the sport. Contradictory notions of class play out within skiing, where images of rustic luxury coexist with claims that skiing is open to everybody. The operation of social power through skiing rarely appears as obvious acts of exclusion or discrimination. Rather, power moves through the "capillaries" of skiing and subtly shapes cultural understandings of which social groups should inhabit and manage the mountain environments where skiing takes place.[1]

Outdoor Sport and Social Power

Race, Ethnicity, and Outdoor Sport
Power relations based on race and ethnicity operate through outdoor sport. Media representations of surfing, rock climbing, and skiing typically favour images of whiteness, which produces a "racialized outdoor

leisure identity" and defines wilderness as white space.[2] In his analysis of media representations of wilderness recreation, Bruce Braun observes, "Within mainstream American culture, *taking* risks is understood as an individuating activity associated with whiteness. One takes risks when one chooses to. Being *at* risk is commonly viewed as a property that belongs to someone else, the *racial* subject."[3]

Mountaineering, for example, is routinely done to perform risk-seeking forms of masculinity associated with "the hegemonic male adventure hero – white, heterosexual, bourgeois, athletic, courageous, risk taking, imperialist, and unmarked."[4] The history of British nationalism and mountaineering on Mount Everest illustrates this connection between sport and ethnicity. As sport historian Susan Birrell notes, "Although Everest was located in a desolate area which was never within bounds of the British Empire ... most Britons considered it a British peak."[5] The history of Canadian mountaineering was similarly intertwined with the colonial project of mapping and redefining First Nations territory as Canadian territory and "emptying the land of the presence of First Nations."[6] This research illustrates how outdoor sport produces places where whiteness is taken for granted and naturalized.

This dynamic plays out in skiing as well as in mountaineering. Historian Annie Gilbert Coleman argues that skiing created a version of the American Rockies characterized by normalized whiteness and the transformation of Native American and Hispanic histories of inhabitation into "sanitized objects for consumption" for tourists. However, the ski resorts of the American Rockies have been undergoing an important labour market shift that is changing this social dynamic. Hal Rothman traces the emergence of ski resort tourism in Idaho, Colorado, and Wyoming and follows its development throughout the postwar period. Ski resort towns developed on top of older communities as new arrivals, or "neonatives," took over resource communities located in the mountains. Over time, ski resort towns were divided by class, as rich home owners lived at the centre, while a struggling labouring class was forced out to the periphery. This class hierarchy is increasingly racialized, with white Americans dominating the tourist centre, Latino and Black workers populating the poorly paid service class. This pattern leads Lisa Park and David Pellow to characterize ski resorts as places of environmental privilege, defined by beautiful vistas, clean air, and unpolluted water, in juxtaposition to spaces of environmental pollution and risk typically examined by environmental justice scholars.[7]

Skiing in British Columbia intersects with issues of colonialism and First Nations claims to the landscape. Nature-based tourism has long played a role in asserting the right of settler populations to move freely through colonized places in Canada.[8] In the early twentieth century, for example, tourism was used to lure new settlers to British Columbia and assert colonial ownership of the landscape. Later, First Nations ethnicity was packaged as spectacle to entertain tourists in a manner that rendered this history of colonization invisible. As Michael Dawson writes, "Having contributed directly to the colonial process in its first phase, tourism promotion then contributed to a process of selective amnesia in its second phase – a process that ... encouraged both visitors and hosts to reimagine the 'resettlement' of British Columbia as benign, comforting, and con-·sumable fare."[9]

Gender and Outdoor Sport

Research on snowboarding, surfing, canoeing, mountaineering, and windsurfing documents how participants construct the meaning of masculinity and femininity through outdoor sport. This research also demonstrates that outdoor sport produces, maintains, and transforms gendered power relations. Practices that privilege male-oriented versions of outdoor sport limit women's participation. For example, Kristin Anderson argues that snowboarders use several practices to assert the masculinity of their sport, such as incorporating fashion and music associated with black male youth subcultures, adopting aggressive modes of personal interaction, and emphasizing their heterosexuality. Susan Frohlick's analysis of mountain film festivals documents the invisibility of women in the cinematic imaginary of mountaineering, even though women often attend these film festivals as spectators. Donna Little and Erica Wilson similarly draw on interviews with female adventure sport participants to document how women struggle with typical images of the male adventurer who is "physically tough, mentally alert and aloof" as they "leave behind family and friends to pursue their dreams" through outdoor sport.[10]

A counterpoint in this literature is that participants may use outdoor sport to pose a limited challenge to dominant gender norms. Skiing initially permitted a "natural" freedom that was becoming harder to find in the industrial landscape of early-twentieth-century America. In the 1920s and 1930s, female skiers connected the notion of freedom through skiing with new ideas about the meaning of womanhood. Coleman argues that "women across the economic spectrum found themselves enamoured with skiing downhill, which could offer them a liberating taste of speed, exhilaration, and danger."[11] The image of the "snow bunny" – with its emphasis on fashion and the sexualization of female skiers for a male gaze – limited women's participation in skiing for much of the twentieth century. The emergence of snowboarding, however, renewed the promise of snow riding as a site for female athleticism. "The unusual combination of girly looks, rap music, and fearless athleticism came together in the image of the Shred Betty that these women embodied and promoted. When they launched themselves off that big jump, they contested the masculinity of the space as well as their competitors' skills."[12]

Sport sociologist Holly Thorpe also describes how women snowboarders carve out space to participate on a relatively equal basis with men, in comparison with many other sports. Embodying the pop culture discourse of girl power, female snowboarders "found space to creatively resist mainstream culture and to define and redefine their own roles."[13] However, snowboarders largely failed to redefine the relationship between gender and sport. As Thorpe observes, "The dominant style of snowboarding has become more aggressive, perilous and exhibitionist" as the sport has evolved.[14] Individual women continue to participate and compete successfully alongside men, but styles of riding characterized as masculine are more highly valued. The commodification of snowboarding has similarly transformed the subcultural setting where participants could challenge traditional gender norms. As a result, "the female boarder is increasingly ... situated within a commercialized variant of heterosexual femininity."[15]

In their analysis of female snowboarding and skydiving, Jason Laurendeau and Nancy Sharara distinguish between "reproductive" and "resistant" agency as strategies for addressing gender inequality in sport.[16] The former refers to individual attempts to manage gender inequality, whereas the latter refers to attempts to transform gendered power relations. Strategies of reproductive agency are used much more frequently, as female snowboarders and skydivers downplay the importance of their gender, avoid certain spaces, or attempt to blend in by wearing gender-neutral styles of clothing. Despite individual women using sport to transform their own experience of gender, Laurendeau and Sharara are pessimistic about the possibilities for fundamentally reshaping relations of gender inequality through sport.

The physical spaces of outdoor sport also reinforce dominant discourses about gender and sport participation. According to both Henning Eichberg and Patricia Vertinsky, the modernist architecture of stadiums, gymnasia, and similar sportscapes creates places oriented toward masculinized forms of athletic performance.[17] Outside the modernist confines of stadiums and gymnasia, "natural" sportscapes are similarly defined in gendered terms. Drawing attention to the interplay of space, gender, and power in surfing, Gordon Waitt writes, "For men-who-surf, the white-water is spoken as a boundary, dividing heterosexual from non-heterosexual male board-riders." Aggressive surfing at the surf break allows surfers to perform a highly valued form of masculinity. Athletic performances within the physical context of the surf break solidify dominant understandings of surf masculinity by stabilizing "gender within the conventional binary scripts of land-ocean, culture-nature, man-woman and straight-gay."[18] Big wave riding is used to assert a valorized version of surf masculinity that is attainable for only the most risk-seeking surfers. This style of surfing takes place far from shore among huge, dangerous waves. It represents a "return to the heroic masculinities of the early days of surfing" by "carving out ... new territory" that separates hard-core male riders from women and less skilled men.[19]

Skiing, Cultural Capital, and Economic Capital

Pierre Bourdieu asserts that sport is a site where economic capital is required for entry and where cultural capital is built up and exercised. Skiing is an example of how social class and cultural capital intersect within a specific field. Participation requires money for specialized gear, as well as lift tickets, but there are also "hidden entry requirements, such as family tradition and early training, and also the obligatory clothing, bearing and techniques of sociability which keep these sports closed to the working classes."[20] While Bourdieu writes of skiing and cultural capital in the context of Europe, Gerry Veenstra includes skiing in his description of a West Coast lifestyle that works as a form of cultural capital in British Columbia.[21] This lifestyle includes hiking, skiing, yoga, cycling, and kayaking as forms of recreation and bodily fitness. The West Coast lifestyle is strongly linked to the province's professional class. Skiing requires economic capital for participation; it is also a site for accumulating cultural capital.

Edward Richey's history of Aspen, Colorado, offers an alternative to historical narratives of waning authenticity in skiing, which is particularly attentive to the class dynamics of ski culture. While people moved to Aspen as an escape from postwar, middle-class America, he argues that skiers routinely performed a masking of their privileged class backgrounds. He writes, "In Aspen, members of the American elite, the men and women with considerable personal or family wealth, often played at, or pretended temporarily to be of a lower class."[22] For these skiers, cultural capital was invested in a working-class ski bum identity that rejected the conspicuous consumption that was dominant in postwar America. This account contrasts with Bourdieu's and Veenstra's observations about skiing as a form of cultural capital. Instead, skiers from wealthy backgrounds took on seasonal work at ski hills, restaurants, and hotels. They lived in rundown miners' shacks and dressed as inhabitants of a frontier town. The golden age of skiing described by ski historians was marked by a wilful denial of class dynamics within ski communities.

Joanne Kay and Suzanne Laberge draw on Bourdieu in their textual analysis of Warren Miller's ski film *Freeriders*. They argue that this film, which is representative of many ski films, asserts an "imperialistic construction of freedom," which is imposed on other people and places.[23] The film defines freedom as the ability to move freely through the postmodern tourist economy and the ability to abdicate wage labour in favour of a life of leisure. The freedom promoted in ski films is an illusory freedom that is "found in mobility" and is limited to those with the financial capital to pursue skiing full time.[24] This imperialistic construction of freedom is a form of symbolic violence against the foreign cultures that are subject to the cinematic skiing gaze. Those who lack the economic and cultural capital required to enter the world of skiing abdicate their claims to freedom.

Haraway and Social Power

Donna Haraway offers a model of social power that challenges critical theory narratives of class struggle and ideological domination. The social world can no longer be understood according to a binary logic of ruling class versus working class. Other theories of domination based on binaries of gender (men versus women), race (white versus non-white), or species (human versus non-human) are also increasingly untenable. This is not to say that class, ethnicity, and gender no longer have social relevance. Discourses of class, ethnicity, and gender are routinely taken up and expressed through social interactions. Haraway suggests treating class, ethnicity, and gender less as objects than as processes. Like Foucault, Haraway emphasizes the relational and discursive characteristics of social power. Power works through everyday interaction, while it also coheres in political and economic structures.

Haraway departs from Foucault in her insistence on the permeability of boundaries between humans and animals, society and nature, and the organic and the technological within contemporary social life. The purity of the human, the social, and the organic is increasingly called into question, resulting in the prevalence of cyborg subject positions. We do not only identify as members of a class, a gender, a nation, or an ethnic group but take on multiple identities that overlap and intersect. Haraway writes, "So my cyborg myth is about transgressed boundaries, potent fusions, and dangerous possibilities."[25] Class-based, racialized, and gendered systems of power intersect and continue to be relevant. Skiing is characterized by ideas of "rustic luxury," normalized whiteness and masculinity, the marginalization of First Nations from skiing landscapes, and gendered differences in participants' experiences.

The Selective Visibility of First Nations

Skiing and White Culture

Ski magazines and ski resort websites typically depict risk-seeking young, white, male skiers. These representations define skiing landscapes as places of white culture, where non-white skiers rarely gain entry as natural inhabitants of the mountainous sublime.[26] The consistency of images of white skiers is rarely disturbed in ski magazines or on websites. When ethnicity explicitly enters ski discourse, it comes as a surprise. For example, an article from *SBC Skier* magazine focuses on a speed-skiing event at Sun Peaks. In speed skiing, skiers use extra-long skis and wear form-fitting, aerodynamic clothing to race down a run in a straight line, achieving extremely high speeds. The article describes one of the racers as follows:

> [The outfit's] a pretty mackin' look, too, none more so than [that of] Ross Anderson of Ruidoso, New Mexico, whose helmet is painted like an elaborate native headdress. A Mescalero Apache, Anderson lives the dream as a casino greeter at Ski Apache and a part-time pro speed skier. His official banner hangs proudly at the finish line, bearing an unforgettable tag line: "The Fastest American Indian on Mother Earth: 236.07 km/h."[27]

Anderson is the only racer whose ethnicity is highlighted by the article. Episodes of making ethnicity visible are rare. They highlight the hegemonic whiteness of skiing texts, taking Raymond Williams's definition of hegemony as cultural beliefs ingrained in everyday common sense that produce power effects.[28]

First Nations, Skiing, and Contentious Politics

Ski industry discourse links skiing to images of nature and a pro-environmental standpoint. Environmentalist challenges to this interpretation of skiing focus on impacts to wildlife and wilderness. By contrast, First Nations protesters at Sun Peaks and Melvin Creek describe ski resort expansion and new resort development as an infringement upon unceded First Nations land. By making skiing the object of "contentious politics," First Nations protesters question the social legitimacy of the ski industry's use of mountainous nature.[29]

While the ski industry uses environmental discourse to position itself as a pro-environmental manager of mountain environments, signs of First Nations presence are less visible within skiing landscapes. At Whitewater, skiers' attention is drawn to the mining history of the region through old signs and props in the pub and lodge. This representation of the past is marked by the invisibility of Sinixt or Ktunaxa indigenous occupation of the Kootenay landscape. The history of the skiing landscape appears to begin with the nineteenth-century arrival of European mining prospectors on wooden skis with leather bindings. Whistler Blackcomb similarly uses mountain man imagery and evokes mythologies of wilderness, the Canadian hinterland, and early European exploration. The Squamish and Lil'wat Nations are becoming increasingly visible at Whistler, through the construction of a Squamish Lil'wat Cultural Centre (designed as a museum and tourist site) and through the two groups' participation in the 2010 Olympics. During field observation in 2006-07, however, I saw few signs of Squamish or Lil'wat presence within the Whistler Blackcomb sportscape. The selective incorporation of First Nations into cultural representations of skiing landscapes recalls Coleman's observation that skiing tourism in Colorado reinforces images of a white West. Through the construction of simulated Alpine villages and Wild West towns, whiteness is normalized, and the participation of Hispanic and American Indian people in the social worlds of the historic West is made invisible, or else they are turned into "sanitized objects for consumption" at tourist sites.[30] Similar processes of symbolic marginalization and the selective incorporation of First Nations play out in Canada as nature tourism embodies the freedom to move through colonized landscapes.

When First Nations become visible within skiing, it often happens through eruptions of social movement activity. This illustrates how First Nations are often selectively visible within British Columbia, appearing within the limited contexts of protests and performances of cultural tradition, while fading into the background for many non–First Nations people.[31] Ongoing land claims disputes between First Nations groups and the BC government are a key area of selective visibility. Most of

British Columbia was never ceded by treaty. Over the past few decades, First Nations groups have become increasingly vocal in their demands for redistribution of land and social resources in recognition of historical injustices. Through protests and blockades of highways and forestry operations, First Nations protesters brought their political demands onto the provincial agenda. In response, the NDP provincial government of the 1990s began negotiating modern treaties, which were meant to settle the question of land control and ownership in the province.

Despite establishing modern land claims negotiations, many specific sites remain contentious and serve as focal points for First Nations activism. Members of the Secwepemc, for example, have protested the expansion of Sun Peaks Resort near Kamloops. First Nations protesters assert their presence in the landscape and challenge Sun Peaks' power to occupy and manage the mountain environment. A dominant theme in Secwepemc protesters' online communication is that the resort expansion infringes on unceded land:

> The Secwepemc never relinquished this territory to either the provincial or federal governments by either land claim or treaty. Nevertheless, the provincial government granted a master lease for the mountains to Sun Peaks, a resort that presently encompasses three mountains and hosts over 3,600 skiable acres of terrain.[32]

Social movement scholars Doug McAdam, Sidney Tarrow, and Charles Tilly use the term "repertoires of contention" to describe the tactics used by social movement groups. They write, "We can think of the repertoire as performances – as scripted interactions in the improvisatory manner of jazz or street theatre rather than the more repetitious routines of art songs or religious rituals."[33] At Sun Peaks, repertoires of contention include setting up a camp and physically reoccupying traditional territory. Protesters also mount large banners and signs in the area, with slogans such as Unceded Secwepemc Territory and Where's Your Deed? Another sign reads Sun Peaks Kills, claiming that displacement of First Nations communities from unceded land is a form of cultural genocide.[34]

Ski hill development does not only raise questions about land ownership. The redevelopment of mountain environments risks disrupting established relationships between members of First Nations communities and non-human nature. In her examination of Coast Salish relationships to rivers and mountains in British Columbia and Washington State, Crisca Bierwert emphasizes that continuing to engage in traditional modes of fishing sustains relationships between the Coast Salish and non-human nature. First Nations often oppose development that risks severing these relationships. As Bierwert writes, "It is not that difference is resisted for its own sake, but that the people's occupation in the fullest sense of the term would become discontinuous with past performance, putting their ways of knowing at risk."[35] Secwepemc protesters similarly perform traditional forms of drumming and singing to assert their ongoing relationship to land claimed by Sun Peaks. The Secwepemc protest camp is also used as a site to gather, share food, and listen to elders, often in the company of non-Native supporters from Canada and elsewhere. The camp is a focal point for physically performing the claims to the landscape that circulate through websites and other texts produced by the Skwelkwek'welt Protection Centre, Assembly of First Nations, Union of BC Indian Chiefs, and Turtle Island News (a First Nations news website).

Secwepemc protesters also use protest marches to enter the tourist spaces of Sun Peaks village. Like the protest camp, marches disrupt the normal flow of ski hill personnel, skiers, and tourists. As protest strategies, marches and roadblocks challenge taken-for-granted assumptions about the rights of non-Natives to move freely through post-colonial Canada.[36] The BC Supreme Court granted an injunction against the Sun Peaks protesters, which gave the RCMP the incentive to arrest protesters and physically remove the camp. A 2002 issue of the *Skwelkwek'welt Newsletter*, published online in Turtle Island News, describes Chief Arthur Manuel's response to the injunction:

> "The judges [sic] reasoning in granting the injunction," Chief Manuel said, "were the balance of convenience – but sadly, in this case it means putting the convenience of snowboarders and corporate profits above the convenience of our Elders and land-users having an adequate diet. This is our land and these are areas where our people have always gone to hunt and we were not preventing one skier from

going down the mountain. But they are evicting Secwepemc women and children from their homes. It is shameful."[37]

Chief Manuel asserts that provincial courts protect the "convenience of snowboarders" from protesters who question the taken-for-granted right of skiers to use this mountain environment. By preventing protesters from occupying the land, the courts and police sever pre-existing connections between the Secwepemc and the mountain landscape. This illustrates how the creation and expansion of skiing collectives produce power effects by privileging certain social groups as managers and users of mountain environments (the resort corporation, skiers, and tourists), while excluding others from these places.

Environmental groups occasionally reinforce claims about skiing's encroachment upon First Nations land and connect these to a discourse of environmental protection. For example, environmental groups who oppose Jumbo Glacier Resort cite Ktunaxa Nation opposition to the project.[38] An anthology about the Purcell Mountains also includes Sinixt and Ktunaxa voices alongside environmentalist opposition to the proposed Jumbo Resort.[39] First Nations and environmentalist concerns are similarly combined at Melvin Creek, the location of the proposed Cayoosh resort. For example, the Wilderness Committee website reads,

> The BC Liberals are furthermore pushing for the construction of a ski resort city high up in the Melvin Creek drainage. All in all the Liberal plan is a death sentence for the wildlife and wilderness in St'at'imc territory as well as being very damaging to the St'at'imc culture and way of life. In stark contrast to the government's land use plan, the St'at'imc's land use plan has a very strong conservation theme, identifying large portions of their territory as "Protection Areas" where industrial developments such as road building, logging, mining and mineral exploration are prohibited.[40]

Although not the dominant theme within either First Nations or environmentalist websites, there are periodic attempts to link First Nations political interests and environmental discourse in opposition to ski resort development and expansion. As illustrated by the Wilderness Committee website, this discourse often relies on troublesome images of wilderness as unspoiled and uninhabited by modern humans, which may sit uneasily alongside with First Nations' demands for control over their traditional territories.[41] Despite tensions between environmentalist and First Nations interpretations of mountain landscapes, this discourse suggests a variant of environmental justice that is concerned with which social actors hold decision-making power over mountain environments. The notion of environmental justice was originally developed to describe the mis-distribution of environmental risks and harms according to race and ethnicity. In British Columbia, however, connections between environmentalism and social justice more often orient toward questions about the distribution of environmental resources such as forests or fish, rather than the distribution of environmental harms.[42]

Mass Media Representations of First Nations Protest

In mass media coverage, when First Nations enter skiing landscapes, it is often as an unwelcome, intrusive presence. This is consistent with the notion that media coverage of First Nations relies on a "limited repertory of storylines" that focus on "conflict and Indian antisocial behaviour."[43] A recurring theme delegitimizes First Nations protest by asserting that the government is the appropriate target of political action, not the ski industry. This is illustrated in a 2005 article about St'at'imc opposition to the proposed Cayoosh ski resort at Melvin Creek. Developer Al Raine asserts that Native land claims should be taken up with the provincial government, not with the resort:

> "I've spent a couple of million dollars and I have a legal right under the act, I can request an extension," he said, noting his original cer-tificate [for the development] expires Aug. 16. He hopes to hear about his extension request before that date.
>
> What bothers him most about the situation is that native chiefs are dictating what happens on land that's under the province's control.[44]

According to Raine, the mountains around Melvin Creek come under the jurisdiction of the province. His company has acted legally within the structures of land ownership and management in British Columbia. Raine invokes his substantial financial commitment and legal legitimacy to position himself against First Nations protesters who act in an "anti-social" manner by attempting to circumvent established systems of land management and who are "dictating" what happens on provincial land. In this account, skiing appears as an apolitical form of economic development that has been unfairly drawn into the realm of politics.

The notion that First Nations protest against skiing focuses on the wrong target is further illustrated when skiers are interviewed as news sources. The *Kamloops Daily News* draws on the experience of a tourist from Washington to convey the message that Sun Peaks protesters unfairly disrupt skiers' enjoyment of their sport:

> Chris Colella came to Sun Peaks from Washington State to enjoy the skiing. He said protesters were blaming tourists for their problems.
>
> "It's not our fault. We never would have known this was Native land if the protest hadn't happened. I'm just a bystander."
>
> At that point a protester dressed in fatigues marched past yelling "You're not a bystander, you're a contributor."
>
> Colella disagreed.
>
> "People come up here and they paid good money to be here. I think a protest like this puts people in a bad mood and they don't deserve it. It's not their fault."[45]

Through his comments, Colella emphasizes that skier-tourists are unaware of the issue they have walked into, which sets skiers apart from the conflict between the Secwepemc protesters and Sun Peaks. He goes on to state he never would have known he had entered a disputed space if the protest had not happened, inadvertently highlighting the success of the protest at breaching the taken-for-granted invisibility of First Nations within recreational landscapes. Like Raine, Colella invokes his financial commitment to maintain the legitimacy of his presence in this place. Within an attractive economy, money purchases the ability to occupy and use recreational environments. The protesters, who have not paid for access to Sun Peaks, become a disruptive presence.

First Nations and environmentalists appear in mass media accounts of social movement opposition to skiing in quite different ways. News about First Nations often focuses on the criminalization of protest. For example, we are told in a front-page story in the *Kamloops Daily News* that the RCMP "have maintained a presence at Sun Peaks throughout the busy holiday season because of concerns aboriginal protesters might try to interfere with the ski hill's business."[46] Police subject protesters to surveillance because they threaten to disrupt the normal flow of skier-tourists who pay for access to this mountain environment. An article from *The Province*, a Vancouver daily with provincial distribution, similarly quotes a RCMP spokesperson, who describes the potential for violence inherent in Native protests:

> "There have been some confrontations. There's a tremendous amount of intimidation of locals passing through, people wearing camouflage, giving fictitious names. I don't want to see anyone get hurt, but if people start pushing other people's buttons like this, a confrontation could easily happen."[47]

First Nations protesters become subjects of police surveillance and are arrested and jailed. News stories of criminalization define these protests as outside the boundaries of acceptable political action. News coverage of the Sun Peaks conflict illustrates how media discourse of First Nations protest often focuses on "their" disruption of "our" everyday lives, often drawing on the language and imagery of combat. In her analysis of the Gustafsen Lake standoff between First Nations protesters and the RCMP, Sandra Lambertus argues that media discourse "reinforces the social dichotomy of us against them that has persisted since the colonial era. It encourages media audiences to lump all Native protests into a generalized, but restrictive schema."[48]

Environmentalist opposition to skiing, on the other hand, generally appears to be within the boundaries of appropriate political action. The repertoires of protest in the Jumbo Pass campaign, or in Wildsight's campaign on mechanized backcountry access, include protest marches, public meetings, education and outreach, and letter writing. News coverage of these campaigns focuses less on protest actions than on the substantive ecological questions environmentalists raise about ski development. Exceptions to this pattern include a few stories about protests against highway expansion for the 2010 Olympics. During these protests, Betty Krawczyk, a well-known BC environmentalist, was arrested for contempt of court, tried, and imprisoned. Coverage from the *Globe and Mail* adopts a significantly different tone:

> The long arm of the law has caught up once again with British Columbia's raging great-granny. Adding to a string of previous prison terms that has given her the status of legend among many environmental activists, 78-year-old Betty Krawczyk was sentenced to 10 months behind bars yesterday for trying to stop an Olympics-related road-building project.[49]

In contrast with articles on First Nations protest, this story of criminalization characterizes Krawczyk as a great-grandmother and a social movement celebrity. The threat of disruption or violence that justifies the RCMP surveillance of First Nations protesters is absent. Referring to the police as "the long arm of the law," or referring to Krawczyk's time "behind bars" (rather than "in prison") downplays the seriousness of the confrontation between police and protesters. This is language that evokes television and film clichés about sympathetic – even lovable – bandits, not camouflaged militants.

Media stories of First Nations protest also invoke protesters' clothing as a signifier of risk and unruly behaviour. This recalls Roland Barthes's observation that fashion does important symbolic work. "This is ... the fundamental status of clothes: an item of clothing that is purely functional is conceivable only outside of any notion of society – as soon as an item is actually manufactured, it inevitably becomes an element in semiology." Cultural criminologist Jeff Ferrell similarly describes how clothing is used to do boundary-work between subcultures and mass culture by making members *"stylistically visible"* to people around them. Clothing becomes a way for members of subcultural groups to express their own identity. It is also invoked in dominant discourse as a sign of deviance and criminality.[50]

News accounts of Sun Peaks protests repeatedly draw attention to protesters' use of camouflage clothing, which connotes radicalism, social threat, and disorder. For example,

> The group marched through the village, banging ceremonial drums and chanting "Sun Peaks hell no." Some wore camouflage army fatigues and covered their faces with ski masks. Others carried video cameras and recorded the march. Several police cars followed the group at a distance.[51]

Descriptions of camouflage as a signifier of radicalism and social threat further undermine First Nations protest as legitimate political action. This is further illustrated in the following news story excerpt:

> Provincial court Judge William Sundhu said the natives were on their way to becoming militants because they wore camouflage and masks and behaved in a hostile manner.
>
> He also placed each of the four on 18 months probation after jail, with terms requiring they not be within 10 kilometres of Sun Peaks Resort, or wear camouflage clothes or military fatigues.[52]

Camouflage is invoked to define First Nations protesters as militants and to question their political legitimacy, whereas environmentalists' clothing is not described in news coverage of their opposition to skiing. Similarly, First Nations protesters' online accounts of campaigns against ski development focus on land control issues, not on their clothing. Where protesters describe police surveillance and arrests, it is the actions of the police, not the clothing of activists, that matters. The focus on protest tactics, clothing, and criminalization differentiates media accounts of First Nations opposition to skiing from stories about environmental conflict over ski development. This discourse distracts readers' attention from substantive issues raised by First Nations protesters about the legitimacy of ski resort control and management of mountainous nature.

"Turns Are for Girls": Gender and Skiing

Skiing and Gendered Sportscapes

Ski magazines and resort websites connect youthful, adventurous masculinity to risk-seeking as key elements of the "gendered risk regime" of skiing.[53] As Gordon Waitt writes about surfers' interactions with the ocean, "Understood as sublime, the surf is respected as [a] worthy opponent, and becomes a 'testing' ground, enabling acts of heroic masculinity."[54] Wilderness environments have historically been sites where men perform masculinity through sports like mountaineering. The cultural construction of skiing and masculinity carries gendered power effects, as it marginalizes women's participation and makes it seem exceptional rather than normal.

Through the combination of risk, masculinity, and the mountainous sublime, skiing landscapes appear as masculine places. Women are not unwelcome, but they are often marginal to cultural representations of the sport. Ski magazines occasionally feature professional female skiers in articles or ads, and *Powder* has published a special women-centred issue, titled *Powder Girl*. A feature article from *Kootenay Mountain Culture* about "she bums" (female ski bums) describes highly committed female skiers this way:

> Their life choices of jobs, accommodations and home bases all come down to what quenches their thirst for powder. These are women who rip through fresh tree lines while pregnant, face shots at each turn, inspiring onlooking guys to mutter, "I want to ski like a girl." Without them, a bloke's ski-bumming fantasy shrivels up fast. Because no matter how much you live to shred, after awhile you get tired of holding your dick in your hands.[55]

This is a provocative passage that illustrates how women – when not marginalized from ski discourse – are depicted as competent, athletic skiers. At the same time, the she bum is sexualized as a necessary presence for the male ski-bumming fantasy.

Based on field observation at Whitewater and Whistler Blackcomb, male skiers and boarders make up a majority at both resorts, though not to the extent suggested by the imagery of ski magazines and resort websites. A 2007-08 Whistler Blackcomb guest survey found that 64 percent of visitors were male and 36 percent were female.[56] Statistics for Canada as a whole estimate that 43 percent of skiers and 32 percent of boarders are women.[57] The most visible parts of the skiing sportscape, including chairlift lines, lodges, and intermediate terrain, feel relatively gender-neutral, both in terms of number of participants and in how men and women use these spaces.

More pronounced gender imbalances appear among hard-core skiers and riders, who show up early in the morning to line up for the first chairlift so that they can compete for fresh tracks on unskied terrain. The gender gap is also more obvious in difficult terrain, where male riders make up more of a majority than elsewhere. Spanky's Ladder, the Horstman Glacier bowls, and the steep cliffs above the Peak Chair offer the most challenging terrain at Whistler Blackcomb. These areas are high in the alpine, with dramatic views of the surrounding Coast Mountains. They are stark landscapes of snow, rock, and steep chutes where falls can lead to serious injury. They are also places where proficient male skiers perform the high-risk, technically demanding styles of skiing associated with valorized forms of masculinity.

While waiting for the Peak Chair at Whistler, I repeatedly saw male skiers drop over cliffs into the steep chutes overlooking this popular chairlift. When these jumps are performed well, they are met with cheers and the clanging of ski poles from fellow skiers waiting in line for the chairlift. These spectacular performances of risk-taking masculinity are notable because they are directed at the spectatorship of other skiers, in contrast to less public forms of risk-seeking that occur in "experts only" areas out of sight of large audiences. This practice recalls Iain Borden's discussion of how skateboarding masculinity is established through performance for an audience of fellow male boarders. These cliffs, like the abandoned swimming pools used by young male skateboarders, provide spaces for "initiation, dangerous ... places where [predominantly] young men might prove themselves to their peers."[58] This practice also illustrates how outdoor sport participants engage in "edgework" through interaction with specific environments. The edge is not only a psychological space "between order and disorder" but is formed by snow, ice, rocks, and the warning signs that physically mark the boundaries between safety and risk.[59] The specific qualities of these places permit male skiers to perform and reproduce the sport's dominant "gendered risk regime."[60] Just as the surf break works as a physical marker of authentic surf masculinity, the double-black-diamond signs and "experts only" warnings separate these masculine places from the rest of the skiing sportscape.

Less risky places within skiing landscapes, such as beginner areas and family zones, are used by a large number of children, who are more often accompanied by female skiers than by male skiers. In these places, female skiers embody a skiing femininity oriented toward caretaking. Corina is a female snowboard instructor who lives in Whistler and works primarily with children. As she tells me, the allocation of work for professional skiing and snowboarding instructors also defines these places as feminine. She describes the kids' zones at the resort as follows:

> There's actually a trail through the trees that takes you in, and you come out and there's a castle built, and it has this little drawbridge and everything. And the kids can climb up in there, and there's two slides, so they can go down ... Whistler Kids hires people to shovel the stairs and make sure it's safe for kids. And then on Whistler there's the Tree Fort that's built off Bear Cub.

Female ski instructors make up most of the staff at the Whistler Blackcomb children's area, whereas male instructors more often work with intermediate and advanced adult skiers. As Corina says, "In Whistler Kids, most of the managers, the supervisors, management, everything, is female." The children's area is a safe and fun playground, rather than a place for risk-seeking or demonstrating athletic prowess. Despite their demonstrated ability as skiers (through certification as instructors), many female instructors are channelled into caretaking work in this safe place. The routine practices of skiers and snowboarders at Whistler Blackcomb and Whitewater define skiing sportscapes as gendered places. High-risk advanced terrain is associated with risk-seeking forms of masculinity, whereas family zones are connected with caretaking forms of femininity.

Women are not excluded from mountain environments but often occupy feminized places within larger sportscapes.

Skiers' Interpretations of Gendered Sportscapes

A key theme related to gender and skiing that emerges from skiers' interview talk focuses on the divide between the ski hill and the back-country. For many participants, the backcountry is interpreted as a particularly masculine space. Men tend to exercise backcountry expertise and leadership more than women do. Judith illustrates this theme:

> I don't know if it has to do with being a woman, or just who ... I am, or with the experience that I've had. In terms of my backcountry experience, most of the times that I've gone out as a group, the person who has been more in charge, or more knowledgeable, has been a man. So I don't know if I was a man, perhaps I might have taken more of that role.

Interview participants also note that men tend to be more comfortable with technologies of mobility, like snowmobiles, used for backcountry access. Roberta, a female skier from Nelson, describes this:

> But in the backcountry I have really noticed it's harder to find skilled women who have the avalanche knowledge, and safety ... They do exist, certainly. Like, there's definitely really knowledgeable women out there, but less so ... This area it seems, access in the backcountry is gotten through using snowmobiles, and they're very heavy, awkward, unwieldy machines. And so, not that women don't have the strength, but I think that there's definitely an intimidation with machinery. Like, how to deal with the machinery. So, a lot of the women that I have toured with tour off the hill. Or tour with their partners. So yeah, that's definitely a factor, I think, for me. In terms of how it's shaped my experience as a woman, I think it's given me less confidence in the backcountry as a result of that.

Skiers and ski magazines often define the backcountry as a riskier landscape than the ski hill. The backcountry represents uncontrolled nature where skiers can get lost or risk setting off an avalanche. The construction of the backcountry as masculine space reinforces gendered power relations. Women are not excluded from the backcountry, but male leadership and expertise typically mediate their backcountry experience. As Judith and Roberta suggest, the technological mediations of backcountry skiing and reliance on male guidance can erode female skiers' confidence in their own abilities and create barriers to entering cherished skiing environments.

The backcountry is perceived as a riskier sportscape, yet it also resembles the mountainous sublime more than ski resorts do. Crowds of people, chairlifts, and lodge buildings characterize ski resorts. Backcountry landscapes, on the other hand, allow skiers to be with small groups of friends, surrounded only by mountains. For many skiers, the backcountry provides a more authentic skiing experience than resorts do. As Judith and Roberta note, female skiers typically enter the backcountry under the guidance of male expertise. As in the imagery of ski magazines, male skiers appear as the natural and privileged inhabitants of the mountainous sublime, thereby defining it as a "masculine sublime."[61]

Although skiers repeatedly describe the backcountry as a masculine sportscape, a few female skiers talk about backcountry skiing in all-women groups, which allows them to hone their skills in a supportive environment. Roberta continues telling me about her backcountry experience:

> Recently, I've met more girlfriends that are into backcountry skiing and seem to have more knowledge in the area. And we actually have been talking about going on some woman tours. Which is very appealing to me, because I think that it would be a lot of fun and, yeah, it would be a good environment to learn more and kind of feel comfortable in that setting.

The strategy of skiing in women-only groups challenges the notion that the backcountry is a masculine place. It brings to mind the increasing visibility of women-only skiing and snowboarding camps at ski resorts.

This strategy might be interpreted as a "practice of freedom," which defies models of skiing femininity that are subordinate to male expertise.[62]

This mode of backcountry skiing might challenge gendered power relations within the sport, but only a few women talk about using this strategy. For these women, it is an individual means to negotiate the gendered power dynamics of skiing. Like the creation of women-only snowboarding media examined by Holly Thorpe, this practice is unlikely to displace dominant discourses of gender, skiing, and nature. As Thorpe writes, "Although female snowboarding films can act as a practice of freedom by expanding the limitations of what it means to be a woman in the snowboarding culture, the dominant discourses of femininity in the snowboarding media continue to hold strong."[63] Individual resistance to dominant understandings of skiing, gender, and place is useful for many female skiers. Such strategies need to become more widespread, however, in order to shift the structure of gendered power relations within skiing.

Gender and Skiing Style

Skiers' interview talk repeatedly invokes the idea that men and women approach skiing differently. This discourse defines good skiing according to masculine norms, while devaluing female skiing styles. Skiers characterize a "male style" of skiing as aggressive, fast, individualistic, and risk-seeking. This model of skiing masculinity recalls Stephen Lyng's concept of edgework, which is a means of seeking out and playing with "the boundary between order and disorder, form and formlessness," where failure to navigate the edge carries the threat of injury, or even death.[64] Jeffrey describes the link between aggression and a "good" (i.e., male) skiing style as follows:

> I think most times men are stronger, or– I'd say, more aggressive. And to be a good rider, either one, you have to be aggressive. You can't be timid and [make progress]. And I'm always amazed when I do see a very aggressive girl riding with us.

As Jeffrey illustrates, many skiers view women as inherently timid compared with men. Being a good rider means performing according to an idealized model of masculinity that valorizes strength and aggression. This echoes Thorpe's discussion of dominant forms of "aggressive, perilous" masculinity within snowboarding, as well as Frohlick's description of the positioning of male athletes as "courageous, risk taking" adventurers.[65] Women are not excluded from skiing, but they are interpreted as less likely to excel. This discourse of skiing masculinity privileges men's skiing experience while devaluing women's participation.

Several skiers describe women's style as less aggressive and risk-taking than men's, but more relaxed, supportive, and group-oriented. As Kendra describes it,

> I think women in general are probably more likely to say that they're [more] keen on the social aspects of skiing than the steep lines and the crazy pow [deep powder snow]. And I think that that's probably true of most women I know. I ski ... with lots of women, and I think that lots of us are into skiing, but we're also really into the social aspects of getting out and skiing with friends.

Kendra also illustrates how women are not excluded from skiing but often approach it differently from men. The steep lines that demand technical expertise, strength, and risk-taking are less important to her than the social aspects of skiing. By claiming that this social approach to skiing is true of most women she knows, Kendra reproduces a binary division between male and female skiing styles. Unlike many skiers, however, Kendra's understanding of this dichotomy does not imply the superiority of a male style. Asserting that the two approaches are distinct but equally valid may be an example of reproductive agency, wherein female skiers negotiate and adapt to gendered power relations.[66]

Many skiers offer biological accounts of difference as a means of explaining skiing style. This naturalizes the dominant discourse of skiing masculinity and devalues women's participation. For example, Jess invokes the biological presence of testosterone to explain his own aggressive skiing style:

My girlfriend thinks I'm more aggressive than necessary. And I think that is probably in part due to a high level of testosterone that a man is more likely to have than a woman.

Ana brings up the idea of girl days: if a male skier is too tired to perform skiing's idealized version of masculinity, he may choose to go out with his wife or girlfriend instead of male ski partners:

> So, I think, just physically, that women tend to be better matched with other women friends. I think the local guys call it "girl days." So if they've, if they're tired and they've had a bunch of days, they have a day when they invite their partners and they have a girl day.

The presence of a wife or girlfriend becomes an excuse to relax and ski in a female style. Taking a so-called girl day is a way for male skiers to cross over and perform a female skiing style without disturbing the binary construction of skiing masculinity and femininity. As another example of reproductive agency, it is a technique for men to manage the dominant discourse of skiing masculinity without challenging its validity.

Biological accounts naturalize gender differences in how skiers interact with mountain environments. Cultural interpretations of gender difference came up less frequently in skiers' interview talk. For example, Sofia talks about a culture of lower expectation for women in sport that affects her skiing experience:

> Because if I had started out male, I would have had higher expectations of myself. I was completely surprised when I became a good skier. But I was also not an athlete before I started. But I just fell in love with skiing and kept going. But women's expectations of their own ability have been shaped by ... a low expectation in many different arenas for a long time.

Sofia's account highlights dominant cultural beliefs that discourage women from aspiring to the aggressive and risk-seeking qualities that characterize "good" (i.e., male) skiing. This excerpt is consistent with the critical gender perspective repeatedly demonstrated by Sofia. She also spoke about the marginality of women within skiing media, as well as the sexualization of women who do appear. Sofia's cultural account of gender difference is a minority counter-discourse that rejects naturalized distinctions between male and female styles.[67]

Multiple forms of masculinity coexist within outdoor sport subcultures. Male skiers often reinforce the dominant discourse of skiing masculinity that valorizes strength, aggression, and risk-taking. A couple of male participants also articulate counter-discourses that challenge dominant gender norms. Tim is a male skier from Whistler who describes how cultural norms around masculinity devalue women's participation:

> Well, in the old days, back in the day when I was a kid, [it] was like "tuck it or fuck it; turns are for girls," right? And so that was a misogynistic statement that would degrade women, and I guess in some ways, would challenge women, and push them to overcome that stereotype. But in other ways, you know, it might be limiting.

Tim acknowledges that the binary division between male and female styles is a cultural stereotype that limits women's participation in the sport, rather than something rooted in biological difference. Despite retaining a masculine definition of "good" skiing, Tim sees no inherent reason why women cannot perform according to the ideals of a male skiing style.

By contrast, Peter is one of the only participants who question the validity of dominant models of skiing masculinity: "Like many men, I think I'm encouraged to look at fear and danger in a physical sense and push through it. And if I don't, then I'm not maybe being, quote, manly." Peter notes that risk-taking is an important aspect of skiing masculinity, and those who fail to "push through" their fear are perceived as less manly. As sport sociologist Jason Laurendeau notes, risk-taking in sport is a gendered activity: "The acceptance (even embracement) of risk is an integral part of the versions of masculinity that occupy hegemonic positions in sport ... [It] is one of the central ways in which sport acts as a proving ground for masculinity."[68] The intersection of sport, gender, and risk leads him to write of "gendered risk regimes" and argue that "edgework might be experienced differently by men and women, young and old, gay and straight."[69] Peter illustrates this process when he describes how failing to perform to the risk-seeking standards of skiing masculinity raises doubts about his manhood.

Female skiers are not subject to the same expectations to engage in risk-seeking through skiing. However, just as men cross over into a female style by taking girl days, individual women negotiate skiing's dominant gender discourse by crossing over into male skiing styles. A few women told me that they prefer to ski or snowboard with men than with women. For example, Stephanie says,

> I normally [backcountry ski] tour with men. Usually it has to do with fitness levels and skill level. I find them more an even match. Because I'm a strong skier and I'm quite physically fit, I prefer skiing with men.

Stephanie defines herself as more skilled and stronger than many women she knows. As a result, she crosses over into a male style characterized by physical strength and technical skill. She demonstrates how exceptional women negotiate skiing's gendered power relations. Peg further illustrates how women perform in a male style, telling me that she "grew up in many ways like a tomboy, or with guys. So, that helped me push my ability. And I think that influenced me in having perhaps more of a male style." Like the women that sport historian Annie Gilbert Coleman describes, these skiers embrace the "liberating taste of speed, exhilaration, and danger" of a male style as they reject dominant models of skiing femininity.[70]

Several male skiers also offer qualifications about exceptional women they ski with. After explaining that skiing is generally male-dominated, Malcolm offers this caveat:

> I've skied with some women before that just smoked me. That totally left me behind, you know [laughs]. So there's some real talent out there, but I think at this point, it's a rarity.

Like many skiers, Malcolm defines good skiing in masculine terms. He acknowledges that women can perform according to ideals of skiing masculinity, but these women appear as anomalies within the normal gender binary of skiing. Belinda Wheaton and Alan Tomlinson make similar observations about gender within windsurfing subcultures. Men accept and respect women who demonstrate commitment and proficiency. Despite the accomplishments of individual women, however, "the naturalness of the association between masculinity and windsurfing [is] extremely effective in marginalizing women's involvement."[71]

Skiing and Rustic Luxury

Ski resort websites provide a valuable entry point for examining class and skiing. Two themes often appear close together within these texts, though they are in tension with each other. One discourse describes hotels, restaurants, and resort real estate in terms such as "rustic luxury," "rustic elegance," and "simple luxury." These terms refer to architecture that relies heavily on natural building materials like wood and stone but which also includes fireplaces and hot tubs as luxury features. As the Big White website describes it,

> When you walk into one of the ... 3,030 sq. ft. homes, you'll know the true meaning of luxury. It starts with heated slate floors in the entry and bathrooms. You'll be inspired to relax at the massive main floor windows that let you soak up incredible ski slope or Monashee Mountains views. Then there's the warm feeling of natural comfort you'll get from the luster of distressed hardwood flooring set against a floor-to-ceiling fireplace built of intricately set stone complete with granite hearth.[72]

Ski resorts devote large amounts of their online presence to real estate advertising. Large, expensive homes are sold as retreats from everyday urban life for family vacations. Norbert Elias describes kitsch as art that is produced for the sake of being sold, rather than for its own sake.[73] The word "kitsch" originated in early-twentieth-century Munich, where it was used to refer to sketches drawn specifically for tourists. The aesthetic of Whistler is a sort of three-dimensional sketch designed for tourist consumption that joins together Canadiana, wilderness, and an idealized mountain town for a tourist gaze. This focus on second-home sales also demonstrates that ski resorts work as spaces of environmental privilege, as they provide access to clean air, beautiful scenery, and outdoor sport opportunities to those with sufficient economic and cultural capital to gain access.[74]

Ski resort websites also work to define skiing as an accessible activity, regardless of economic status. For example, the Kicking Horse website tells readers,

> With an ever increasing selection of accommodation and activity options at Kicking Horse Mountain Resort and in the surrounding communities of Golden, Kicking Horse Central's local experts will customize a vacation package that matches any budget for style and taste.[75]

The notion that Kicking Horse Resort vacations can match any budget frames skiing in class-neutral language. In this discourse, skiing landscapes are open and accessible to everyone. The Whistler Blackcomb website also contains a large section focused on accommodation.[76] This includes a photo of the village at dusk, which provides a sense of alpine tranquility, with warm yellow light pouring out of shop windows, Christmas lights on trees, snow-covered mountains in the background, and a few people walking cobblestone streets. In language that defines Whistler as a place where class does not matter, readers are told that the resort offers everything from luxurious mountain chalets to economical hotels that make the skiing experience universally available. Ski resort websites provide conflicting images of skiing landscapes. They are characterized by an aesthetic of rustic luxury but are also accessible to visitors of every budget. Prolific advertisements for season passes, early bird deals, and family packages, where economy is stressed over luxury, also work against understanding skiing landscapes as places of environmental privilege.

A variation on the idea of skiing as an unclassed mode of interaction with nature appears in the conflict over ski development at Jumbo Pass. Through their website, the resort developers claim that Jumbo Glacier

Resort is not designed to cater exclusively to the wealthy but will make wilderness available to a wider spectrum of the public. According to the developers, they want to make the glaciers and peaks of the Jumbo valley accessible to "average" Canadians who lack the financial capital needed for heli-skiing or cat-skiing. In response to environmentalist critiques of the resort, the developers argue,

> JCCS [Jumbo Creek Conservation Society] claims the resort will be an "exclusive" playground for the wealthy. By contrast, the "fact" is that the ski resort is not exclusive, but is open to everyone and will give "average" Canadians the only readily available access to a 3,000 metre glacier in the country.[77]

The website disputes environmentalist claims that the resort will create a poor imitation of a European ski village, thereby destroying the wilderness value of the BC landscape. Instead, it argues that it is sad that many Canadian children visit the West Edmonton Mall or Disneyland, but few experience the "3,000 meter glaciers of our own backyard." Environmentalist opposition to development is reframed as an elitist attempt to deny people a unique mountain experience. Referring to hikers and backcountry skiers, the resort website asks, "Should all of BC's vast high alpine continue to remain the exclusive domain of a privileged few?"[78] In this discourse, environmentalists become the elitists who wish to restrict access to mountain environments to those who can afford backcountry skiing via helicopters or snowcats.

Although a tension around class pervades ski industry discourse, notions of rustic luxury characterize some resorts more than others. For example, Whistler Blackcomb, Kicking Horse, and Big White emphasize rustic luxury more than do Whitewater, Fernie, and Mount Washington. The degree to which specific skiing landscapes work as classed places is variable. This is illustrated by a comparison between Whistler and Whitewater.

The aesthetic of rustic luxury characterizes the architecture of Whistler Village (see Figure 5.1). The village is dominated by hotels, ski gear stores, restaurants, bars, and shops selling tourist paraphernalia. The focus of

Figure 5.1 Rustic luxury at Whistler Blackcomb

the village is on enabling conspicuous consumption rather than providing the essentials of everyday life. Whistler is also characterized by the ubiquitous presence of relatively new ski gear, as well as skiers wearing new, fashionable clothing. Skiers with older gear or clothing look out of place in this setting. Drawing on Barthes's insights into fashion, clothing and gear do more than facilitate interactions between skiers and nature.[79] Clothing and gear carry symbolic weight, pointing to the economic and cultural capital required for participation in the sport. Obvious signs of economic disparity or poverty are also invisible in the village. Panhandlers, street drug dealers, or other abject figures of urban life are absent from this mountain town. Luxury cars and SUVs are common in Whistler parking lots and on the Sea to Sky Highway between Whistler and Vancouver. Whistler Blackcomb may be interpreted

Figure 5.2   Rustic, but less luxurious, Whitewater

as a rural, mountainous version of a fantasy city, which foregrounds entertainment, consumerism, and riskless risk for those with sufficient economic means to gain entry to this "themed environment."[80]

By contrast with the rustic luxury of Whistler, Whitewater feels more socially inclusive. School buses are often at the hill, carrying children from local public schools. Whereas Whistler skiers typically wear newer outdoor sport clothing, at Whitewater there is a greater presence of sub-cultural styles associated with hippie and youth subcultures. Skiers with older gear and wearing older ski clothing also appear more often. The Whitewater landscape is less explicitly focused on consumerism, and it feels rustic, without creating an aesthetic of rustic luxury. If it is possible to decouple skiing from economic class, given the significant economic capital required to buy ski gear and lift passes, Whitewater is a *relatively* unclassed skiing landscape in comparison with Whistler Blackcomb (see Figure 5.2).

Conclusion: Social Power and Skiing

Images that circulate through skiing discourse shape cultural understandings of who legitimately inhabits the mountain environments where skiing takes place. The archetypal skiers of magazines and websites are white, male, and heterosexual, with sufficient economic capital to participate in the sport and to travel in search of new skiing experiences. Skiing discourse may be interpreted as a form of white culture that marginalizes skiers who do not fit dominant images of normalized whiteness.[81] First Nations claims to skiing landscapes occasionally disrupt this normalized whiteness, but media coverage of protest generally frames it as social disorder. Ski texts also produce and reinforce images of a mode of adventurous hegemonic masculinity.[82] The mountainous sublime of ski magazines and websites is typically inhabited by young, fit, risk-seeking men. When gender comes up in interviews, skiers also describe differences between guys' style, which valorizes aggression, speed, and risk-seeking, and girls' style of skiing. This model of skiing masculinity devalues women's experience and participation in the sport. In terms of class, there is a tension between two discourses. An aesthetic of rustic luxury is promoted on many ski resort websites and defines the architecture of Whistler. This coexists with a discourse of skiing as an unclassed activity that allows anyone to experience mountainous nature. This image of skiing neglects the economic barriers to participation, as well as class distinctions between skiing participants and the multitude of low-waged workers required to run ski hill equipment and staff resort bars, restaurants, and boutiques. Skiing requires a steady and significant output of economic capital for equipment, lift tickets, and gas. Although skiing is part of the British Columbian West Coast lifestyle, access to this lifestyle is not available to everyone.[83]

Beyond these relations of social power, skiing texts also reinforce normalized heterosexuality. Rainbow flags marking a Gay Pride ski week at Whistler were the only signs that disrupted this normalized heterosexuality throughout my textual analysis, field observation, and interviews.[84] Ski discourse also tends to focus on young, fit skiers in their twenties and thirties. Children are rarely seen in skiing texts. An occasional older skier may be profiled as a pioneer, but senior skiers exist at the margins of ski discourse. Skiing texts reinforce images of normalized whiteness, masculinity, and heterosexuality, as well as an aesthetic of rustic luxury. Female skiers, non-white skiers, gay and lesbian skiers, younger and older skiers, as well as those who cannot afford access to the sport, occupy the peripheries of discourse about who belongs in mountain environments.

Conclusion   **6**
Toward a Political Ecology of Skiing

> I am not saying that skiing is necessarily a valid goal. But living is.
> Living in a particular place in a real relationship with the earth and
> the sky and the living beings around you ... Community is sharing a
> particular physical place, an environment, not only with other people
> but the other beings of the place and fully realizing that the needs
> of all the beings of that place affect how you live your life.
>
> – Dolores LaChapelle, *Deep Powder Snow:*
> *40 Years of Ecstatic Skiing, Avalanches and*
> *Earth Wisdom*

Dolores LaChapelle's philosophical memoir, *Deep Powder Snow*, connects skiing with deep ecology, an environmentalist belief about the need for "deep" identification with and sympathy for nature. From this perspective, skiing may work to create community among humans and non-humans. Many other skiers also interpret the sport as a meaningful way of engaging in relationships with mountain environments. Through skiing, participants may gain insight into society-environment relations and incorporate environmental values into their sense of self. As such, skiing may work as an ecological technology of the self that leads to greater environmental awareness and pro-environmental action.[1]

Skiing also ties into narratives of a shift from extractive development to attractive development in British Columbia.[2] Extractive industries, such as logging, mining, and fishing, traditionally dominated the provincial economy and valued the environment primarily as a source of raw materials for capitalist production. Since Expo '86 "introduced ... the province to the world," outdoor sport and nature tourism have assumed an increasingly important role in the BC economy.[3] As historian Jean Barman writes, "The attributes of natural beauty and opportunities for outdoor recreation that exist in abundance across the province became increasingly valued around the world, heightening British Columbia's appeal as a holiday destination."[4] From its origins as a mining town in the provincial hinterland, Nelson recreated itself as a "heritage town" focused on tourism, skiing, hiking, and mountain biking.[5] The Sea to Sky corridor has similarly transformed from a forestry-dependant region into outdoor "sports country," led by the rapid growth of Whistler Blackcomb from the 1980s onward.[6] Skiing is central to the attractive economy of British Columbia, where the experience of being in nature is sold as the object of tourist travel. This story of a shift from extractive to attractive development interprets skiing as a more ecologically benign mode of interaction with mountain environments than forestry or mining.

This ecologically benign image of skiing circulates through ski resort websites, ski magazines, and the mass media. The ski industry maintains this image through the use of both discursive and material resources. However, environmental ambiguities underlie pro-environmental interpretations of skiing. Skiing depends on deforestation for ski runs, water for snow-making, and energy to run chairlifts, snowmobiles, and helicopters. Ski resorts create waste, soil and water pollution, noise pollution, and permanent infrastructure that displaces animals and damages alpine vegetation. Social movement groups disrupt the pro-environmental discourses of skiing when they challenge the sport's ecological and social legitimacy, thereby bringing skiing into our political ecology.

Many skiers who participated in this research articulate pro-environmental values, practise pro-environmental behaviour, and engage in environmental self-reflection about the impacts of their chosen forms of outdoor recreation. This is consistent with prior survey research that suggests that skiers score as high as, or higher than, the general public on measures of environmental values.[7] Interview participants appreciate how the sport allows them to physically engage with mountainous nature. This echoes John Fry's observation that "among the foremost reasons that people give for wanting to ski is the desire to be in a natural environment and to enjoy the mountain scenery."[8] This interpretation of skiing resonates with industry discourse of skiing as an environmentally benign mode of interaction with mountain environments.

Skiers repeatedly give voice to the ecopolitical ambiguities at the heart of skiing. Participants repeatedly talk about energy use to power chairlifts and describe wildlife displacement through resort development and mechanized backcountry access. They express skepticism about claims to sustainability by the 2010 Olympics, hosted by Vancouver and Whistler. Ski industry discourse generally neglects connections between skiing, automobility networks, and climate change, but this ecologically ironic relationship does not pass unnoticed by many skiers. Environmentally aware skiers participate in the sport despite acknowledging its environmental ambiguities and contradictions. A possible explanation is that discourses that link skiing, nature, and environmental values, combined with the exciting kinesthetic sensations of interacting with mountain environments, is more powerful and pervasive than counter-discourses of environmentalists or the self-reflection of skiers. Another explanation is that ecological ironies – the gaps between pro-environmental belief and anti-ecological behaviour – permeate contemporary capitalist societies.[9] If ecological irony is commonplace, then it may be noticed and commented upon, without being sufficient to provoke a shift in ecologically harmful practices.

The meaning of mountains is not innate in nature, not universal, not fixed. The meaning of mountains is flexible and is articulated by different social groups, including the ski industry, skiers, First Nations, environmentalists, and the mass media. The meaning of mountains is constructed, but it is not only *socially* constructed. It is co-constructed by humans, chairlifts, cars, explosives, bears, whisky jacks, snow, trees, wind, and various other non-human actants that inhabit mountain environments. Skiing provides an entry point to examine outdoor recreation and nature tourism as discursively mediated, embodied practices that build complex connections among humans and non-humans.

The meaning of mountains intersects with power relations among humans and non-humans. Ski resort websites and ski magazines link images of the mountainous sublime with athletic, risk-seeking masculinity, normalized whiteness, and an aesthetic of rustic luxury. Those who embody these traits become perceived as the "natural" inhabitants of mountainous nature, while others' experience is devalued and marginalized. Mountains and their inhabitants also enter political struggles over who controls and who can access recreational landscapes. Jumbo Glacier Resort, a proposed development in southeastern British Columbia, is challenged by environmentalists primarily on the basis of wildlife impacts. Wildsight, an East Kootenay environmental organization, campaigns against the expansion of heli-skiing tenures because of impacts to endangered caribou populations. Ski resort development at Melvin Creek and the expansion of Sun Peaks Resort near Kamloops were contested by First Nations protesters concerned about land claims issues. Conflict over ski development is not unique to British Columbia. Similar questions about the ecological and social legitimacy of skiing have been raised in the American Rockies, the European Alps, and New Zealand.

Mythology, according to Roland Barthes, is a style of communication that works by removing signs from their historical and political context: "Myth does not deny things, on the contrary its function is to talk about them; simply, it purifies them, it makes them innocent ... it gives them a clarity which is not that of an explanation but that of a statement of fact."[10] Myth distorts meaning but does not erase meaning. The ski industry's presentation of itself is a mythology that joins skiing to mountainous nature and a pro-environmental standpoint. The skiing landscape often appears as a sublime mountain wilderness, and animals also enter skiing discourse as symbols of nature. Skiing assumes a pro-environmental posture through animal habitat management, recycling, educational signs about climate change, or the use of alternative energy. Through these pro-environmental practices, the ski industry engages in a project of ecological modernization where environmental sustainability is sought within existing social structures of consumer capitalism.[11] This pro-environmental interpretation of skiing is often taken up by interview participants, who view the sport as a means of interacting with nature and learning to care for mountain environments. As they echo ski industry discourse, these skiers suggest the ski industry is successful at constructing a pro-environmental mythology for the sport.

Although attempts by the ski industry to improve its environmental practices are valuable, the pro-environmental interpretation of skiing is a myth, in Barthes's sense, that removes skiing from political ecology. Environmental groups disrupt this mythology when they speak against the ski industry on behalf of non-human animals. If the Jumbo Glacier Resort is allowed to develop, or if heli-skiing tenures are expanded, grizzly bears and mountain caribou risk displacement from their pre-existing collectives. This interpretive framework accuses skiing of transforming wilderness landscapes into cultural places where tourism and recreation dominate at the expense of ecological well-being.

First Nations protesters also occasionally disrupt the apolitical mythology of skiing. In mass media news coverage and through the Internet, members of the Secwepemc and St'at'imc Nations argue that skiing development creates profound transformation of First Nations places that have not been ceded by treaty. At Melvin Creek and Sun Peaks, First Nations protesters question the expansion of skiing as they demand recognition for their relationship to the BC landscape. These protests illustrate how skiing inherits a historical legacy of outdoor recreation and nature tourism as a means to affirm ownership over colonized landscapes. Social movement discourse highlights the ways in which new skiing development produces power effects as developers and the province disrupt pre-existing collectives of humans and non-humans for the sake of attractive development.

The Dialogue between Sport and Environmental Sociology

This research uses skiing in British Columbia as an entry point to expand the limited dialogue between environmental sociology and sociology of sport. By applying Foucauldian and actor-network theoretical perspectives to the political ecology of skiing, this project offers a model for future research on the intersections of environmentalism and outdoor sport. In their agenda-setting piece for environmental sociology, Riley

Dunlap and William Catton set out three core areas for the subdiscipline: environmental values and environmental movements, natural resource use and conflicts, and "wildland recreation."[12] Environmental sociologists expend a great deal of effort examining the first two areas but pay less attention to outdoor recreation and nature tourism. Skiing works as a mode of human-environment interaction that intersects with eco-political power relations. The present analysis suggests the political ecology of outdoor sport and nature tourism deserves greater attention from environmental sociologists.

Sport sociologists examine outdoor sports such as snowboarding, windsurfing, and skateboarding, but these analyses typically focus on how sport is linked to gender, race, ethnicity, or class. Despite two recent special issues of the *Journal of Sport and Social Issues* focusing on the environmental dimensions of sport, non-human nature has often been neglected, as sport is treated as an essentially social activity. This research highlights the active presence of non-human nature in outdoor sport. Mountains, weather systems, technologies, trees, and animals shape skiing as a discursively mediated, embodied activity. Non-human nature influences skiers' experiences and is affected by skiers' presence in mountain environments. Just as environmental social scientists could take greater notice of outdoor sport as a field of inquiry, so might sport sociologists place greater emphasis on understanding the connections between sport and nature.

Research on society-environment interaction in British Columbia traditionally focuses on conflicts over natural resource use (forestry and fisheries) or on environmental movement participation. Outdoor recreation and nature tourism are becoming increasingly important within the provincial economy. This process is accompanied by political rhetoric about how tourism and outdoor recreation work as strategies for economic diversification, which allows for environmentally sustainable interactions with provincial landscapes. Writing about the intense conflicts over old-growth forestry in Clayoquot Sound during the 1990s, Timothy Luke and Catriona Sandilands have each cast a critical gaze on the attractive economy. Both authors argue for the need to attend to the role of ecotourism within environmental conflicts, as well as the ways in which environmental conflict transforms rural landscapes into eco-tourist sites.[13] The present research further contributes to a sociology of the attractive economy. Attractive development is often interpreted as an environmentally benign alternative to economies based on the extraction of timber, minerals, and oil. Social science research on outdoor sport and nature tourism provides much-needed critical reflection on this interpretation by highlighting environmental tensions and ambiguities within recreational modes of society-environment interaction.

Implications for an Ecopolitics of Skiing

There is more to skiing than simply having fun in the snow. Skiing involves flows of power among humans and non-humans, and it should be seen as part of our political ecology, where the purified boundaries between human politics and non-human nature break down. Like the ecological harms of forestry, mining, or the oil industry, the impacts of recreational and tourist development deserve attention from environmental organizations, environmentally aware citizens, and federal and provincial governments.

By defining skiing as an unproblematic part of an attractive economy, we miss a large part of the picture.[14] Skiing, whether at resorts or in the backcountry, involves environmental withdrawals and additions.[15] Skiing withdraws from the environment through energy use to access terrain (through chairlifts, snowmobiles, and cars), through water use for snow-making, and through deforestation to create ski runs. Additions include resort waste and pollution. As ski companies present themselves as pro-environmental stewards of mountain landscapes, they mask the ecologically harmful aspects of their daily operations. Despite this, many skiers articulate environmental critiques of their sport when asked about skiing and sustainability. It is important for ski resort owners and managers to own up to the ecological ironies inherent in skiing.[16] Acknowledging the gap between pro-environmental discourse and the material additions and withdrawals required for skiing would be a meaningful step toward mitigating the harmful effects of the ski industry's use of mountain environments. However, this is unlikely without the further provocation of skiers and environmental organizations.

The ski industry often presents itself as pro-environmental through its habitat stewardship, as well as through its technological innovation and adaptation. Whistler Village uses the Natural Step Framework to move toward environmental sustainability. Elsewhere, the National Ski Areas Association adopted the Sustainable Slopes Program as a voluntary program for greening North American ski resorts.[17] These are positive steps toward the ecological modernization of the sport, and the ski industry should continue to adopt energy efficiency and alternative energy technologies to reduce the impacts of chairlifts and resort infrastructure. Ski resorts should also implement and improve waste management and recycling practices to reduce the waste stream of ski hill lodges and restaurants. They might also incorporate ski run design that requires less deforestation and animal habitat disruption.

Although the ski industry has taken positive steps toward ecological modernization, it largely fails when it comes to addressing the environmental implications of its intimate connections with mobility. Ski magazines and resort websites normalize automobility and aeromobility – the assemblies of vehicles and infrastructure related to car and airplane travel – as means of accessing nature.[18] These mobility networks produce their own environmental withdrawals (i.e., fossil fuels) and additions (i.e., greenhouse gases), which extend the ecological impacts of skiing beyond local mountain environments. Places like Whistler Blackcomb and Whitewater depend on flows of tourism. This is the essence of an attractive economy, and it is unlikely to change in the foreseeable future. Given the connections between mobility and climate change, the failure of the ski industry to address this relationship is ecologically ironic, in Szerszynski's sense of the gulf between pro-environmental values and ecologically harmful practices.[19] The ski industry is a canary in the coal mine for climate change. In the winter of 2006/2007, media stories proliferated about the potential demise of skiing in the European Alps. Media accounts also discuss receding glaciers at Whistler Blackcomb and other North American ski resorts. Indeed, the constant stream of traffic between Vancouver and Whistler serves as testimony to the ski industry's contributions to global climate change.

Several environmental education campaigns specifically target skiers on the issue of climate change. With names like "Protect Our Winters" and "Save Our Snow," these campaigns attempt to make skiers into good ecological citizens and ask them to take personal responsibility for their environmental impacts (for example, by reducing their energy consumption).[20] Such approaches are important and deserve support, but they are limited, as they individualize responsibility for action on climate change and neglect the large-scale political and economic transformations required to address this issue. The ski industry does incorporate pro-environmental discourses into its self-representation, but it has been timid about entering formal networks of environmental politics. The ski industry might consider taking a more activist stance on climate change. For example, ski industry organizations like the Canadian Ski Council might partner with environmental organizations like the David Suzuki Foundation to push for more aggressive Canadian climate change policy. Ski industry participation in such initiatives is unlikely without the encouragement of skiers and social movement organizations. Such initiatives would, however, give skiers a higher level of political efficacy than can be achieved through individual responses to climate change.

Skiers often express misgivings about the car use required to access mountain environments. Individual responses to this reliance on automobility include carpooling, car sharing, and driving Smart cars or hybrid vehicles. Individual actions are worthwhile, but they do not address the need for structural changes to automobility networks. The ski industry could engage more directly with transportation policy debates and encourage the development of viable public transportation between ski resorts and nearby cities and towns. Several skiers decry the decision of the provincial Liberal government to upgrade the Sea to Sky Highway, instead of rebuilding rail service in the region, as a failed opportunity to demonstrate a commitment to environmental sustainability for the 2010 Winter Olympics. Skiers, environmental groups (such as Whistler's AWARE), and Whistler Blackcomb might become more vocal in demanding the revitalization of rail service along the Whistler to Vancouver corridor as an alternative mode of transportation.

Skiers who participated in this research generally demonstrate a pro-environmental orientation, which is consistent with previous work on skiers and environmental values.[21] Given the apparent pro-environmental inclinations of skiers, the ski industry should be attentive to the critiques of environmental groups and respond to these criticisms seriously. It may be time for the ski industry to reconsider the logic of growth that guides new resort development and the expansion of mechanized back-country access (cat-skiing or heli-skiing). For example, proposed developments like Jumbo Glacier Resort and Cayoosh Creek are opposed by environmentalists and First Nations groups and are questioned by many skiers. Are these new resorts necessary additions to the skiing landscape of the province? Would it make more sense from an ecopolitical perspective to concentrate on supporting and developing existing resorts rather than adhering to an expansionist vision for the ski industry in British Columbia?

Skiing enters the agenda of BC environmental groups when new development threatens valued wilderness areas. Wilderness discourse, which focuses on protecting unspoiled nature from development, was integral to environmentalist efforts to protect old-growth forests from clear-cut logging in British Columbia. Environmental groups also use this discourse to challenge ski industry expansion. The notion of wilderness may ultimately be counterproductive for the environmental movement.[22] It reinforces a binary relationship between humans and non-human nature by parcelling out parts of the natural world for protection, while the normal, unsustainable operation of capitalism continues outside the borders of protected areas. The focus on wilderness risks diverting us from questions of how best to inhabit our environments and cohabit with non-humans.

Environmental ambiguities will remain at the heart of skiing. Creating and supporting environmental organizations that monitor the ongoing performance of the ski industry would help mitigate the harmful effects of skiers' interactions with mountainous nature. Groups like the Ski Areas Citizens' Coalition present a different model for the political ecology of skiing. This American environmental organization attempts to provide more rigorous evaluations of ski industry environmental practices than the voluntary Sustainable Slopes Program. In Europe, organizations like Alp Action and Mountain Wilderness also work to make the ecological costs of skiing and tourism in the Alps visible to the public.[23] These groups provide templates for social movements to engage the ski industry on the impacts of their everyday operations. Ongoing pressure from social movement organizations would ensure that the ecological modernization of skiing is viewed as an ongoing process rather than as a finished project.

A political ecology of skiing should account for the social justice dimensions of ski development. Skiing is occasionally problematized as an infringement on unceded First Nations land in British Columbia. Elsewhere, the Save the Peaks Coalition makes similar claims about the environmental and human rights issues associated with the San Francisco Peaks ski development in Arizona. As the coalition's website states, "The proposed development will further the desecration of this sacred site, increase threats to endangered species, and cause environmental destruction."[24] Questions about who controls and who has access to mountain environments join together environmental and social justice concerns. As Myron Floyd and Cassandra Johnson observe, a broader conception of environmental justice is necessary to understand the relationship between social justice and non-human nature in the context of outdoor recreation.[25] The established environmental justice perspective, which emerged through American-based research, is primarily concerned with the misdistribution of environmental harms such as exposure to toxic waste. A different model may be called for in the BC context, where political conflict often focuses on the equitable distribution of environmental "goods" as well as "bads." Suggestions that the ski industry become more environmentally self-aware apply equally to social justice concerns about who enjoys the so-called environmental privilege to access and inhabit the mountain sportscapes of British Columbia.[26] Environmentalists and First Nations groups concerned about the negative social and ecological impacts of ski development should consider how they might productively work with each other. Recognizing outdoor sport and nature tourism as elements of our political ecology is a key step toward building ecologically sound and socially equitable forms of attractive development in British Columbia and elsewhere.

Epilogue
The 2010 Olympics and the Ecopolitics of Snow

Vancouver and Whistler hosted the Winter Olympics and Paralympics in February and March 2010. Media coverage described a lack of winter weather, surges of Canadian patriotism, and a record haul of Canadian gold medals. If Expo '86 marked an early turning point in British Columbia's shift toward attractive development, the 2010 Olympics further accelerated the reorganization of British Columbia as a global destination for outdoor sport and nature tourism. As the data for this project were collected in 2006 and 2007, I have not discussed the Olympics in detail here. However, a brief examination of the Olympics suggests that many processes already described were at play during the games.

Like the images of the mountainous sublime used in skiing discourse, CTV coverage of the Olympics repeatedly drew upon (computer-enhanced) imagery of the Coast Mountains to link the games to the BC wilderness. The opening ceremonies included images of orca whales swimming through BC Place stadium. These animals also connected the Olympics to non-human nature for a global audience. Claims to environmental sustainability circulated in the lead up to the games and during Olympic media coverage, including discussions of "green" building techniques used to construct athletes' residences. The Olympics also embody environmental ambiguities, though these are masked by pro-environmental discourse and nature imagery. The mass movement of

tourists from around the globe to Vancouver involved significant ecological withdrawals and additions through fossil fuel consumption and
greenhouse gas emissions. Prior to the games, environmentalists were
arrested for blockading work to upgrade the Sea to Sky Highway linking
Vancouver and Whistler, arguing that construction would disrupt important bird habitat.[1] Just as interview participants recognize environmental ambiguities within skiing, so do they give voice to environmental
tensions within the Olympics, using the decision to upgrade the highway
rather than revitalize rail service as evidence that bolsters their skepticism about Olympics claims to environmental sustainability.

The 2010 Olympics also illustrated how non-human nature can behave
as an unpredictable, sometimes unruly, actant. Despite media imagery
of snow-covered mountains, the weather often failed to cooperate with
games organizers, appearing in accounts of the games as a non-human
"trouble-maker."[2] Lack of snow, as well as fog and rain, were persistent
problems during skiing and snowboarding events. At Cypress Mountain,
thousands of tickets were cancelled and refunded as rain limited the space
available for event spectators. The lack of snow at Cypress Mountain also
led organizers to fly in snow by helicopter to construct snowboarding
terrain. This resulted in further ecological withdrawals and additions
associated with the games.

The opening and closing ceremonies also worked to construct Canadian collective identity for a global media gaze. Canadian ex-pat celebri-
ties, including William Shatner and Neil Young, were incorporated into
the performance, as were star athletes such as Wayne Gretzky and Nancy
Greene. In contrast to the routine invisibility of First Nations within
skiing landscapes, the four "host nations" were incorporated into the
games through performances of First Nations culture and through a
First Nations pavilion. The inclusion of French- and English-language
performances further worked to construct an idealized multicultural
Canada for a global audience (an image that contrasts with the whiteness
of most Canadian winter athletes). As Himani Bannerji notes, the type
of official multiculturalism embodied by the games glosses over unequal
power relations among ethnic groups in Canada and transforms ethnicity
into a purely cultural phenomenon.[3]

Performances of a multicultural Canadian collective identity, which link sport, nature, and nationalism, define a national "us" that is distinct from the out-group of protesters who were separated from the sites and symbols of the games, such as the Olympic cauldron and opening ceremonies, by police and metal fences. Protesters' claims about the inequity of hosting a costly mega-event in a city with chronic homelessness received relatively little media attention. Protesters' slogan No Olympics on Stolen Land was also meant to draw attention to unresolved land claims in British Columbia and to disrupt taken-for-granted assumptions about the right of tourists to move freely through colonized landscapes. Concerns about the environmental impacts and social justice implications of the Olympics were marginal to most media narratives of the games. Protesters were consistently overshadowed by performances of Canadian patriotism and multiculturalism within the urban and mountain landscapes of British Columbia.

Notes

Chapter 1: Introduction

1 Peter W. Williams, *Tracking the Future*.
2 Ferguson and Ferguson, *How to Be a Canadian*.
3 Escobar, "After Nature"; Latour, *Politics of Nature*.
4 Luke, "On the Political Economy."
5 John Gow Consultants, *Ski Market Study*, 1.
6 Macnaghten and Urry, *Contested Natures*.
7 For an overview of this debate see Burningham and Cooper, "Being Constructive"; Buttel, "Environmental and Resource Sociology"; Lidskog, "The Re-Naturalization of Society?"; Murphy, "Ecological Materialism."
8 Franklin, "Burning Cities"; Haraway, *When Species Meet*; Latour, *Reassembling the Social*; Michael, *Reconnecting Culture, Technology and Nature*; White and Wilbert, *Technonatures*.
9 Mol and Spaargaren, "Ecological Modernisation Theory."
10 Szerszynski, "The Post-Ecologist Condition."
11 Foucault, *History of Sexuality*, vol. 1, *An Introduction*; Foucault, *"Society Must Be Defended"*; Foucault, *Hermeneutics of the Subject*.
12 For example, see Anderson, "Snowboarding"; Coleman, *Ski Style*; Frohlick, "'That Playfulness of White Masculinity'"; Gilchrist, "Motherhood, Ambition and Risk"; Laurendeau and Sharara, "'Every Bit as Good'"; Martin, "Apartheid in the Great Outdoors"; Schrepfer, *Nature's Altars*; Stedman, "From Gidget to Gonad Man"; Thorpe, "Beyond 'Decorative Sociology.'"
13 Coleman, *Ski Style*; Rothman, *Devil's Bargains*.
14 Dunlap and Catton, "Environmental Sociology."
15 In contrast with research in sport sociology, sport geographers have paid greater attention to the spatial/environmental dimensions of outdoor sport. Particularly valuable work includes Bale, *Landscapes of Modern Sport*; Ford and Brown, *Surfing and Social Theory*; Waitt, "'Killing Waves.'"

16   Canadian Ski Council, *Facts and Stats.*
17   Whistler Blackcomb, http://www.whistlerblackcomb.com.
18   Mansbridge, *Hollyburn*, 33.
19   Ibid., 40.
20   Armitage, *Around the Sound;* Vogler, Kawano, and Makarevicz, *Top of the Pass.*
21   Barman, *The West Beyond the West*, 370.
22   Ibid., 359.
23   Armitage, *Around the Sound.*
24   Vogler, Kawano, and Makarevicz, *Top of the Pass*, 71.
25   Hannigan, *Fantasy City*, 3-4; Armitage, *Around the Sound,* 171.
26   AWARE, http://www.awarewhistler.org.
27   Barman, *The West Beyond the West*, 403.
28   Whitewater Winter Resort, http://www.skiwhitewater.com.
29   Mansbridge, *Hollyburn.*
30   Whitewater Winter Resort, "History."
31   Ibid.
32   Ibid.
33   Bardati, "Participation, Information, and Forest Conflict"; Pryce, *"Keeping the Lakes' Way."*
34   Data collection for this project occurred prior to this recent environmental conflict over ski resort expansion at Whitewater, so this issue is not examined in depth here. As noted in an email from the West Kootenay EcoSociety to its mailing list, January 19, 2010, environmentalists voice concern about the displacement of mountain caribou (an endangered species) and grizzly bears. They also argue that expanding the resort will have negative impacts in terms of water use and sewage treatment. In response to public concern, resort management withdrew its application to exempt Whitewater from the provincial Caribou Habitat Legal Order and cancelled plans to expand into the Qua Basin. Although applauding the move, EcoSociety continues to call for the removal of the Qua Basin from any future consideration for ski resort expansion, as noted in an email to the West Kootenay EcoSociety mailing list, February 21, 2010.
35   John Scott, *Social Network Analysis.*
36   Intrawest, "Company Overview."
37   Ibid.
38   CBC News Online, "Intrawest, Creditors Reach Deal"; CBC News Online, "Intrawest Sells Panorama Resort"; Grant, "How Did Intrawest Rack Up So Much Debt?"; Willis and Erman, "Colorado's Vail Tops List of Bidders."
39   Mansbridge, *Hollyburn.*
40   Boyne Resorts, "Boyne Resorts History."
41   Robertson, *Imagining Difference.*
42   Kennedy, "Cominco Doles Out Pink Slips"; Parkinson, "Creditors Approve Bailout Plan"; Resorts of the Canadian Rockies, "Company Overview."
43   Sun Peaks Resort, "Who We Are."
44   Red Mountain Resort, "The History of Red Mountain Resort."
45   Mount Seymour, "Seymour 411."
46   Carroll, "From Canadian Corporate Elite."
47   Sheller and Urry, "Places to Play."
48   BC Stats, "Special Focus."
49   Allen, *From Skisport to Skiing.*
50   Ibid., 171.

51 Ibid., 96, 171.
52 Rothman, *Devil's Bargains*, 370.
53 Coleman, *Ski Style*, 2.
54 Ibid., 118.
55 Hannigan, *Fantasy City*, 71.
56 Urry and Larsen, *The Tourist Gaze 3.0*.
57 Joosse, "Leaderless Resistance."
58 Grafton, Pendleton, and Nelson, *Dictionary of Environmental Economics*, 271.
59 Hay, *Western Environmental Thought*.
60 Adkin, *Politics of Sustainable Development*; Luke, "System of Sustainable Degradation."
61 Fry, *The Story of Modern Skiing*, 291, 306.
62 Fry, "Exactly What Are Their Environmental Attitudes?"; Rockland, "The Environment and Your Customer," 40, 58.
63 Weiss et al., "Ski Tourism and Environmental Problems"; Hudson, *Snow Business*, 133.
64 Chernushenko, *Greening Our Games*; Sachs, "National Perspective."
65 Rivera and de Leon, "Is Greener Whiter?"; Rivera, de Leon, and Koerber, "Is Greener Whiter Yet?"
66 Rivera and de Leon, "Is Greener Whiter?" 433.
67 Clifford, *Downhill Slide*.
68 Spaargaren and Mol, "Sociology, Environment, and Modernity."
69 Foucault, *History of Sexuality*, vol. 1, *An Introduction*; Foucault, "Politics and the Study of Discourse"; Foucault, *"Society Must Be Defended"*; Macdonald, *Exploring Media Discourse*; Prior, "Following in Foucault's Footsteps."
70 Kvale, *InterViews*; Rubin and Rubin, *Qualitative Interviewing*. The quota sample was divided into four strata of nearly equal size, defined by gender and location (eleven male and eleven female skiers in the Vancouver/Whistler region; eleven male and twelve female skiers in the Nelson region). To recruit respondents for the interviews, I posted notices on public bulletin boards and in local newspapers in both locations.
71 Macnaghten and Urry, *Contested Natures*; Milton, "Land or Landscape"; Schama, *Landscape and Memory*.
72 Franklin, "Burning Cities"; Haraway, *Simians, Cyborgs, and Women*; Haraway, *When Species Meet*; Latour, *Politics of Nature*; Latour, *Reassembling the Social*.
73 Foucault, *History of Sexuality*, vol. 1, *An Introduction*; Foucault, *"Society Must Be Defended"*; Luke, *Ecocritique*; Rutherford, "Entry of Life into History."
74 Foucault, "Technologies of the Self"; Foucault, *Hermeneutics of the Subject*; Markula and Pringle, *Foucault, Sport and Exercise*; Thorpe, "Foucault."
75 MacCannell, *Empty Meeting Grounds*.
76 Laurendeau, "'Gendered Risk Regimes.'"
77 Veenstra, "Social Space."
78 Foucault, "Truth and Juridical Forms."

Chapter 2: Skiing Naturecultures and the Mountainous Sublime

1 Bale, *Landscapes of Modern Sport*.
2 Macnaghten and Urry, *Contested Natures*.
3 Gieryn, "A Space for Place in Sociology," 465.
4 Allen, *From Skisport to Skiing*.
5 Macnaghten and Urry, *Contested Natures*, 176.
6 Ring, *How the English Made the Alps*, 9; Tuan, *Topophilia*, 122.

7   Schama, *Landscape and Memory*, 450.
8   Urry and Larsen, *The Tourist Gaze 3.0.*
9   Urry, *The Tourist Gaze*, 129.
10 Franklin, *Tourism*, 213; Sheller and Urry, "Places to Play," 1; Baerenholdt et al., *Performing Tourist Places*, 101.
11 Macdonald, *Exploring Media Discourse*, 10; emphasis in original.
12 Foucault, *Discipline and Punish*, 27.
13 Foucault, *History of Sexuality*, vol. 1, *An Introduction*, 27.
14 Foucault, "Truth and Juridical Forms."
15 Foucault, *History of Sexuality*, vol. 1, *An Introduction*, 94.
16 Ibid., 95.
17 Foucault, "Subject and Power."
18 Foucault, *Discipline and Punish*, 26.
19 Foucault, *History of Sexuality*, vol. 1, *An Introduction*, 45.
20 Hansen, "British Mountaineering, 1850-1914," 22.
21 Lyotard, *The Postmodern Condition*, 77.
22 Lyng, "Edgework," 857.
23 Kicking Horse Mountain Resort, http://www.kickinghorseresort.com; Whitewater Winter Resort, http://www.skiwhitewater.com.
24 Spricenieks, "The Imperative," 44.
25 Baerenholdt et al., *Performing Tourist Places*, 2.
26 *SBC Skier,* "Open House."
27 Sheller and Urry, "Places to Play."
28 Frohlick, "'That Playfulness of White Masculinity,'" 179.
29 Schrepfer, *Nature's Altars.*
30 MacCannell, *Empty Meeting Grounds*, 129.
31 Canadian Ski Council, *Facts and Stats.*
32 Kay and Laberge, "Oh Say, Can You Ski?"
33 Whistler Blackcomb field notes, February 9, 2007.
34 For example, see Philo and Wilbert, *Animal Spaces, Beastly Places;* Wolch and Emel, *Animal Geographies.*
35 Cypress Mountain, http://www.cypressmountain.com; Kicking Horse Mountain Resort, http://www.kickinghorseresort.com.
36 Big White Ski Resort, http://www.bigwhite.com; Fernie Alpine Resort, http://www. skifernie.com; Sun Peaks Resort, http://www.sunpeaksresort.com.
37 Mount Washington Alpine Resort, http://www.mountwashington.ca; Whistler Blackcomb, http://www.whistlerblackcomb.com; Cascade Environmental Resource Group, *Environmental Review.*
38 Franklin, "Burning Cities"; Haraway, *When Species Meet.*
39 Pogge, "Sounds of Ski-lence," 25.
40 Big White Ski Resort, http://www.bigwhite.com.
41 Whistler Blackcomb field notes, November 24, 2006.
42 Chic Scott, "Hans Gmoser 1932-2006," 79.
43 Sheller and Urry, "The New Mobilities Paradigm," 209.
44 Petterson, "Iran Unveiled."
45 Gannett, "Manali Muse."
46 Kay and Laberge, "Oh Say, Can You Ski?"
47 Ibid., 384.

48 Barthes, *Mythologies*, 95; Urry, "The 'System' of Automobility," 26.

49 Elliot, *Mediating Nature*.

50 Baerenhòldt et al., *Performing Tourist Places*, 69.

51 Douglas Booth, "(Re)Reading the Surfers' Bible."

52 According to surveys, men make up an estimated 94 percent of *Powder*'s readership. Action Sports Group, "*Powder* Magazine Media Kit."

53 Stebbins, *Challenging Mountain Nature*.

54 Frohlick, "'That Playfulness of White Masculinity,'" 179.

55 Thorpe, "Foucault," 204.

56 Hall, "Encoding/Decoding."

57 Macnaghten and Urry, *Contested Natures*.

58 Ibid., 115-16.

59 Mitchell Scott, "Emotional Exports," 46.

60 England, "Connections," 43.

61 Tuan, *Topophilia*, 10.

62 Midol and Broyer, "Towards an Anthropological Analysis," 207.

63 Rose, *The Politics of Life Itself*. Douglas Coupland captures the connection between skiing, landscape, and somatic selfhood in his novel *JPod*, writing: "We were soon on Highway 99, headed up Howe Sound into the Coast Mountains. The alpine environment was already making me feel healthier than I really am – which I believe is the secret allure of skiing as a sport." Coupland, *JPod*, 449.

64 Franklin, *Tourism;* Thrift, "Still Life in Nearly Present Time."

65 Murphy, *Leadership in Disaster*, 43.

66 MacCannell, *The Tourist*, 3.

67 Fry, *The Story of Modern Skiing*, 306.

68 Nash, *Wilderness and the American Mind*, 3.

69 Jumbo Creek Conservation Society, "Jumbo Wild"; West Coast Environmental Law, http://www.wcel.org.

70 Sierra Club of Canada, http://www.sierraclub.ca.

71 Wildsight, http://www.wildsight.ca.

72 Szerszynski, "The Post-Ecologist Condition," 342.

73 Woods, "Fantastic Mr. Fox?" 182.

74 Loo, *States of Nature*, 3.

75 Skwelkwek'welt Protection Centre, http://www.skwelkwekwelt.net. Originally accessed September 29, 2006. Much of the same material can now be found at the First Nations Land Rights and Environmentalism in British Columbia website, http://www.firstnations.de/development/secwepemc-skwelkwekwelt.htm.

76 Assembly of First Nations, "Resolution No. 59."

77 Ibid.

78 Western Canada Wilderness Committee, http://www.wildernesscommittee.org; Sierra Legal Defence Fund, "Environmentalists and St'at'imc Nation Oppose Olympic Spin-Off Development."

79 Wilcocks, "Major Political Battle Brewing," 4.

80 Hewlett, "Native Protest Hits Resort," A1.

81 *Nelson (BC) Daily News*, "$70m B.C Ski Resort Expansion Protested," 3.

82 Davidson, "Jumbo Glacier Resort," 2.

83 Hume, "The People of the Kootenays," A15.

84 Ericson, Baranek, and Chan, *Negotiating Control*, 396.

85   Castells, *The Power of Identity*, vol. 2, *The Information Age*, 370.
86   Cottle, "Reporting Demonstrations."
87   Macnaghten and Urry, *Contested Natures*.
88   Luke, "On the Political Economy."
89   Connell, *Masculinities*, 77; Connell and Messerschmidt, "Hegemonic Masculinity."
90   Foucault, "Truth and Juridical Forms."
91   Loo, *States of Nature*, 3.
92   Hannigan, *Fantasy City*.
93   Murphy, "Disaster or Sustainability."
94   Franklin, *Tourism;* Thrift, "Still Life in Nearly Present Time."

Chapter 3: Cyborg Skiers and Snowy Collectives

1   Murphy, *Leadership in Disaster*, 38.
2   Ibid., 42-43.
3   Haraway, *Simians, Cyborgs, and Women*.
4   Franklin, "Burning Cities"; Haraway, *When Species Meet*.
5   Latour, *We Have Never Been Modern*.
6   Latour, *Pandora's Hope*, 178.
7   Latour, *Politics of Nature*, 71.
8   Latour, *Pandora's Hope*, 179.
9   Ibid., 183.
10   Ibid., 209.
11   Latour, "*The Prince* for Machines as Well as for Machinations," 22.
12   Latour, *Reassembling the Social*, 68.
13   Haraway, *Simians, Cyborgs, and Women*.
14   Haraway, "The Promises of Monsters," 66.
15   Gane and Haraway, "When We Have Never Been Human," 139.
16   Foucault, "Truth and Juridical Forms"; Foucault, *History of Sexuality*, vol. 1: *An Introduction*.
17   Michael, *Reconnecting Culture, Technology and Nature*, 4.
18   Michael, "These Boots Are Made for Walking," 115.
19   Fry, *The Story of Modern Skiing*, 74.
20   Atkinson and Wilson, "Bodies, Subcultures and Sport," 385.
21   Borden, *Skateboarding, Space and the City*, 97.
22   Bauman, *Liquid Life*, 82.
23   Atomic, "You Think I Like Working Nights at Burger World?" 155.
24   Fry, *The Story of Modern Skiing*, 89-90.
25   Taylor, "Intro," 15.
26   Michael, "These Boots Are Made for Walking," 119.
27   Bauman, *Liquid Life*.
28   White and Wilbert, *Technonatures*.
29   Szerszynski, "The Post-Ecologist Condition," 342.
30   Latour, *We Have Never Been Modern*.
31   Schnaiberg and Gould, *Environment and Society*.
32   Michael, "The Cellphone-in-the-Countryside," 86.
33   Urry and Larsen, *The Tourist Gaze 3.0*.
34   Macnaghten and Urry, *Contested Natures*, 122.
35   Urry, "The 'System' of Automobility."

36 Sheller and Urry, "The New Mobilities Paradigm," 209.
37 Barthes, *Mythologies*, 95.
38 Philpott, "Consuming Colorado."
39 Armitage, *Around the Sound*, 192.
40 Lassen, "Aeromobility and Work."
41 Szerszynski, "The Post-Ecologist Condition."
42 Urry, *Global Complexity*.
43 Whistler Blackcomb field notes, March 16, 2007.
44 Murphy, *Leadership in Disaster*.
45 Ibid., 324.
46 Haraway, *When Species Meet*.
47 Haraway, *The Companion Species Manifesto*, 8.
48 Ibid., 11-12.
49 Franklin, "Tourism as an Ordering," 279.
50 Franklin, *Tourism*.
51 Verchere, *VON 1B0*.
52 Bauman, *Liquid Life*.
53 Coleman, *Ski Style*, 173.
54 Rothman, *Devil's Bargains*.
55 Bauman, *Liquid Life*.
56 Park and Pellow, *Slums of Aspen*.
57 Franklin, "Burning Cities"; Haraway, *When Species Meet*; White and Wilbert, *Technonatures*.
58 Bale, *Landscapes of Modern Sport*, 13.
59 Hannigan, *Fantasy City*.
60 Nash, *Wilderness and the American Mind*, 3. Selected examples of critiques of this image of wilderness include Cannavo, *The Working Landscape*; Cronon, "The Trouble with Wilderness"; Luke, *Ecocritique*.
61 Nash, *Wilderness and the American Mind*, 6.
62 MacCannell, *The Tourist*.
63 Elliott and Urry, *Mobile Lives*; Sheller and Urry, "The New Mobilities Paradigm."
64 Urry, "The 'System' of Automobility"; Lassen, "Aeromobility and Work."
65 Schnaiberg and Gould, *Environment and Society*.

Chapter 4: Environmental Subjectivity and the Ecopolitics of Skiing

1 Foucault, "Subject and Power," 331.
2 Foucault, "Technologies of the Self," 225.
3 Foucault, *Hermeneutics of the Subject*, 11.
4 Foucault, *History of Sexuality*, vol. 3, *The Care of the Self*, 41.
5 Ibid., 45.
6 Foucault, *Hermeneutics of the Subject*, 176.
7 Markula and Pringle, *Foucault, Sport and Exercise*; Ravel and Rail, "The Lightness of Being 'Gaie'"; Thorpe, "Foucault," 204.
8 Thrift, "I Just Don't Know," 83.
9 Foucault, "Society Must Be Defended," 247.
10 Foucault, *History of Sexuality*, vol. 1, *An Introduction*, 139.
11 Ibid., 141.
12 Foucault, "Society Must Be Defended," 245.

13 Rutherford, "Entry of Life into History"; Luke, "Eco-Managerialism," 104.
14 For example, see Brechin, "Objective Problems, Subjective Values"; Brechin, "Comparative Public Opinion and Knowledge"; Dietz, Dan, and Shwom, "Support for Climate Change Policy"; Dietz, Kalof, and Stern, "Gender, Values, and Environmentalism"; Dunlap et al., "Measuring Endorsement"; Dunlap and York, "Globalization of Environmental Concern"; Kalof et al., "Race, Gender and Environmentalism"; Stern et al., "Value-Belief-Norm Theory of Support."
15 Dunlap and Catton, "Environmental Sociology"; Dunlap, "Paradigms, Theories, and Environmental Sociology"; Dunlap, "New Environmental Paradigm Scale."
16 Tindall, Davies, and Mauboulès, "Activism and Conservation Behavior."
17 This application of network analysis techniques to qualitative data is inspired by Mische, *Partisan Publics;* Mohr, "Measuring Meaning Structures"; Reiter et al., "Global Justice Movement in Italy."
18 Slocum, "Polar Bears and Energy-Efficient Lightbulbs," 420.
19 Ibid., 430-31.
20 Schnaiberg and Gould, *Environment and Society.*
21 Spaargaren and Mol, "Greening Global Consumption," 351.
22 Ibid., 357.
23 Gould, Pellow, and Schnaiberg, *The Treadmill of Production,* 24; Szasz, *Shopping Our Way to Safety.*
24 Bauman, *Liquid Life,* 82.
25 Urry, *Global Complexity.*
26 Tindall, "Social Networks, Identification and Participation."
27 Castells, *The Power of Identity,* vol. 2, *The Information Age,* 6.
28 Ibid., 8.
29 Fry, "Exactly What Are Their Environmental Attitudes?"; Rockland, "The Environment and Your Customer"; Weiss et al., "Ski Tourism and Environmental Problems."
30 Whistler Blackcomb, http://www.whistlerblackcomb.com.
31 Ibid.
32 Castells, *The Power of Identity,* vol. 2, *The Information Age,* 168.
33 Mol and Spaargaren, "Ecological Modernisation Theory."
34 Chernushenko, *Greening Our Games;* Sachs, "National Perspective."
35 Mount Washington Alpine Resort, http://www.mountwashington.ca.
36 Foucault, *Security, Territory, Population,* 126.
37 Ibid., 166-67.
38 Loo, *States of Nature,* 212.
39 Turner, *The Abstract Wild,* 118.
40 Hannigan, *Fantasy City.*
41 Barthes, *Mythologies.*
42 Warner, "Jumbo on Display," 1.
43 Boyd, *Unnatural Law.*
44 Jumbo Glacier Resort's efforts to use provincial environmental assessment approval to narrow the field of "meaningful" discussion recalls the critique of deliberative democracy articulated by Iris Marion Young, "Activist Challenges to Deliberative Democracy." Proponents of deliberative democracy assert that increased dialogue among diverse political actors is likely to lead to consensual and satisfactory outcomes. Young argues that this account is often based on overly optimistic assumptions. Where debate is prematurely narrowed, for example, activism outside official public input processes (such

as those managed by the provincial government or by ski resort developers) may be more important than participation within these processes.

45 *Nanaimo (BC) Daily News,* "Global Warming Threatens Global Skiing," A1.

46 Efron, "Schussing on Slush," T1.

47 Mol and Spaargaren, "Ecological Modernisation Theory."

48 Foucault, *History of Sexuality,* vol. 1, *An Introduction.*

49 Szerszynski, "The Post-Ecologist Condition."

50 Booth and Cullen, "Managing Recreation and Tourism"; Chernushenko, *Greening Our Games;* Clifford, *Downhill Slide;* Haimayer, "Glacier-Skiing Areas in Austria"; Hamr, "Disturbance Behaviour of Chamois"; Hudson, *Snow Business;* Price, "Impacts of Recreational Activities"; Ries, "Landscape Damage by Skiing."

51 Mount Washington Alpine Resort, http://www.mountwashington.ca.

52 Stifler, "Paradox in Paradise," 28.

53 Wildsight, http://www.wildsight.ca.

54 Mitchell Scott, "Jumbo or Dumbo? 28.

55 Foucault, *Hermeneutics of the Subject.*

56 Heywood and Montgomery, "Ambassadors of the Last Wilderness?"; Laviolette, "Green and Extreme"; Wheaton, "Identity, Politics, and the Beach."

57 Mitchell Scott, "Jumbo or Dumbo?"

58 Bauman, *Liquid Life,* 10.

59 Urry, *Global Complexity.*

60 Lenskyj, *Olympic Industry Resistance,* 62.

61 Luke, "On the Political Economy."

62 Mol and Spaargaren, "Ecological Modernisation Theory."

63 Schnaiberg and Gould, *Environment and Society.*

64 Bale, *Landscapes of Modern Sport.*

65 Clifford, *Downhill Slide,* 168.

66 Foucault, *Abnormal,* 43.

67 Midol and Broyer, "Towards an Anthropological Analysis," 208; Schrepfer, *Nature's Altars.*

68 Heywood and Montgomery, "Ambassadors of the Last Wilderness?"; Laviolette, "Green and Extreme"; Wheaton, "Identity, Politics, and the Beach."

69 Foucault, *Hermeneutics of the Subject.*

70 Urry, "The 'System' of Automobility"; Lassen, "Aeromobility and Work."

71 Szerszynski, "The Post-Ecologist Condition."

Chapter 5: Skiing and Social Power

1 Foucault, "Truth and Juridical Forms."

2 Martin, "Apartheid in the Great Outdoors."

3 Braun, "'On the Raggedy Edge of Risk,'" 198; emphasis in original.

4 Frohlick, "'That Playfulness of White Masculinity,'" 178-79.

5 Birrell, "Approaching Mt. Everest," 14.

6 Erickson, "Colonial Climbs of Mount Trudeau," 74.

7 Coleman, *Ski Style,* 171; Rothman, *Devil's Bargains;* Park and Pellow, *Slums of Aspen.*

8 Dawson, *Selling British Columbia;* Jasen, *Wild Things;* Mawani, "Genealogies of the Land."

9 Dawson, *Selling British Columbia,* 176.

10 Anderson, "Snowboarding"; Frohlick, "'That Playfulness of White Masculinity'"; Little and Wilson, "Adventure and the Gender Gap," 194.

11 Coleman, *Ski Style,* 60.

12   Coleman, "From Snow Bunnies to Shred Betties," 211.
13   Thorpe, "Beyond 'Decorative Sociology,'" 221.
14   Thorpe, "Jibbing the Gender Order," 81.
15   Thorpe, "Beyond 'Decorative Sociology,'" 221.
16   Laurendeau and Sharara, "'Every Bit as Good.'"
17   Eichberg, "New Spatial Configurations of Sport?"; Vertinsky, "Locating a 'Sense of Place.'"
18   Waitt, "'Killing Waves,'" 81.
19   Ford and Brown, *Surfing and Social Theory,* 107.
20   Bourdieu, "Sport and Social Class," 370.
21   Veenstra, "Social Space."
22   Richey, "Living It Up in Aspen," 2.
23   Kay and Laberge, "Oh Say, Can You Ski?" 382.
24   Ibid., 384.
25   Haraway, *Simians, Cyborgs, and Women,* 154.
26   MacCannell, *Empty Meeting Grounds.*
27   Brooker, "The Slow Lane," 84.
28   Raymond Williams, *Marxism and Literature.*
29   McAdam, Tarrow, and Tilly, *Dynamics of Contention.*
30   Coleman, *Ski Style,* 171.
31   Bruce Miller, pers. comm., May 27, 2008; also see Robertson, *Imagining Difference.*
32   Skwelkwek'welt Protection Centre, http://www.skwelkwekwelt.net.
33   McAdam, Tarrow, and Tilly, *Dynamics of Contention,* 49.
34   Skwelkwek'welt Protection Centre, http://www.skwelkwekwelt.net.
35   Bierwert, *Brushed by Cedar,* 281.
36   Blomley, "'Shut the Province Down.'"
37   Turtle Island News, "The People Will Never Retreat."
38   Jumbo Creek Conservation Society, "Jumbo Wild."
39   Kivi, *The Purcell Suite.*
40   Western Canada Wilderness Committee, http://www.wildernesscommittee.org.
41   Tensions between environmentalists' use of wilderness discourse and First Nations claims to sovereignty over traditional territories in British Columbia are not unique to skiing. Throughout the 1980s and 1990s, First Nations and environmentalists made sporadic attempts at alliances, which often highlighted profound differences in their respective interpretations of the provincial landscape. Selected accounts of political affinities and tensions between First Nations and environmental organizations in British Columbia include Hipwell, "Environmental Conflict and Democracy"; Robinson et al., "Support for First Nations' Land Claims"; Shaw, "Clearcut Identities"; Torgerson, "Images of Place"; Willems-Braun, "Buried Epistemologies."
42   Agyeman et al., *Speaking for Ourselves;* Page, "Salmon Farming"; Stoddart, "Open for Business."
43   Miller, "Indian-White Relations."
44   Michele Young, "Chiefs Take Stand," A7.
45   Hewlett, "Native Protest Hits Resort," A1.
46   Koopmans and Youds, "Natives' Blockade Lasts Just Minutes," A1.
47   Fournier, "Natives Block Sun Peaks Construction Road," A4.
48   Lambertus, *Wartime Images, Peacetime Wounds,* 200.
49   Mickleburgh, "B.C. Woman Sent to Jail," A6.

50 Barthes, *The Language of Fashion*, 42; Ferrell, "Style Matters," emphasis in original.
51 Hewlett, "Native Protest Hits Resort," A1.
52 *Victoria Times-Colonist*, "Four Natives Jailed," A5.
53 Laurendeau, "'Gendered Risk Regimes.'"
54 Waitt, "'Killing Waves,'" 84.
55 Richardson, "Rise of the She Bum," 38.
56 M. Kemp, email message to author, April 13, 2009.
57 Canadian Ski Council, *Facts and Stats*.
58 Borden, *Skateboarding, Space and the City*, 52.
59 Lyng, "Edgework."
60 Laurendeau, "'Gendered Risk Regimes.'"
61 Schrepfer, *Nature's Altars*, 6.
62 Markula and Pringle, *Foucault, Sport and Exercise*, 153.
63 Thorpe, "Foucault," 223.
64 Lyng, "Edgework," 858.
65 Thorpe, "Jibbing the Gender Order"; Frohlick, "'That Playfulness of White Masculinity.'"
66 Laurendeau and Sharara, "'Every Bit as Good.'"
67 Thorpe, "Foucault."
68 Laurendeau, "'Gendered Risk Regimes,'" 296.
69 Ibid., 295.
70 Coleman, *Ski Style*, 60.
71 Wheaton and Tomlinson, "The Changing Gender Order in Sport?" 269.
72 Big White Ski Resort, http://www.bigwhite.com.
73 Elias, "The Kitsch Style."
74 Park and Pellow, *Slums of Aspen*.
75 Kicking Horse Mountain Resort, http://www.kickinghorseresort.com.
76 Whistler Blackcomb, http://www.whistlerblackcomb.com.
77 Jumbo Glacier Resort, http://www.jumboglacierresort.com.
78 Ibid.
79 Barthes, *The Language of Fashion*.
80 Hannigan, *Fantasy City*, 84.
81 MacCannell, *Empty Meeting Grounds*.
82 Connell, *Masculinities*.
83 Veenstra, "Social Space."
84 Although this was the only explicit sign of the disruption of normalized heterosexuality, the fact that Whistler celebrates a Gay Pride ski week at all may be viewed as a sign that the community of Whistler is more socially progressive than many towns of similar size in British Columbia, where the declaration of Gay and Lesbian Pride days often remain contentious. Alternatively, given that many gay male skiers might feel comfortable within skiing's culture of normalized whiteness, masculinity, and rustic luxury, this also might be seen as a clever marketing strategy on the part of Whistler Blackcomb.

Chapter 6: Conclusion

1 Foucault, *Hermeneutics of the Subject*.
2 Luke, "On the Political Economy."
3 Barman, *The West Beyond the West*, 393.
4 Ibid., 395.

5 DeGrace, Thornton, and Gluns, *Nelson British Columbia in Photographs.*
6 Armitage, *Around the Sound.*
7 Fry, "Exactly What Are Their Environmental Attitudes?"; Rockland, "The Environment and Your Customer"; Sachs, "National Perspective"; Weiss et al., "Ski Tourism and Environmental Problems."
8 Fry, *The Story of Modern Skiing,* 291.
9 Szerszynski, "The Post-Ecologist Condition."
10 Barthes, *Mythologies,* 156.
11 Mol and Spaargaren, "Ecological Modernisation Theory"; Spaargaren and Mol, "Sociology, Environment, and Modernity," 323-44.
12 Dunlap and Catton, "Environmental Sociology."
13 Luke, "On the Political Economy"; Sandilands, "Between the Local and the Global."
14 Luke, "On the Political Economy."
15 Schnaiberg and Gould, *Environment and Society.*
16 Szerszynski, "The Post-Ecologist Condition."
17 For a critical evaluation of the Sustainable Slopes Program, see Rivera and de Leon, "Is Greener Whiter?"; Rivera, de Leon, and Koerber, "Is Greener Whiter Yet?"
18 Urry, "The 'System' of Automobility"; Lassen, "Aeromobility and Work."
19 Szerszynski, "The Post-Ecologist Condition."
20 Adkin, "Ecology, Citizenship, Democracy"; Spaargaren and Mol, "Greening Global Consumption."
21 Fry, "Exactly What Are Their Environmental Attitudes?"; Rockland, "The Environment and Your Customer"; Sachs, "National Perspective"; Weiss et al., "Ski Tourism and Environmental Problems."
22 This argument is explored in depth in Cannavo, *The Working Landscape;* Cronon, "The Trouble with Wilderness"; Luke, *Ecocritique.*
23 Hudson, *Snow Business,* 128-29.
24 Save the Peaks Coalition, "Protect and Respect the Mountain and Our Children!"
25 Floyd and Johnson, "Coming to Terms with Environmental Justice."
26 Park and Pellow, *Slums of Aspen.*

Epilogue: The 2010 Olympics and the Ecopolitics of Snow

1 Lenskyj, *Olympic Industry Resistance.*
2 Latour, *Politics of Nature.*
3 Bannerji, *The Dark Side of the Nation.*

Bibliography

Action Sports Group. "*Powder* Magazine Media Kit." http://www.actionsportsgroup. net/.

Adkin, Laurie E. "Ecology, Citizenship, Democracy." In *Environmental Conflict and Democracy in Canada*, edited by L.E. Adkin, 1-15. Vancouver: UBC Press, 2009.

–. *The Politics of Sustainable Development*. Montreal: Black Rose Books, 1998.

Agyeman, Julian, Peter Cole, Randolph Haluza-Delay, and Pat O'Reiley, eds. *Speaking for Ourselves: Environmental Justice in Canada*. Vancouver: UBC Press, 2009.

Allen, E. John B. *From Skisport to Skiing*. Amherst: University of Massachusetts Press, 1993.

Anderson, Kristin L. "Snowboarding: The Construction of Gender in an Emerging Sport." *Journal of Sport and Social Issues* 23, 1 (1999): 55-79.

Armitage, Doreen. *Around the Sound: A History of Howe Sound-Whistler*. Madeira Park, BC: Harbour, 1997.

Assembly of First Nations. "Resolution No. 59." http://www.afn.ca/.

Atkinson, Michael, and Brian Wilson. "Bodies, Subcultures and Sport." In *Theory, Sport and Society*, edited by J. Maguire and K. Young, 375-95. Amsterdam: Elsevier Science, 2002.

Atomic. "You Think I Like Working Nights at Burger World?" *Skiing*, November 2006, 155.

AWARE. http://www.awarewhistler.org.

Baerenholdt, Jorgen Ole, Michael Haldrup, Jonas Larsen, and John Urry. *Performing Tourist Places*. Aldershot, UK: Ashgate, 2004.

Bale, John. *Landscapes of Modern Sport*. Leicester, UK: Leicester University Press, 1994.

Bannerji, H. *The Dark Side of the Nation*. Toronto: Canadian Scholars' Press, 2000.

Bardati, Darren R. "Participation, Information, and Forest Conflict in the Slocan Valley of British Columbia." In *Environmental Conflict and Democracy in Canada*, edited by L.E. Adkin, 103-22. Vancouver: UBC Press, 2009.

Barman, Jean. *The West Beyond the West: A History of British Columbia*. 3rd ed. Toronto: University of Toronto Press, 2007.

Barthes, Roland. *The Language of Fashion*. Edited by A. Stafford and M. Carter. Translated by A. Stafford. Oxford: Berg, 2006.

–. *Mythologies*. Translated by A. Lavers. London: Paladin, 1973.

Bauman, Zygmunt. *Liquid Life*. Cambridge, UK: Polity Press, 2005.

BC Stats. "Special Focus: Skiing in Whistler." *Tourism Sector Monitor*, August 2005, 4-7.

Beck, Ulrich. *Risk Society: Towards a New Modernity*. Translated by M. Ritter. London: Sage, 1992.

Bierwert, Crisca. *Brushed by Cedar, Living by the River: Coast Salish Figures of Power*. Tucson: University of Arizona Press, 1999.

Big White Ski Resort. http://www.bigwhite.com.

Birrell, Susan. "Approaching Mt. Everest: On Intertextuality and the Past as Narrative." *Journal of Sport History* 34, 1 (2007): 1-22.

Blomley, Nicholas. "'Shut the Province Down': First Nations Blockades in British Columbia, 1984-1995." *BC Studies* 111 (Autumn 1996): 5-35.

Booth, Douglas. "(Re)Reading the Surfers' Bible: The Affects of Tracks." *Continuum: Journal of Media and Cultural Studies* 22, 1 (2008): 17-35.

Booth, Kay L., and Ross Cullen. "Managing Recreation and Tourism in New Zealand Mountains." *Mountain Research and Development* 21, 4 (2001): 331-34.

Borden, Iain. *Skateboarding, Space and the City*. Oxford: Berg, 2001.

Bourdieu, Pierre. "Sport and Social Class." In *Rethinking Popular Culture: Contemporary Perspectives in Cultural Studies*, edited by C. Mukerji and M. Schudson, 357-73. Berkeley: University of California Press, 1991.

Boyd, David R. *Unnatural Law: Rethinking Canadian Environmental Law and Policy*. Vancouver: UBC Press, 2003.

Boyne Resorts. "Boyne Resorts History." http://www.boyneresorts.com/.

Braun, Bruce. "'On the Raggedy Edge of Risk': Articulations of Race and Nature after Biology." In *Race, Nature, and the Politics of Difference*, edited by D.S. Moore, J. Kosek, and A. Pandian, 175-203. Durham, NC: Duke University Press, 2003.

Brechin, Steven R. "Comparative Public Opinion and Knowledge on Global Climatic Change and the Kyoto Protocol: The U.S. versus the World?" *International Journal of Sociology and Social Policy* 23, 10 (2003): 106-34.

–. "Objective Problems, Subjective Values, and Global Environmentalism: Evaluating the Postmaterialist Argument and Challenging a New Explanation." *Social Science Quarterly* 80, 4 (1999): 793-809.

Brooker, Kevin. "The Slow Lane: Sun Peaks in Kamloops, B.C., Is the Home of Speed Skiing's Last Stand in North America; Apparently, This Comes as No Surprise." *SBC Skier,* Spring 2006, 80-85.

Burningham, Kate, and Geoff Cooper. "Being Constructive: Social Constructionism and the Environment." *Sociology* 33, 2 (1999): 297-316.

Buttel, Frederick H. "Environmental and Resource Sociology: Theoretical Issues and Opportunities for Synthesis." *Rural Sociology* 61, 1 (1996): 56-76.

Canadian Ski Council. *2007-2008 Canadian Skier and Snowboarder Facts and Stats.* Craigleith, ON: Canadian Ski Council, 2008.

Cannavo, Peter F. *The Working Landscape: Founding, Preservation, and the Politics of Place.* Cambridge, MA: MIT Press, 2007.

Carroll, William K. "From Canadian Corporate Elite to Transnational Capitalist Class: Transitions in the Organization of Corporate Power." *Canadian Review of Sociology and Anthropology* 44, 3 (2007): 265-88.

Cascade Environmental Resource Group. *Environmental Review: Whitewater Resort Plan for Expansion and Improvement.* Nelson, BC: Whitewater Winter Resort, 2002.

Castells, Manuel. *The Power of Identity.* 2nd ed. Vol. 2, *The Information Age: Economy, Society, and Culture.* Malden, MA: Blackwell, 2004.

CBC News Online. "Intrawest, Creditors Reach Deal: Report." March 1, 2010. http://www.cbc.ca/money/story/.

–. "Intrawest Sells Panorama Resort." January 28, 2010. http://www.cbc.ca/money/story/.

Chernushenko, David. *Greening Our Games: Running Sports Events and Facilities That Won't Cost the Earth.* Ottawa, ON: Centurion Publishing and Marketing, 1994.

Clifford, Hal. *Downhill Slide: Why the Corporate Ski Industry Is Bad for Skiing, Ski Towns, and the Environment.* San Francisco: Sierra Club Books, 2002.

Coleman, Annie Gilbert. "From Snow Bunnies to Shred Betties: Gender, Consumption, and the Skiing Landscape." In *Seeing Nature through Gender,* edited by V.J. Scharff, 194-217. Lawrence: University Press of Kansas, 2003.

–. *Ski Style: Sport and Culture in the Rockies.* Lawrence: University Press of Kansas, 2004.

Connell, R.W. *Masculinities.* 2nd ed. Berkeley: University of California Press, 2005.

Connell, R.W., and James W. Messerschmidt. "Hegemonic Masculinity: Rethinking the Concept." *Gender and Society* 19, 6 (2005): 829-59.

Cottle, Simon. "Reporting Demonstrations: The Changing Media Politics of Dissent." *Media, Culture and Society* 30, 6 (2008): 853-72.

Coupland, Douglas. *JPod.* Toronto: Vintage, 2007.

Cronon, William. "The Trouble with Wilderness: Or, Getting Back to the Wrong Nature." In *Uncommon Ground: Toward Reinventing Nature*, edited by W. Cronon, 69-90. New York and London: W.W. Norton, 1995.

Cypress Mountain. http://www.cypressmountain.com.

Davidson, Darren. "Jumbo Glacier Resort Gets Environmental Sign-Off: Many Hurdles Still Must Be Cleared before Development of Controversial Project Can Begin." *Cranbrook (BC) Daily Townsman*, October 15, 2004.

Dawson, Michael. *Selling British Columbia: Tourism and Consumer Culture, 1890-1970*. Vancouver: UBC Press, 2004.

DeGrace, Anne, Steve Thornton, and David R. Gluns. *Nelson British Columbia in Photographs*. 2nd ed. Nelson, BC: Ward Creek Press, 2001.

Dietz, Thomas, Amy Dan, and Rachael Shwom. "Support for Climate Change Policy: Social Psychological and Social Structural Influences." *Rural Sociology* 72, 2 (2007): 185-214.

Dietz, Thomas, Linda Kalof, and Paul C. Stern. "Gender, Values, and Environmentalism." *Social Science Quarterly* 83, 1 (2002): 353-64.

Dunlap, Riley E. "The New Environmental Paradigm Scale: From Marginality to Worldwide Use." *Journal of Environmental Education* 40, 1 (2008): 3-18.

–. "Paradigms, Theories, and Environmental Sociology." In *Sociological Theory and the Environment: Classical Foundations, Contemporary Insights*, edited by R.E. Dunlap, F.H. Buttel, P. Dickens, and A. Giswijt, 329-50. Lanham, MD: Rowman and Littlefield, 2002.

Dunlap, Riley E., and William R. Catton Jr. "Environmental Sociology." *Annual Review of Sociology* 5 (1979): 243-73.

Dunlap, Riley E., Kent D. Van Liere, Angela G. Mertig, and Robert Emmet Jones. "Measuring Endorsement of the New Ecological Paradigm: A Revised NEP Scale." *Journal of Social Issues* 56, 3 (2000): 425-42.

Dunlap, Riley E., and Richard York. "The Globalization of Environmental Concern and the Limits of the Postmaterialist Values Explanation: Evidence from Four Multinational Surveys." *Sociological Quarterly* 49, 3 (2008): 529-63.

Efron, Sarah. "Schussing on Slush (or Worse): Is Whistler's Wet Year a Freak Occurrence? Many Researchers Say Ski Resorts Across North America and Europe Face Rising Snow Lines and Erratic Weather." *Globe and Mail*, March 9, 2005.

Eichberg, Henning. "New Spatial Configurations of Sport? Experiences from Danish Alternative Planning." *International Review for the Sociology of Sport* 28, 2/3 (1993): 245-62.

Elias, Norbert. "The Kitsch Style and the Age of Kitsch." In *The Norbert Elias Reader: A Biographical Selection*, edited by J. Goudsblom and S. Mennell, 26-35. Oxford, UK: Blackwell, 1998.

Elliot, Nils Lindahl. *Mediating Nature*. London: Routledge, 2004.

Elliott, Anthony, and John Urry. *Mobile Lives*. London: Routledge, 2010.

England, Mike. "Connections: The Shared Psyche of Skiers." *Powder*, February 2005, 42-43.

Erickson, Bruce. "The Colonial Climbs of Mount Trudeau: Thinking Masculinity through the Homosocial." *Topia* 9 (Spring 2003): 67-82.

Ericson, Richard V., Patricia M. Baranek, and Janet B.L. Chan. *Negotiating Control: A Study of News Sources*. Toronto: University of Toronto Press, 1989.

Escobar, Arturo. "After Nature: Steps to an Antiessentialist Political Ecology." *Current Anthropology* 40, 1 (1999): 1-30.

Ferguson, Will, and Ian Ferguson. *How to Be a Canadian*. 2nd ed. Vancouver: Douglas and McIntyre, 2007.

Fernie Alpine Resort. http://www.skifernie.com.

Ferrell, Jeff. "Style Matters." In *Cultural Criminology Unleashed*, edited by J. Ferrell, K. Hayward, W. Morrison, and M. Presdee, 61-63. London: Glasshouse Press, 2004.

Floyd, Myron F., and Cassandra Y. Johnson. "Coming to Terms with Environmental Justice in Outdoor Recreation: A Conceptual Discussion with Research Implications." *Leisure Sciences* 24, 1 (2002): 59-77.

Ford, Nick, and David Brown. *Surfing and Social Theory: Experience, Embodiment and Narrative of the Dream Glide*. London: Routledge, 2006.

Foucault, Michel. *Abnormal: Lectures at the College De France, 1974-1975*. Edited by V. Marchetti and A. Salomoni. Translated by G. Burchell. New York: Picador, 2003.

–. *Discipline and Punish*. New York: Vintage Books, 1977.

–. *The Hermeneutics of the Subject: Lectures at the College De France, 1981-82*. Edited by F. Gros. Translated by G. Burchell. New York: Picador, 2005.

–. *The History of Sexuality*. Vol. 1, *An Introduction*. Translated by R. Hurley. New York: Vintage Books, 1978.

–. *The History of Sexuality*. Vol. 3, *The Care of the Self*. Translated by R. Hurley. New York: Vintage Books, 1986.

–. "Politics and the Study of Discourse." In *The Foucault Effect: Studies in Governmentality*, edited by G. Burchell, C. Gordon, and P. Miller, 53-72. Translated by C. Gordon. Chicago: University of Chicago Press, 1991.

–. *Security, Territory, Population: Lectures at the College De France, 1977-1978*. Edited by M. Senellart. Translated by G. Burchell. New York: Palgrave Macmillan, 2007.

–. *"Society Must Be Defended": Lectures at the College De France, 1975-1976*. Edited by M. Bertani and A. Fontana. Translated by D. Macey. New York: Picador, 2003.

–. "The Subject and Power." In *Power*. Vol. 3 of *Essential Works of Foucault 1954-1984*. Edited by J. Faubion, 326-48. Translated by R. Hurley. New York: The New Press, 2000.

–. "Technologies of the Self." In *Ethics: Subjectivity and Truth*. Edited by P. Rabinow, 223-52. New York: The New Press, 1997.

–. "Truth and Juridical Forms." In *Power*. Vol. 3 of *Essential Works of Foucault 1954-1984*. Edited by J. Faubion, 1-89. Translated by R. Hurley. New York: The New Press, 2000.

Fournier, Suzanne. "Natives Block Sun Peaks Construction Road." *Vancouver Province*, June 5, 2001.

Franklin, Adrian. "Burning Cities: A Posthumanist Account of Australians and Eucalypts." *Environment and Planning D: Society and Space* 24, 4 (2006): 555-76.

–. *Tourism: An Introduction*. London: Sage, 2003.

–. "Tourism as an Ordering: Towards a New Ontology of Tourism." *Tourist Studies* 4, 3 (2004): 277-301.

Frohlick, Susan. "'That Playfulness of White Masculinity': Mediating Masculinities and Adventure at Mountain Film Festivals." *Tourist Studies* 5, 2 (2005): 175-93.

Fry, John. "Exactly What Are Their Environmental Attitudes?" *Ski Area Management*, November 1995, 45-47.

–. *The Story of Modern Skiing*. Hanover: University Press of New England, 2006.

Gane, Nicholas, and Donna Haraway. "When We Have Never Been Human, What Is to Be Done? Interview with Donna Haraway." *Theory, Culture and Society* 23, 7-8 (2006): 135-58.

Gannett, Alison. "Manali Muse: Following Historical Footsteps in the Himalayas." *Powder Girl: A Special All Women's Edition*, 2006, 34-36.

Gieryn, Thomas F. "A Space for Place in Sociology." *Annual Review of Sociology* 26 (2000): 463-96.

Gilchrist, Paul. "Motherhood, Ambition and Risk": Mediating the Sporting Hero/ine in Conservative Britain. *Media, Culture and Society* 29, 3 (2007): 395-414.

Gould, Kenneth A., David N. Pellow, and Allan Schnaiberg. *The Treadmill of Production: Injustice and Unsustainability in the Global Economy*. Boulder, CO: Paradigm, 2008.

Grafton, R. Quentin, Linwood H. Pendleton, and Harry W. Nelson. *A Dictionary of Environmental Economics, Science, and Policy*. Cheltenham, UK: Edward Elgar, 2001.

Grant, Tavia. "How Did Intrawest Rack Up So Much Debt?" *Globe and Mail*, January 21, 2010.

Haimayer, Peter. "Glacier-Skiing Areas in Austria: A Socio-Political Perspective." *Mountain Research and Development* 9, 1 (1989): 51-58.

Hall, Stuart. "Encoding/Decoding." In *Culture, Media, Language: Working Papers in Cultural Studies, 1972-79*, edited by S. Hall, 128-38. London: Hutchinson Centre for Contemporary Cultural Studies, University of Birmingham, 1980.

Hamr, Joseph. "Disturbance Behaviour of Chamois in an Alpine Tourist Area of Austria." *Mountain Research and Development* 8, 1 (1988): 65-73.

Hannigan, John A. *Fantasy City: Pleasure and Profit in the Postmodern Metropolis*. London: Routledge, 1998.

Hansen, Peter Holger. "British Mountaineering, 1850-1914." PhD diss., Harvard University, 1991.

Haraway, Donna. *The Companion Species Manifesto: Dogs, People, and Significant Otherness*. Chicago: Prickly Paradigm, 2003.

–. "The Promises of Monsters: A Regenerative Politics for Inappropriate/D Others." In *The Haraway Reader*, 63-124. New York: Routledge, 2004 [1992].

–. *Simians, Cyborgs, and Women: The Reinvention of Nature*. New York: Routledge, 1991.

–. *When Species Meet*. Minneapolis: University of Minnesota Press, 2008.

Hay, Peter. *Main Currents in Western Environmental Thought*. Bloomington: Indiana University Press, 2002.

Hewlett, Jason, "Native Protest Hits Resort: First Nations Group Sets Up at Sun Peaks." *Kamloops (BC) Daily News*, December 22, 2003.

Heywood, Leslie, and Mark Montgomery. "'Ambassadors of the Last Wilderness'? Surfers, Environmental Ethics, and Activism in America." In *Tribal Play: Subcultural Journeys through Sport*, edited by M. Atkinson and K. Young, 153-72. Bingley, UK: JAI Press, 2008.

Hipwell, William T. "Environmental Conflict and Democracy in Bella Coola: Political Ecology on the Margins of Industria." In *Environmental Conflict and Democracy in Canada*, edited by L.E. Adkin, 140-58. Vancouver: UBC Press, 2009.

Hudson, Simon. *Snow Business: A Study of the International Ski Industry*. London: Cassell, 2000.

Hume, Mark. "The People of the Kootenays Don't Want Another Whistler." *Globe and Mail*, March 9, 2004.

Intrawest. "Company Overview." http://www.intrawest.com/.

Jasen, Patricia Jane. *Wild Things: Nature, Culture, and Tourism in Ontario, 1790-1914*. Toronto: University of Toronto Press, 1995.

John Gow Consultants. *Ski Market Study*. Victoria: Government of Canada, Department of Regional Industrial Expansion; Province of British Columbia, Ministry of Tourism, Recreation and Culture; and Province of British Columbia, Ministry of Economic Development, 1987.

Joosse, Paul. "Leaderless Resistance and Ideological Inclusion: The Case of the Earth Liberation Front." *Terrorism and Political Violence* 19, 3 (2007): 351-68.

Jumbo Creek Conservation Society. "Jumbo Wild." http://www.keepitwild.ca.

Jumbo Glacier Resort. http://www.jumboglacierresort.com.

Kalof, Linda, Thomas Dietz, Gregory Guagnano, and Paul C. Stern. "Race, Gender and Environmentalism: The Atypical Values and Beliefs of White Men." *Race, Gender and Class* 9, 2 (2002): 112-30.

Kay, Joanne, and Suzanne Laberge. "Oh Say, Can You Ski? Imperialistic Construction of Freedom in Warren Miller's *Freeriders*." In *To the Extreme: Alternative Sports Inside and Out*, edited by R. Rinehart and S. Sydnor, 381-400. New York: SUNY, 2003.

Kennedy, Peter. "Cominco Doles Out Pink Slips at B.C. Mine." *Globe and Mail*, September 28, 2000.

Kicking Horse Mountain Resort. http://www.kickinghorseresort.com.

Kivi, K. Linda, ed. *The Purcell Suite: Upholding the Wild*. Nelson, BC: Maa Press, 2007.

Koopmans, Robert, and Mike Youds. "Natives' Blockade Lasts Just Minutes: Police Quickly Arrive to End Protest on the Road to Ski Resort." *Kamloops (BC) Daily News*, December 29, 2001.

Kvale, Steinar. *InterViews: An Introduction to Qualitative Research Interviewing*. Thousand Oaks, CA: Sage, 1996.

LaChapelle, Dolores. *Deep Powder Snow: 40 Years of Ecstatic Skiing, Avalanches and Earth Wisdom*. Durango, CO: Kivaki Press, 1993.

Lambertus, Sandra. *Wartime Images, Peacetime Wounds*. Toronto: University of Toronto Press, 2004.

Lassen, Claus. "Aeromobility and Work." *Environment and Planning A* 38 (2006): 301-12.

Latour, Bruno. *Pandora's Hope*. Cambridge, MA: Harvard University Press, 1999.

–. *Politics of Nature: How to Bring the Sciences into Democracy*. Translated by C. Porter. Cambridge, MA: Harvard University Press, 2004.

–. *"The Prince* for Machines as Well as for Machinations." In *Technology and Social Process*, edited by B. Elliott, 20-43. Edinburgh: Edinburgh University Press, 1988.

–. *Reassembling the Social: An Introduction to Actor-Network-Theory*. Oxford: Oxford University Press, 2005.

–. *We Have Never Been Modern*. Translated by C. Porter. Cambridge, MA: Harvard University Press, 1993.

Laurendeau, Jason. "'Gendered Risk Regimes': A Theoretical Consideration of Edgework and Gender." *Sociology of Sport Journal* 25, 3 (2008): 293-309.

Laurendeau, Jason, and Nancy Sharara. "'Women Could Be Every Bit as Good as Guys': Reproductive and Resistant Agency in Two 'Action' Sports." *Journal of Sport and Social Issues* 32, 1 (2008): 24-47.

Laviolette, Patrick. "Green and Extreme: Free-Flowing through Seascape and Sewer." *Worldviews* 10, 2 (2006): 178-204.

Lenskyj, Helen. *Olympic Industry Resistance: Challenging Olympic Power and Propaganda*. Albany: State University of New York Press, 2008.

Lidskog, Rolf. "The Re-Naturalization of Society? Environmental Challenges for Sociology." *Current Sociology* 49, 1 (2001): 113-36.

Little, Donna E., and Erica Wilson. "Adventure and the Gender Gap: Acknowledging Diversity of Experience." *Society and Leisure* 28, 1 (2005): 185-208.

Loo, Tina. *States of Nature*. Vancouver: UBC Press, 2006.

Luke, Timothy W. *Ecocritique: Contesting the Politics of Nature, Economy, and Culture*. Minneapolis: University of Minnesota Press, 1997.

–. "Eco-Managerialism: Environmental Studies as a Power/Knowledge Formation." In *Living with Nature: Environmental Politics as Cultural Discourse*, edited by F. Fischer and M.A. Hajer, 103-20. New York: Oxford University Press, 1999.

–. "On the Political Economy of Clayoquot Sound: The Uneasy Transition from Extractive to Attractive Models of Development." In *A Political Space: Reading the Global through Clayoquot Sound*, edited by W. Magnusson and K. Shaw, 91-112. Montreal and Kingston: McGill-Queen's University Press, 2002.

–. "The System of Sustainable Degradation." *Capitalism, Nature, Socialism* 17, 1 (2006): 99-112.

Lyng, Stephen. "Edgework: A Social Psychological Analysis of Voluntary Risk Taking." *American Journal of Sociology* 95, 4 (1990): 851-86.

Lyotard, Jean-Francois. *The Postmodern Condition: A Report on Knowledge*. Translated by G. Bennington and B. Massumi. Minneapolis: University of Minnesota Press, 1984 [1979].

MacCannell, Dean. *Empty Meeting Grounds: The Tourist Papers*. London: Routledge, 1992.

–. *The Tourist: A New Theory of the Leisure Class*. New York: Schocken Books, 1976.

Macdonald, Myra. *Exploring Media Discourse*. London: Arnold, 2003.

Macnaghten, Phil, and John Urry. *Contested Natures*. Thousand Oaks, CA: Sage, 1998.

Mansbridge, Francis. *Hollyburn: The Mountain and the City*. Vancouver: Ronsdale Press, 2008.

Markula, Pirkko, and Richard Pringle. *Foucault, Sport and Exercise: Power, Knowledge and Transforming the Self*. London: Routledge, 2006.

Martin, Derek Christopher. "Apartheid in the Great Outdoors: American Advertising and the Reproduction of a Racialized Outdoor Leisure Identity." *Journal of Leisure Research* 36, 4 (2004): 513-35.

Mawani, Renisa. "Genealogies of the Land: Aboriginality, Law, and Territory in Vancouver's Stanley Park." *Social Legal Studies* 14, 3 (2005): 315-39.

McAdam, Doug, Sidney Tarrow, and Charles Tilly. *Dynamics of Contention*. Cambridge: Cambridge University Press, 2001.

Michael, Mike. "The Cellphone-in-the-Countryside: On Some of the Ironic Spatialities of Technonatures." In *Technonatures: Environments, Technologies, Spaces, and Places in the Twenty-First Century*, edited by D.F. White and C. Wilbert, 85-104. Waterloo, ON: Wilfred Laurier University Press, 2009.

–. *Reconnecting Culture, Technology and Nature: From Society to Heterogeneity*. London: Routledge, 2000.

–. "These Boots Are Made for Walking ... Mundane Technology, the Body and Human – Environment Relations." *Body and Society* 6, 3-4 (2000): 107-26.

Mickleburgh, Rod. "B.C. Woman Sent to Jail over Protest." *Globe and Mail*, March 6, 2007.

Midol, Nancy, and Gerard Broyer. "Towards an Anthropological Analysis of New Sport Cultures: The Case of Whiz Sports in France." *Sociology of Sport Journal* 12, 2 (1995): 204-12.

Miller, Bruce. "The Press, the Boldt Decision, and Indian-White Relations." *American Indian Culture and Research Journal* 17, 2 (1993): 75-97.

Milton, Kay. "Land or Landscape: Rural Planning Policy and the Symbolic Construction of the Countryside." In *Rural Development in Ireland*, edited by M. Murray and J. Greer, 129-50. Avesbury, UK: Aldershot, 1993.

Mische, Ann. *Partisan Publics: Communication and Contention Across Brazilian Youth Activist Networks*. Princeton, NJ: Princeton University Press, 2008.

Mohr, John W. "Measuring Meaning Structures." *Annual Review of Sociology* 24 (1998): 345-70.

Mol, Arthur P.J., and Gert Spaargaren. "Ecological Modernisation Theory in Debate: A Review." In *Ecological Modernization around the World: Perspectives and Critical Debates*, edited by A.P.J. Mol and D.A. Sonnenfeld, 17-49. London: Frank Cass, 2000.

Mount Seymour. "Seymour 411." http://www.mountseymour.com/media-411.

Mount Washington Alpine Resort. http://www.mountwashington.ca.

Murphy, Raymond. "Disaster or Sustainability: The Dance of Human Agents with Nature's Actants." *Canadian Review of Sociology and Anthropology* 41, 3 (2004): 249-66.

–. "Ecological Materialism and the Sociology of Max Weber." In *Sociological Theory and the Environment*, edited by R.E. Dunlap, F. Buttel, P. Dickens, and A. Gijswijt, 73-89. New York: Rowman and Littlefield, 2002.

–. *Leadership in Disaster: Learning for a Future with Global Climate Change*. Montreal and Kingston: McGill-Queen's University Press, 2009.

Nanaimo (BC) Daily News. "Global Warming Threatens Global Skiing." December 3, 2003.

Nash, Roderick Frazier. *Wilderness and the American Mind*. New Haven, CT: Yale University Press, 2001.

Nelson (BC) Daily News. "$70m B.C Ski Resort Expansion Protested." December 23, 2003.

Page, Justin. "Salmon Farming in First Nations' Territories: A Case of Environmental Injustice on Canada's West Coast." *Local Environment* 12, 6 (2007): 616-26.

Park, Lisa Sun-Hee, and David Naguib Pellow. *The Slums of Aspen: Immigrants vs. the Environment in America's Eden*. New York: New York University Press, 2011.

Parkinson, David. "Resort Firm's Creditors Approve Bailout Plan." *Globe and Mail*, August 18, 2001.

Petterson, Jimmy. "Iran Unveiled: Closed Society, Open Boundaries." *Backcountry Magazine*, November 2006, 74-79.

Philo, Chris, and Chris Wilbert, eds. *Animal Spaces, Beastly Places: New Geographies of Human-Animal Relations*. London: Routledge, 2000.

Philpott, William Peter. "Consuming Colorado: Landscapes, Leisure, and the Tourist Way of Life." PhD diss., University of Wisconsin, 2002.

Pogge, Drew. "Sounds of Ski-lence." *Backcountry Magazine*, November 2006, 24-25.

Price, Martin F. "Impacts of Recreational Activities on Alpine Vegetation in Western North America." *Mountain Research and Development* 5, 3 (1985): 263-78.

Prior, Lindsay. "Following in Foucault's Footsteps: Text and Context in Qualitative Research." In *Qualitative Research: Theory, Method and Practice*, edited by D. Silverman, 63-79. London: Sage, 1997.

Pryce, Paula. *"Keeping the Lakes' Way": Reburial and the Re-Creation of a Moral World among an Invisible People*. Toronto: University of Toronto Press, 1999.

Ravel, Barbara, and Geneviève Rail. "The Lightness of Being 'Gaie': Discursive Constructions of Gender and Sexuality in Quebec Women's Sport." *International Review for the Sociology of Sport* 41, 3/4 (2006): 395-412.

Red Mountain Resort. "The History of Red Mountain Resort." http://www.redresort.com/.

Reiter, Herbert, Massimiliano Andretta, Donatella della Porta, and Lorenzo Mosca. "The Global Justice Movement in Italy." In *The Global Justice Movement: Cross-National and Transnational Perspectives*, edited by D. della Porta, 52-78. Boulder, CO: Paradigm, 2007.

Resorts of the Canadian Rockies. "Company Overview." http://www.skircr.com/.

Richardson, Lisa. "Rise of the She Bum." *Kootenay Mountain Culture Magazine*, Winter 2005/2006, 34-41.

Richey, Edward Duke. "Living It Up in Aspen: Post-War America, Ski Town Culture, and the New Western Dream, 1945-1975." PhD diss., University of Colorado, 2006.

Ries, Johannes B. "Landscape Damage by Skiing at the Schauinsland in the Black Forest, Germany." *Mountain Research and Development* 16, 1 (1996): 27-40.

Ring, Jim. *How the English Made the Alps*. London: John Murray, 2000.

Rivera, Jorge, and Peter de Leon. "Is Greener Whiter? Voluntary Environmental Performance of Western Ski Areas." *Policy Studies Journal* 32, 3 (2004): 417-37.

Rivera, Jorge, Peter de Leon, and Charles Koerber. "Is Greener Whiter Yet? The Sustainable Slopes Program after Five Years." *Policy Studies Journal* 34, 2 (2006): 195-221.

Robertson, Leslie. *Imagining Difference: Legend, Curse, and Spectacle in a Canadian Mining Town*. Vancouver: UBC Press, 2005.

Robinson, Joanna L., D.B. Tindall, Erin Seldat, and Gabriela Pechlaner. "Support for First Nations' Land Claims amongst Members of the Wilderness Preservation Movement: The Potential for an Environmental Justice Movement in British Columbia." *Local Environment* 12, 6 (2007): 579-98.

Rockland, David B. "The Environment and Your Customer." *Ski Area Management*, July 1994.

Rose, Nikolas. *The Politics of Life Itself: Biomedicine, Power, and Subjectivity in the Twenty-First Century*. Princeton, NJ: Princeton University Press, 2007.

Rothman, Hal K. *Devil's Bargains: Tourism in the Twentieth-Century American West*. Lawrence: University Press of Kansas, 1998.

Rubin, Herbert J., and Irene Rubin. *Qualitative Interviewing: The Art of Hearing Data*. Thousand Oaks, CA: Sage, 1995.

Rutherford, Paul. "The Entry of Life into History." In *Discourses of the Environment*, edited by E. Darier, 37-62. Oxford, UK: Blackwell, 1999.

Sachs, Bob. "National Perspective on Mountain Resorts and Ecology." *Vermont Law Review* 26 (2001-02): 515-42.

Sandilands, Catriona. "Between the Local and the Global: Clayoquot Sound and Simulacral Politics." In *A Political Space: Reading the Global through Clayoquot Sound*, edited by W. Magnusson and K. Shaw, 139-68. Montreal and Kingston: McGill-Queen's University Press, 2002.

–. "Where the Mountain Men Meet the Lesbian Rangers: Gender, Nation, and Nature in the Rocky Mountain National Parks." In *This Elusive Land: Women and the Canadian Environment*, edited by M. Hessing, R. Raglon, and C. Sandilands, 142-62. Vancouver: UBC Press, 2004.

Save the Peaks Coalition. "Protect and Respect the Mountain and Our Children!" http://www.savethepeaks.org.

SBC Skier. "Open House." *SBC Skier*, December 12-13, 2004.

Schama, Simon. *Landscape and Memory*. London: HarperCollins, 1995.

Schnaiberg, Allan, and Kenneth Alan Gould. *Environment and Society: The Enduring Conflict*. Caldwell, NJ: Blackburn Press, 2000.

Schrepfer, Susan R. *Nature's Altars: Mountains, Gender, and American Environmentalism*. Lawrence: University Press of Kansas, 2005.

Scott, Chic. "Hans Gmoser 1932-2006: A Tribute to Canada's Mountain Pioneer." *Kootenay Mountain Culture Magazine*, Winter 2006/2007, 78-79.

Scott, John. *Social Network Analysis: A Handbook*. 2nd ed. London: Sage, 2000.

Scott, Mitchell. "Emotional Exports: BC's Newest Resource Economy May End Up Overseas, but this Time Nature Gets to Stay Behind." *Kootenay Mountain Culture Magazine*, Winter 2006/2007, 46-51.

–. "Jumbo or Dumbo? BC's Newest Uber-Resort Serves Up a Slew of Controversy." *Powder*, February 2005, 28.

Shaw, Gary C. "Clearcut Identities: Tracking Shape-Shifters in Clayoquot Sound." In *A Political Space: Reading the Global through Clayoquot Sound*, edited by W. Magnusson and K. Shaw, 209-62. Montreal and Kingston: McGill-Queen's University Press, 2002.

Sheller, Mimi, and John Urry. "Places to Play, Places in Play." In *Tourism Mobilities: Places to Play, Places in Play,* edited by M. Sheller and J. Urry, 1-10. London: Routledge, 2004.

–. "The New Mobilities Paradigm." *Environment and Planning A* 38 (2006): 207-26.

Sierra Club of Canada. http://www.sierraclub.ca.

Sierra Legal Defence Fund. "Environmentalists and St'at'imc Nation Oppose Olympic Spin-Off Development." http://www.sierralegal.org/.

Skiing. "The American Wild: Discover What's Out There in a 4Runner." November 2006, 157.

Skwelkwek'welt Protection Centre. http://www.skwelkwekwelt.net. Originally accessed September 29, 2006. Much of the same material can now be found at the First Nations Land Rights and Environmentalism in British Columbia website, http://www.firstnations.de/development/secwepemc-skwelkwekwelt.htm.

Slocum, Rachel. "Polar Bears and Energy-Efficient Lightbulbs: Strategies to Bring Climate Change Home." *Environment and Planning D: Society and Space* 22 (2004): 413-38.

Spaargaren, Gert, and Arthur P.J. Mol. "Greening Global Consumption: Redefining Politics and Authority." *Global Environmental Change* 18, 3 (2008): 350-59.

–. "Sociology, Environment, and Modernity: Ecological Modernization as a Theory of Social Change." *Society and Natural Resources* 5, 4 (1992): 323-44.

Spricenieks, Ptor. "The Imperative." *Kootenay Mountain Culture Magazine,* Winter 2005/2006, 43-44.

Stebbins, Robert A. *Challenging Mountain Nature: Risk, Motive, and Lifestyle in Three Hobbyist Sports.* Calgary: Detselig Enterprises, 2005.

Stedman, Leanne. "From Gidget to Gonad Man: Surfers, Feminists and Post-Modernisation." *Journal of Sociology* 33, 1 (1997): 75-90.

Stern, Paul C., Thomas Dietz, Troy Abel, Gregory A. Guagnano, and Linda Kalof. "A Value-Belief-Norm Theory of Support for Social Movements: The Case of Environmentalism." *Human Ecology Review* 6, 2 (1999): 81-97.

Stifler, Emily. "Paradox in Paradise: Will Helicopter-Assisted Ski Touring Change the Sport?" *Backcountry Magazine,* November 2006, 28.

Stoddart, Mark C.J. "'British Columbia Is Open for Business': Environmental Justice and Working Forest News in the *Vancouver Sun.*" *Local Environment* 12, 6 (2007): 663-74.

Sun Peaks Resort. http://www.sunpeaksresort.com.

–. "Who We Are." http://www.sunpeaksresort.com/.

Szasz, Andrew. *Shopping Our Way to Safety: How We Changed from Protecting the Environment to Protecting Ourselves.* Minneapolis: University of Minnesota Press, 2007.

Szerszynski, Bronislaw. "The Post-Ecologist Condition: Irony as Symptom and Cure." *Environmental Politics* 16, 2 (2007): 337-55.

Taylor, Derek. "Intro." *Powder,* November 2006, 15.

Thorpe, Holly. "Beyond 'Decorative Sociology': Contextualizing Female Surf, Skate, and Snow Boarding." *Sociology of Sport Journal* 23, 3 (2006): 205-28.

–. "Foucault, Technologies of Self, and the Media: Discourses of Femininity in Snowboarding Culture." *Journal of Sport and Social Issues* 32, 2 (2008): 199-229.

–. "Jibbing the Gender Order: Females in the Snowboarding Culture." *Sport in Society* 8, 1 (2005): 76-100.

Thrift, Nigel. "I Just Don't Know What Got into Me: Where Is the Subject?" *Subjectivity* 22, 1 (2008): 82-89.

–. "Still Life in Nearly Present Time: The Object of Nature." In *Bodies of Nature,* edited by P. Macnaghten and J. Urry, 34-57. London: Sage, 2001.

Tindall, David B. "Social Networks, Identification and Participation in an Environmental Movement: Low-Medium Cost Activism within the British Columbia Wilderness Preservation Movement." *Canadian Review of Sociology and Anthropology* 39, 4 (2002): 413-52.

Tindall, David B., Scott Davies, and Céline Mauboulès. "Activism and Conservation Behavior in an Environmental Movement: The Contradictory Effects of Gender." *Society and Natural Resources* 16, 10 (2003): 909-32.

Torgerson, Douglas. "Images of Place in Green Politics: The Cultural Mirror of Indigenous Traditions." In *Living with Nature: Environmental Politics as Cultural Discourse,* edited by F. Fischer and M.A. Hajer, 186-203. New York: Oxford University Press, 1999.

Tuan, Yi-Fu. *Topophilia: A Study of Environmental Perception, Attitudes, and Values.* New York: Columbia University Press, 1990 [1974].

Turner, Jack. *The Abstract Wild.* Tucson: University of Arizona Press, 1996.

Turtle Island News. "The People Will Never Retreat from Their Homeland," January 8, 2002. http://www.theturtleislandnews.com/.

Urry, John. *Global Complexity.* Cambridge, UK: Polity Press, 2003.

–. "The 'System' of Automobility." *Theory, Culture and Society* 21, 4/5 (2004): 25-39.

–. *The Tourist Gaze.* 2nd ed. London: Sage, 2002.

Urry, John, and Jonas Larsen. *The Tourist Gaze 3.0.* 3rd ed. Los Angeles: Sage, 2011.

Veenstra, Gerry. "Social Space, Social Class and Bourdieu: Health Inequalities in British Columbia, Canada." *Health and Place* 13, 1 (2007): 14-31.

Verchere, Ian. *V0N 1B0: General Delivery, Whistler, B.C.* Vancouver: Douglas and McIntyre, 2006.

Vertinsky, Patricia. "Locating a 'Sense of Place': Space, Place and Gender in the Gymnasium." In *Sites of Sport: Space, Place, Experience,* edited by P. Vertinsky and J. Bale, 8-24. London: Routledge, 2004.

Victoria Times-Colonist. "Four Natives Jailed for Resort Blockade." December 18, 2002.

Vogler, Stephan, Toshi Kawano, and Bonny Makarevicz. *Top of the Pass: Whistler and the Sea-to-Sky Country*. Madeira Park, BC: Harbour, 2007.

Waitt, Gordon. "'Killing Waves': Surfing, Space and Gender." *Social and Cultural Geography* 9, 1 (2008): 75-94.

Warner, Gerry. "Jumbo on Display at Open House: Protesters Renting Buses to Travel to Invermere for the Event." *Cranbrook (BC) Daily Townsman*, January 3, 2006.

Weiss, Otmar, Gilbert Norden, Petra Hilscher, and Bart Vanreusel. "Ski Tourism and Environmental Problems." *International Review for the Sociology of Sport* 33, 4 (1998): 367-79.

West Coast Environmental Law. http://www.wcel.org.

Western Canada Wilderness Committee. http://www.wildernesscommittee.org.

Wheaton, Belinda. "Identity, Politics, and the Beach: Environmental Activism in Surfers against Sewage." *Leisure Studies* 26, 3 (2007): 279-302.

Wheaton, Belinda, and Alan Tomlinson. "The Changing Gender Order in Sport? The Case of Windsurfing Subcultures." *Journal of Sport and Social Issues* 22, 3 (1998): 252-74.

Whistler Blackcomb. http://www.whistlerblackcomb.com.

White, Damian F., and Chris Wilbert, eds. 2009. *Technonatures: Environments, Technologies, Spaces, and Places in the Twenty-First Century*. Waterloo, ON: Wilfred Laurier University Press.

Whitewater Winter Resort. http://www.skiwhitewater.com.

–. "History." http://www.skiwhitewater.com/.

Wilcocks, Paul. "Major Political Battle Brewing over Jumbo Plan." *Trail (BC) Daily Times*, October 18, 2004.

Wildsight. http://www.wildsight.ca.

Willems-Braun, Bruce. "Buried Epistemologies: The Politics of Nature in (Post) Colonial British Columbia." *Annals of the Association of American Geographers* 87, 1 (1997): 3-31.

Williams, Peter W. *Tracking the Future: Trends in Canadian Ski Industry Markets*. Vancouver: National Ski Industries Association, Simon Fraser University, and Tourism Canada, 1990.

Williams, Raymond. *Marxism and Literature*. New York: Oxford University Press, 1977.

Willis, Andrew, and Boyd Erman. "Colorado's Vail Tops List of Bidders for Intrawest's Whistler Blackcomb." *Globe and Mail*, February 18, 2010.

Wolch, Jennifer, and Jody Emel, eds. *Animal Geographies: Place, Politics, and Identity in the Nature-Culture Borderlands*. London: Verso, 1998.

Woods, Michael. "Fantastic Mr. Fox? Representing Animals in the Hunting Debate." In *Animal Spaces, Beastly Places: New Geographies of Human-Animal Relations*, edited by C. Philo and C. Wilbert, 182-202. London: Routledge, 2000.

Young, Iris Marion. "Activist Challenges to Deliberative Democracy." In *Philosophy of Education Yearbook 2001*, edited by Suzanne Rice, 41-55. Urbana, IL: Philosophy of Education Society, 2001.

Young, Michele. "Chiefs Take Stand against Planned Ski Resort." *Kamloops (BC) Daily News*, July 28, 2005.

Index

Note: "(i)" after a page number indicates an illustration.

Printed and bound in Canada by Friesens

Set in Myriad and Sabon by Artegraphica Design Co. Ltd.

Copy editor: Judy Phillips

Proofreader: Lara Kordic

Indexer: Judith Anderson